Arabic in Modern Hebrew Texts

The Stylistics of Exophonic Writing

Mohamed A. H. Ahmed

EDINBURGH
University Press

Edinburgh University Press is one of the leading university presses in the UK. We publish academic books and journals in our selected subject areas across the humanities and social sciences, combining cutting-edge scholarship with high editorial and production values to produce academic works of lasting importance. For more information visit our website: edinburghuniversitypress.com

Edinburgh University Press Ltd
The Tun – Holyrood Road, 12(2f) Jackson's Entry, Edinburgh EH8 8PJ

First published in hardback by Edinburgh University Press 2019

Typeset in Times New Roman by
Servis Filmsetting Ltd, Stockport, Cheshire, and

A CIP record for this book is available from the British Library

ISBN 978 1 4744 4443 9 (hardback)
ISBN 978 1 4744 4444 6 (paperback)
ISBN 978 1 4744 4445 3 (webready PDF)
ISBN 978 1 4744 4446 0 (epub)

Contents

List of Figures and Tables vi
Acknowledgements viii
Typography, Translations and Transcription x
Transcription xi
List of Abbreviations xiii

Introduction 1
From Baghdad to a Transit Camp 3
Why Study the Use of Arabic in Modern Hebrew Texts? 5
The Structure of the Book 7
Limitations of the Study 9

1 Arabic and Hebrew in One Text: Early Potential, Current Perspective 11
1.1 Judaeo-Arabic: General Remarks 12
1.2 Judaeo-Arabic Texts: Early Potential of Arabic/Hebrew in One Text 13
1.3 Iraqi Judaeo-Arabic 15
1.3.1 Literature Written in Iraqi Judaeo-Arabic 16
1.3.2 The Linguistic Features of Iraqi Judaeo-Arabic: General Remarks 17
1.4 Iraqi Jewish Novelists: From Arabic to Hebrew 18
1.4.1 Shimon Ballas: *Adīb Al-Qaṣṣ* 21
1.4.2 Sami Michael: 'Saleh-Menashe' or 'Samir-Marid'? 22
1.4.3 Eli Amir: *Ibn-'Arab* 23

1.5 The Novels 24
1.5.1 Scapegoat – Eli Amir (1983) 24
1.5.2 All Men are Equal – But Some are More – Sami Michael (1974) 26
1.5.3 The Transit Camp – Shimon Ballas (1964) 28
1.5.4 Farewell Baghdad – Eli Amir (1992) 29
1.5.5 Victoria – Sami Michael (1993) 31
1.5.6 The Other One – Shimon Ballas (1991) 34
1.5.7 What's Left – Eli Amir (2010a) 35
1.5.8 End of the Visit – Shimon Ballas (2008) 36
1.5.9 Diamond from the Wilderness – Sami Michael (2011) 37

2 Exophonic Writing, Stylistics and the Study of Iraqi Jewish Fiction 38
2.1 Stylistics: An Approach to Exophonic Texts 39
2.1.1 Exophonic Texts 39
2.1.2 Approaches to Exophonic Texts 43
2.1.3 Aspects of Non-Code-Switching in Exophonic Texts 47
2.1.4 Towards a New Approach to Exophonic Texts 51
2.2 The Analysis of Arabic Use in the Iraqi Hebrew Novels 57
2.2.1 Data 58
2.2.2 Code-Switching in the Hebrew Novels 60
2.2.3 Syntagmatic/Paradigmatic Deviations 73
2.3 Conclusion 79

3 The Use of Arabic Between Authors and Novels 80
3.1 A Diachronic Analysis of Arabic Use in the Selected Hebrew Novels 81
3.1.1 Early Hebrew Novels, Corpus 1 81
3.1.2 Hebrew Novels Written in the Middle Period, Corpus 2 83
3.1.3 The Late Hebrew Novels, Corpus 3 85
3.1.4 General Remarks on the Diachronic Analysis of Arabic Use 85
3.2 Arabic Use as Compared Between Novels and Authors 87
3.2.1 Shimon Ballas 88
3.2.2 Sami Michael 91
3.2.3 Eli Amir 96

3.3 Iraqi Judaeo-Arabic and Arabic Dialects in the Novels 100
3.3.1 Iraqi Judaeo-Arabic 101
3.3.2 Arabic Dialects 104
3.4 Conclusion 105

4 Final Remarks 107
4.1 Why Arabic? 107
4.1.1 *Ha-ma'abara*: The Narratives of Baghdad and Israel 108
4.1.2 Baghdad 111
4.1.3 Israel 115
4.2 Summary and Concluding Remarks 117
4.2.1 The Model 117
4.2.2 Stylistic Analysis of the Arabic Use of the Iraqi Jewish Authors 120
4.2.3 The Style of Arabic Use According to Each Author 122

Appendices 126
Notes 161
References 166
Index 176

Figures and Tables

Figures

2.1 Suggested approach to exophonic texts 56
2.2 The relationship between the three main elements of the suggested approach 57
3.1 Parts of speech, corpus 1 82
3.2 Parts of speech, corpus 2 84
3.3 Semantic field analysis of Ballas's sample 92
3.4 Contextual settings of Ballas's sample 92
3.5 Semantic field analysis of Michael's sample 94
3.6 Contextual settings in Michael's sample 96
3.7 Semantic field analysis of Amir's sample 99
3.8 Contextual settings in Amir's sample 100

Tables

2.1 Code-switching in the novels 60
3.1 Use of Arabic according to parts of speech, corpus 1 81
3.2 Arabic use strategies, corpus 1 83
3.3 Arabic uses according to parts of speech, corpus 2 84
3.4 Arabic use strategies, corpus 2 85
3.5 Arabic uses according to parts of speech, corpus 3 86
3.6 Arabic use strategies, corpus 3 86
3.7 Arabic parts of speech in Ballas's sample 88
3.8 Arabic use strategies in Ballas's sample 91
3.9 Arabic parts of speech in Michael's sample 92
3.10 Arabic use strategies in Michael's sample 94

Acknowledgements

The idea behind this book was born in Mansoura, Egypt, the book itself was written in Leipzig, Germany and it was revisited for publication in Cambridge, UK. Therefore, thanks are due to these three countries to which the book, and its author, owe gratitude.

I wish to thank the GERLS programme (German Egyptian Long-Term Scholarship – Grant No. A/11/90868) for the financial aid I have received to fund this project, which was also partially funded by The German Academic Exchange Service (DAAD) and the Egyptian Ministry of Higher Education (MoHE). Thanks are due to the Simon Dubnow Institute for Jewish History and Culture at Leipzig University for hosting me and for providing me with a very good academic environment in which to pursue my project during my PhD.

I would like to thank my 'Doktorvater' and supervisor Professor Dan Diner, Simon Dubnow Institut für jüdische Geschichte und Kultur/ Universität Leipzig, for his great support. His ideas and advice were brilliant and essential for this study. I am equally thankful to Professor José Martinez Delgado, Department of Semitic Studies, Granada University, Spain, who helped me so much with the linguistic part of the book. Thanks are due also to Dr Nicolas Berg, Simon Dubnow Institute, for the support he gave to me as a PhD student during my stay in Leipzig. I would also like to thank Professor Dr Anat Feinberg and Dr Natasha Gordinsky for their guidance and support during the early phase of the project.

I am grateful to the many scholars and colleagues who supported this project with ideas and suggestions; special thanks are due to Professor Reuven Snir, Professor Nancy E. Berg, Professor Sasson Somekh and Professor Omar Kamil. I would also like to give special thanks to both

Professor Geoffrey Khan and Dr Esther-Miriam Wagner, University of Cambridge, for their great support and encouragement to publish the book.

Thanks are also due to the publishing team at Edinburgh University Press for their support during the production of the book, including Laura Williamson and Richard Strachan. I give my thanks also to the anonymous reviewers of the proposal and the typescript of the book for their supportive suggestions and comments that helped to make this book happen.

Finally, I would like to thank my wife and children for their patience and understanding.

Typography, Translations and Transcription

All extracted examples of the study are written in plain type, only Arabic instances are written in **bold**. The Arabic and Hebrew extracts from the Hebrew novels of the study, which are integrated within the main text, are in *italics*. When a free translation is needed for certain Arabic or Hebrew words and phrases, the word-for-word translation is given first inside brackets, followed by a free translation like in this example: [word-for-word translation – free translation].

The examples in the study are written as they appear in the original Hebrew texts. This is to highlight the distinct features of each text concerning employing Arabic and how each author has his unique typography.

All the examples in the study are my translations. Quotations from Hebrew novels, which were already translated into English, are cited from those editions. However, I use my translation of some examples so as to elucidate some linguistic features that are not shown in the English editions. The translation into English appears in brackets […].

Transcription

Arabic and Hebrew transliterations follow the Romanisation Tables, Library of Congress, as illustrated below.

The Romanisation of Hebrew Script

Consonants

Vernacular	Romanisation	Vernacular	Romanisation
א	’ (alif) or disregarded	ל	l
בּ	b	מ (final ם)	m
ב	v	נ (final ן)	n
ג	g	ס	s
ד	d	ע	‘ (ayn)
ה	h	פּ	p
ו	ṿ (only if consonant)	פ (final ף)	f
ז	z	צ (final ץ)	ts
ח	ḥ	ק	ḳ
ט	ṭ	ר	r
י	y (only if consonant)	שׁ	sh
כּ (final ך)	k	שׂ	ś
כ (final ך)	kh	ת	t

Vowels

◌ָ ◌ַ	a	◌ֶי / ◌ֵי / ◌ֵ / ◌ֶ	e
◌ְ	e	◌ִי	i
◌ֱ	e	וֹ , ◌ֹ	o
◌ִ	i	וּ , ◌ֻ	u

The Romanisation of Arabic Script

Consonants

Vernacular	Romanisation	Vernacular	Romanisation
ا	omit	ض	ḍ
ب	b	ط	ṭ
ت	t	ظ	ẓ
ث	th	ع	ʿ
ج	g	غ	gh
ح	ḥ	ف	f
خ	kh	ق	q
د	d	ك	k
ذ	dh	ل	l
ر	r	م	m
ز	z	ن	n
س	s	ه	h
ش	sh	و	w
ص	ṣ	ي	y

Vowels

◌َ	a	آ	ā
◌ِى	ī	◌ُ	u
◌ِ	i	◌َى	ay
◌َوْ	aw	◌ُو	ū

Abbreviations

AA-CS	ambiguous-access code-switching
CS	code-switching
EA-CS	easy-access code-switching
EL	embedded language
ET	exophonic text
HA-CS	hard-access code-switching
In.R	insider reader
L1	first language (mother tongue)
L2	second language
MTL	Matrix Text Language
Out.R	outsider reader

Introduction

About thirty years after his immigration from Iraq to Israel, Sami Michael, a well-known Israeli author, said in an interview: 'Today I think only in Hebrew and write only in Hebrew. Many times the pen stops, the brain searches for the word, but the word appears only in Arabic or English' (Michael 1984: 29).

Reflecting on the way Hebrew and Arabic merged in his literary work *Mafriaḥ ha-yonim* (Farewell Baghdad) (1992), Eli Amir says: 'When writing this Hebrew novel, I imagined myself listening in one ear to my father telling it to me in Arabic' (Snir 2005a: 338).

Similar to Amir and Michael is Shimon Ballas. The three authors were born in Baghdad and they share the same cultural, linguistic and transitional experience to a new land and a new language. They portray feelings of switching between Arabic and Hebrew in their literary careers, and they also reflect upon the collective emotional state with regard to the emigrational influx of many Jews from Arab countries who had to leave their mother tongue and their lands during the period of mass immigration to Israel in the 1950s.

Since it was difficult to find empathetic listeners to his silenced voice, Michael (1984: 23) tried to find a solution: 'I was ready to learn new things, but I categorically refused to break with my former self. The upshot of this was that Israeli society was not prepared to listen, and I was unable to make myself heard – I had no Hebrew then'. Amir started writing only in Hebrew once in Israel. Both Michael and Ballas wrote in Arabic at the beginning of their literary careers in Israel before switching to Hebrew. The three authors understood the key importance of acquiring the Hebrew language.

When they encountered this new society, where Hebrew was in the process of being established as the national language, most Iraqi Jewish authors found it impossible to continue writing in Arabic in their new home and thus had to face the literary challenge of switching to another tongue in order to be heard. This complex situation constitutes the historical background of this book, and it sheds light on the sociolinguistic background of the three authors, which is demonstrated by the inner conflict between the mother tongue, i.e. Arabic, and the adopted language in the new country, i.e. Hebrew. This engagement within and between two cultures and two languages resulted not only in bilingualism but also in biculturalism. Although their mother tongue is Arabic, these three Iraqi Jewish authors felt that they needed to write in Hebrew if they were to have successful literary careers in Israel. In addition, the fear of living in 'exile', as Berg (1996) puts it, was among the reasons for most Iraqi Jewish authors to discharge Arabic and adjust to Hebrew with regad to their creativity. (Although there were a few who did not change their mother tongue and continued to write in Arabic.) The decision to shift to Hebrew, however, did not stop the three Iraqis using Arabic in their Hebrew texts.

The phenomenon of writing literature in the non-mother tongue is central to this book. As bilinguals, Iraqi Jewish novelists have employed Arabic in some of their Hebrew literary works. The study of these Iraqi Jewish authors and how they employed Arabic in their Hebrew novels is conducted from the perspective of sociolinguistics, multilingualism and exophonic writing. In this regard, this book shows how and why Arabic was incorporated into modern Hebrew texts.

The main aim of the book is to introduce a model to study exophonic texts (that is, a text composed in the non-mother tongue), looking at the use of Arabic in the Iraqi Hebrew novels as an example of such a phenomenon. Demonstrating an example of exophonic literature from Semitic languages, this book will contribute to the study of bilingualism in literature. By doing so, the book adds to the ongoing research on linguistic features of bilingual literary texts, such as literary code-switching and linguistic stylistics.

The study of these three Iraqi Jewish authors and how they used their native Iraqi Arabic in their literary works in Hebrew, 'language in migration' (Perloff 2010), can provide new insights into literary production by bilingual writers in the Israeli context. In addition, the study aims to introduce an example of exophonic writings outside the European boundary by means of introducing a study of exophonic writings from the Middle Eastern/Semitic languages (Hebrew/Arabic).

The book focuses on nine Hebrew novels by three Iraqi Jewish authors: Sami Michael (born in Baghdad in 1926), Shimon Ballas (born in Baghdad in 1930) and Eli Amir (born in Baghdad in 1937). These three authors, as indicated in Chapter 1, have been selected for this study mainly because they are the most prominent Iraqi novelists from the first generation who decided to write in Hebrew after their immigration to Israel. Unlike Michael and Ballas, Amir never wrote in Arabic. In the Hebrew novels analysed in this book, Arabic is used in many ways, not only in code-switching form, loanwords from classical Arabic and Iraqi dialects or Iraqi Judaeo-Arabic variety, idioms and folk sayings, but also in non-code-switching aspects, such as word order and syntagmatic and paradigmatic deviations.

The book explores the influence of Arabic language and culture on the Hebrew novels of the Iraqis. This influence was primarily the result of a literary phenomenon that exists in the context of bilingualism, namely 'exophonic writing'. Additionally, the study surveys and evaluates the function, meaning and implications of using Arabic in Hebrew novels in the contexts of language choice, language and place and language and symbols of belonging.

It was essential for this book to trace all the uses of Arabic in the Hebrew works selected to represent the three authors. In this regard, the book tries to answer questions such as: How did Iraqi Jewish novelists use Arabic in early Hebrew novels? In what way did the style of Iraqi Jewish novelists change with regard to Arabic over a period of fifty years? Why did Iraqi Jews use Arabic in these particular works? And what is the correlation between language and belonging among Iraqi Jewish novelists?

With regard to theory, this study explores the possibilities and motivations of using stylistics as a theoretical framework in approaching exophonic texts. Since Iraqi Jewish novelists wrote their literary works in Hebrew, one can consider the Hebrew novels selected for analysis as exophonic texts. A suggested linguistic, stylistic, analytical model has been developed and applied to the selected Hebrew novels.

From Baghdad to a Transit Camp

Iraq has a rich Jewish culture and history. For more than 2,000 years, Jews have settled there – the oldest existence of Jews in Iraq dating back to the 7th century BC (Ghunayma 1924: 48–52; Rejwan 1998: 14). Jews were integrated into Iraqi society in modern times as well and came to adopt an Iraqi national identity (Gat 1997: 12–16; Ghunayma 1924: 183–5). Iraqi Jews were well educated; many had studied in the Alliance schools in Baghdad which had a great impact on the level of their education.

Because of their solid education, Iraqi Jews acquired a strong level of proficiency in French, English and Hebrew in addition to Arabic. Due their knowledge of foreign languages, Iraqi Jewish university graduates were successful in finding the best job positions in Iraq, mainly working in banks and the advertising industry (Rejwan 1985: 186–7). Iraqi Jews generally held a good economic situation, especially during the British Mandate in Iraq. They owned a number of banks and international companies with offices outside Iraq (Shiblak 2005: 48; Simon et al. 2003: 363) and Iraqi Jews were active in Iraq's political life. In 1946 there were six Jewish members of the Iraqi parliament (Kiwān 1996: 31). Sir Sassoon Eskell (b. Baghdad, 1860–1932) was a famous statesman and served as the first finance minister in the country from 1920 to 1925 (Kiwān 1996: 30; Simon et al. 2003: 357). In view of this, one can say that Iraqi Jews were well integrated within social, political and cultural life in Iraq before their mass immigration to Israel, which was also the general case with other Jewish communities in the Middle East and North Africa at the time (Behar and Ben-Dor Benite 2013)

The oldest Zionist activities in Iraq, as Rejwan (1985: 200–2) notes, date back to 1890, and the early immigration of some Iraqi Jews to Palestine motivated by religious belief. Starting from 1921, Zionist activities in Iraq increased. The call for immigration to Palestine was among the main activities of the movement (Kūriyah 1998: 108–9). However, this call was not received with much interest among Iraqi Jewry; only a few Iraqi Jews immigrated to Palestine in the 1920s and 1930s. Even after the violence against Jews in Iraq that erupted in June 1941, known as *al-Farhūd*,[1] in which more than 100 Jews were killed, the majority of Iraqi Jews did not wish to emigrate to Palestine.

Earlier on, Mizrahi Jews[2] had not received the same attention from Zionist leaders as the Western Jews: 'The official Zionist bodies in Palestine did not consider the eastern Jews as a pioneering element or as candidates for immigration. The focus of Zionist action was in Europe' (Gat 1997: 14). This changed in 1942, when David Ben-Gurion proposed the 'One Million Plan', which aimed at increasing the number of immigrant Jews to Mandatory Palestine, including the immigration of Jews from Arab lands (Shenhav 2003: 29–34). In March 1950, the Iraqi government announced the right for Jews to emigrate to Israel on the condition of relinquishing their Iraqi citizenship, the so-called *ṭasqīt* law (Shiblak 2005: 104–17).[3] A series of bombings that began in April 1950 and continued on into 1951, resulting in injuries and a number of deaths, also encouraged a growing Jewish exodus; this violence may have been the work of some activists in the Zionist movement in Iraq eager to spur Jewish departure. Between

May 1950 and June 1951, some 100,000 Iraqi Jews emigrated to Israel (Shenhav 2003: 126).

Their exodus was part of a broader mass immigration of Jews to Israel from the Arab world and Iran. As part of the Iraqi intellectual elite, Iraqi Jewish authors contributed to Arabic literature in Iraq at the beginning of the twentieth century. They left behind a great literary cultural heritage that was part of the building of modern Iraq. After their immigration to Israel, Iraqi Jewish writers, like other immigrants to Israel, experienced certain difficulties and hardships during the first years after their arrival (1950–1). The first obstacle they faced in the integration process into the new society was learning its language, Hebrew. Since the three authors investigated in this study left Iraq as young adults during the 1950s, when Arabic was their mother tongue, they had to rebuild their lives in new country and learn new language, i.e. the modern Hebrew language. In Israel, where Hebrew was developing as the national language of the fledgling state, most Iraqi Jewish authors found it impossible to continue writing in Arabic and had to grapple with the literary challenge of switching to Hebrew.

Why Study the Use of Arabic in Modern Hebrew Texts?

The study of Hebrew and Arabic interference after 1948 has been thoroughly investigated. There are a considerable number of studies which examine the influence of Hebrew on the Arabic of the Palestinians in Israel (Amara 1999; Koplewitz 1990; Talmon 2000), while other studies focused on the sociolinguistic terms between Hebrew and Arabic (Amara and Mar‘i 2002; Henkin-Roitfarb 2011; Lefkowitz 2004). The issues of the bilingualism, interference and translation between Hebrew and Arabic, looking at Palestinian authors in Israel who write in Hebrew, have been also widely investigated (Brenner 2001; Hever 1987; Kayyal 2008a, 2008b, 2010, 2011; Levy 2003; Snir 1993, 1995; Somekh 1993; Tannenbaum 2014). Some studies have been conducted on Mizrahi authors who write in Arabic or who use Arabic in their Hebrew texts (Henshke 2013; Snir 1991, 2005a, 2005b, 2015).

Although the phenomenon of using Arabic in some modern literary Hebrew texts constitutes a rich field for linguists, the majority of studies on Iraqi Jewish authors and their works are mainly focused on the literary and socio-political aspects of their works. One of the early studies in this vein by Berg (1996) approaches Iraqi Jewish novelists as writers in exile after their immigration to Israel. She includes a brief discussion about the use of Arabic in early Hebrew novels, which she regards as a cultural translation process, concluding that: ‘The use of Arabic words, phrases, expressions, and formulas in all of these novels is present mostly in the speech of the characters in the literature describing the period shortly after the Iraqis' arrival to Israel' (Berg 1996: 62). Berg also published another book (2005) which deals with the literary works of Sami Michael. Müller et al. (2011) have noted the influence of Arabic on the language in Ballas's Hebrew texts. Another important study conducted by Snir (2005a) focuses on the dilemma of identity in the literary works of Iraqi Jews written either in Arabic or in Hebrew. Gat (1998) has also analysed the reflection of an oriental environment in some Iraqi Jews' novels in Hebrew. Hever (2002, 2007) examines Oriental Jewish writers in general and Iraqi Jewish novelists in particular, Siebers (2010) focused on the transcultural issues in Iraqi Jewish literary works, while Alcalay (1993) gave more attention to cultural and political issues between Jews and Arabs in general, including the status of Iraqi Jewish literature in the canon of modern Hebrew literature.[4] Levy (2006) conducted a literary study on the representation of Baghdad in Iraqi Jewish fiction.

The recent study of Levy (2014) deserves attention, dealing as it does with the question of language in the literary works of first, second and third generations of Mizrahi Jews in Israel, as well as the issue of writing in Hebrew by the Palestinian Israelis. The question of using Arabic and Hebrew by Arabs and Jews in Israel is widely discussed in her book. Her study also involves investigating literary works by Israeli Arabs and Mizrahi Jews from the vantage point of post-colonial literature. Although Levy's study raises general questions regarding language contact and bilingualism in the literary works by both Mizrahi and Palestinian authors, there is a need for a study that is deeply based on linguistic and stylistics theories to deal with such linguistic and literary phenomena resulting from writing in an exophonic mode.

Most of the studies mentioned above concerning the three Iraqi Jewish authors follow mainstream literary and socio-political approaches. Yet if the three authors and their literature are not examined in the light of linguistics and exophonic writing, an important aspect of their creation is overlooked. The present study focuses on the linguistic investigation of Arabic use in a selected number of Hebrew novels as an exophonic practice of bilingual authors who write in the non-mother tongue, suggesting a model for approaching exophonic texts in general. The book uses this model to investigate various aspects of the Arabic used in the selected Hebrew novels, namely code-switching, translation and language interference. Although the authors and the texts selected for this study constitute a good case to investigate the use of mother tongue or first language (L1) in exophonic texts, the model developed in this study for approaching such texts should be applied in further studies to other exophonic texts in languages other than Hebrew and Arabic.

The Structure of the Book

The data for this study are taken from nine Hebrew novels written by three Iraqi Jewish authors: Amir (1983, 1992, 2010a), Ballas (1964, 1991, 2008) and Michael (1974, 1993, 2015). The study relies on manual annotation of the data. All Arabic uses employed by the authors in the selected corpora are extracted and analysed linguistically.

As to the choice of the corpora, it is essential to recall attention to the main research questions, on which the choice of the appropriate corpora depends. The main questions of this book are: (1) How did Iraqi Jewish novelists use Arabic in the early Hebrew novels? (2) In what way has the style of Iraqi Jewish novelists regarding Arabic use been changed? (3) Why did Iraqi Jews use Arabic in the suggested corpora?

As to question (1), with the help of the suggested model of the book based on 'stylistic analysis', in which more than one linguistic level could be examined, the first question is answered using a linguistic analysis of the selected early Hebrew novels. In order to trace the style changes in the Arabic use of the three Iraqi Jewish authors to answer (2), a diachronic study is involved.

The selected novels of the study have been chosen to highlight the historical implications of the Arabic used; the study suggests a diachronic analysis based on three periods in which each period is exemplified by a corpus. The first period is represented through three early novels written in Hebrew by the Iraqi authors at the beginning of their literary career (Amir 1983; Ballas 1964; Michael 1974). The following middle period comprises three Hebrew novels covering the period of the 1990s (Amir 1983; Ballas 1991; Michael 1993), while the late literary works of the three authors denote the third period (Amir 2010a; Ballas 2008; Michael 2015). These three periods are termed as three corpora, and each corpus represents a period; namely: early Hebrew novels constitute corpus 1, the Hebrew novels written during the middle period of the 1990s belong to corpus 2, and corpus 3 contains the three latest Hebrew novels published. In proceeding in this manner, the study is likely to be more representative and the diachronic investigation of Arabic use over approximately fifty years can be achieved.

Question (3) is answered in Chapter 4, in which the concepts of belonging regarding language shift, language conflicts, migration and homeland versus the new land of immigration are discussed. In light of this, the study investigates the correlation between Arabic use as a linguistic phenomenon, as well as the impact, motivation and the influence of using Arabic on the sense of belonging of the three suggested authors.

The book is divided into four chapters: Chapter 1 is an introduction to the phenomenon of Arabic and Hebrew in one text from a historical perspective. This chapter includes a general introduction to the Judaeo-Arabic paradigm, as it represents the typical form of Arabic and Hebrew in one text, and information about the linguistic features of the Iraqi Judaeo-Arabic. In addition, it discusses the process of adopting Hebrew by Iraqi Jewish authors in Israel during the early years after their immigration. It ends with a summary of each of the nine selected Hebrew novels discussed in the study.

Chapter 2 is divided into two main sections. The first section constitutes the theoretical part of the study. In this section, the possibilities and the motivations of using stylistics as a theoretical framework to approach literary texts written by bilingual authors are discussed. It encompasses a review of the literature regarding the different methods with which to approach such literary texts, as well as an interpretation of the possibilities of linking style as a choice to the analysis of literary texts written in the non-mother tongue or second language (L2) of bilingual authors. This first seciton ends with a representation of the suggested model for approaching exophonic texts. The second section of Chapter 2 analyses the style of Arabic used in the nine Hebrew novels in light of the suggested model discussed in section 1. In this second section, the data collected from the nine Hebrew novels are analysed as one corpus without any consideration of the diachronic aspect.

Chapter 3 analyses the diachronic development of Arabic use. The novels are categorised into three main corpora to trace Arabic use from early to late Hebrew novels. In this chapter, the style of each of the three authors is also analysed independently. This means that the style of each of the three authors is investigated according to the model developed in Chapter 2, and other linguistic and literary features of each author associated with Arabic/Hebrew are also discussed.

Chapter 4 concludes the study with two sections. The first section discusses the employment of place as an iconic element in the nine Hebrew novels of the study, looking at the mutual relationship between the geographical location of the narrative setting and the use of Arabic in the novels. The second section constitutes a general summary of the book with its main results.

An appendix is attached to the study. This appendix contains, first, a list of all Arabic instances (excluding proper names, place names) used in the nine Hebrew novels. The list is arranged alphabetically and written in

Hebrew script, exactly as the instances appeared in the texts, and in Arabic script as well. Further, the appendix provides a list of all Arabic code-switching (CS) instances extracted from the novels. The CS instances are arranged according to the two main terminologies of CS suggested by the study: hard-access code-switching (HA-CS) and easy-access code-switching (EA-CS).

Limitations of the Study

Spoken and Written Code-Switching

The study of the spoken code-switching by Mizrahi Jewish immigrants from the first generation is outside the scope of this book. However, the book turns to important studies which discuss bilingualism and code-switching at a spoken level in Chapter 2.

An interesting question is how the code-switching used by the three Iraqi authors in their novels differs to code-switching in spoken Hebrew? Indeed, there are some difficulties in answering such a question. First, the study of code-switching between Arabic and Hebrew in Israel is relatively new. Further, there has been no study on the Arabic code-switching of Iraqi Jews (or Mizrahi Jews) in a spoken medium conducted during the early years after the establishment of Israel (1950s–1970s). Second, recent sociolinguistic studies showed that a lot of Arabic terms became borrowed terms in Israeli Hebrew lexicon (these terms are excluded from my analysis of the late Hebrew novels); as Roni (2011: 61–2) puts it: 'The majority of Hebrew speakers today do not speak Arabic. They do, however, have access to borrowed lexicon items in the domain of slang and vernacular speech that both enriches these registers and provides the speakers with a feeling of being "indigenous" and "belonging" to the social and cultural milieu of the larger environment.' The majority of Arabic speakers discussed by Roni, however, are not Jews. Rather, they are bilingual Palestinian citizens of the state of Israel who speak Arabic and Hebrew. Members of the first-generation Mizrahi Jews (Jews who emigrated from Arab lands and North African countries) were the only Jewish population whose mother tongue was Arabic. Hebrew, and not Arabic, is the first language spoken by second- and third-generation Mizrahi Jews. Therefore, the comparison between spoken/written code-switching between Hebrew/Arabic would not be precise.

Arabic Dictionaries and Extracts from the Novels

The data used in the analysis are extracted manually from the text. The corpora are not digitalised, so the frequencies stated in the study cannot be 100 per cent guaranteed, although great effort has been made in the study to ensure the accuracy of the results.

The book turns to various Hebrew/Arabic and Judaeo-Arabic dictionaries to examine, for instance, the employed Arabic terms in the novels, and to differentiate between the loanwords and the code-switching cases.

1

Arabic and Hebrew in One Text: Early Potential, Current Perspective

> 'Die Frage, wo beginnt die Arabische Literatur der Juden?' ist leicht beantwortet: in Arabien selbst. Die Frage: wann? Wird schwerlich jemals direkt und genau zu erledigen sein. (Steinschneider 1902: 1)

After more than a century, the above question of 'when?' asked by Moritz Steinschneider still, to some extent, requires further investigation in order to uncover a precise answer. Although some scholars claim that Jews were speaking an Arabic Jewish dialect called '*al-Yahūdiyya*' in the pre-Islamic period (Hary 2009: 34–5; Stillman 2005), the early potential existence of Arabic and Hebrew in one single text is difficult to identify precisely. This is due to that fact that the oldest discovered texts written in Judaeo-Arabic date back to the ninth century (Blau 1981: 19). Since the possibility of the presence of Hebrew and Arabic in a single text is related to so-called Judaeo-Arabic, referring to different varieties of using Arabic at written levels by Jews from the pre-Islamic era until modern times, this introductory chapter briefly discusses the history of Judaeo-Arabic in general, with more attention given to Iraqi Judaeo-Arabic. With reference to Judaeo-Arabic, I use Khan's terminology (2007: 526), in which the term Judaeo-Arabic refers to any Arabic medium written in Hebrew script.

In almost all Judaeo-Arabic texts the dominant language is Arabic, although the Hebrew script was mainly and widely used to write these texts. The embedded languages brought into Judaeo-Arabic texts were mainly Hebrew and Aramaic. The linguistic features and the style of Arabic used in these texts were shaped mainly by classical or middle Arabic. Indeed, the potential of Arabic/Hebrew in one text has a long history. The significance of the phenomenon of using Arabic and Hebrew in one text is configured not only by this long history, but also by the diversity and the varieties of themes, style, registers, the portion of languages involved and the different genres employed in these texts. This includes religious texts, as well as secular texts of fiction, poetry, philosophy, medicine and science.

Since the study at hand investigates the way in which Iraqi Jewish authors employ Arabic in their Hebrew texts, the study of history, literature and the linguistic features of Judaeo-Arabic used by Iraqi Jews before immigration to Israel is relevant and essential. In addition, this chapter discusses the process of adapting Hebrew by Iraqi Jewish authors in Israel during the early years after their immigration and the shift to write in Hebrew instead of Arabic. It ends with a summary of the selected Hebrew novels comprising the corpus of the study.

1.1 Judaeo-Arabic: General Remarks

Hebrew and Arabic are two Semitic languages. Hebrew emerged from the Canaanite period as one of other dialects, and it was used by the Jews in Palestine at both spoken and written levels until the Roman period, when Aramaic displaced Hebrew (Goldenberg 2013: 11). As a result of contact between Hebrew and other languages since the dispersion of the Jews, many linguistic varieties were being developed and used by Jews according to the linguistic and geographical locations in which communities resided. These different varieties share the use of Hebrew script as well as lexical borrowing from biblical Hebrew and Aramaic on the one hand, and adopt the lexical, syntactical and grammatical rules of the non-Hebrew language on the other (Hary 1992: 72).[1]

Aramaic was the vernacular language in Syria, Palestine and Babylon long before Islam. This was gradually replaced by Arabic after the emergence of Islam and its spread into these areas. The shift to using Arabic as a lingua franca started to develop as Islam spread. As a result, the languages spoken before Islam in the ancient Near East and North Africa, mainly Aramaic, were displaced gradually by Arabic. Jews were among those who also adapted Arabic in everyday life as a natural process of language shifting that occurred at the time. Due to the fact that the shift from Aramaic to Arabic occurred on a large scale and included almost everything, the religious settings were also conveyed in Arabic: 'Being the literary medium of religious writings, it was replaced by Arabic here too. So, apparently, Arabic had become the language in which the most sacred matters of Judaism were discussed' (Blau 1981: 22).

As pointed out above, Jews in the Arabian Peninsula spoke Arabic before the rise of Islam. Hebrew influenced their Arabic. This is due to the fact that Hebrew was still being used by Jews for religious scholarly activities as well as in Jewish prayers. Thus, their Arabic language was embedded with some Hebrew lexical items (Wulfinsūn 1927: 20). This claim supports the assertion that Arabic and Hebrew might be found in Jewish literature in the pre-Islamic era.

Judaeo-Arabic is considered one of the most important linguistic varieties associated with Jewish history, culture and intellectual life. From a historical perspective, Judaeo-Arabic texts are thought to have emerged from the pre-Islamic era to the modern time, and they spanned a wide geographical areas across the Islamic empire from Spain to Iraq (Hary 1992: 73).

The most obvious feature in these linguistic varieties, according to Hary, is orthographical: the use of Hebrew script. Another important and common trait is the employment of Aramaic and Hebrew lexical elements.

1.2 Judaeo-Arabic Texts: Early Potential of Arabic/Hebrew in One Text

Although the Judaeo-Arabic writing system is believed to have been used by Jews starting from the seventh century, there is no evidence of preserved texts that were written in Judaeo-Arabic before the ninth century (Blau 1981: 19).[2] Therefore, one can assume that the first instance of Arabic and Hebrew in one text as a linguistic literary phenomenon could be found in Judaeo-Arabic texts starting from the ninth century onwards.

Judaeo-Arabic texts in the Middle Ages, although they contain features typical of middle Arabic texts, have two main distinct features in which the Jewish paradigm is reflected, i.e.: the use of Hebrew script instead of Arabic, and the use of code-switching strategies. This also influences the linguistic features of Judaeo-Arabic in general; as Chetrit (2003: 128) puts it: 'Judaeo-Arabic is composed of vocabulary and grammar that is basically Arabic, enriched by Hebrew and Aramaic'. In view of this, the early possibilities of using Arabic side by side with Hebrew in one text are probably found in Judaeo-Arabic texts. Although Arabic is the dominant language in these texts, Hebrew is used in two main forms: the first form is the use of Hebrew script, since the texts are written mainly in Hebrew typescripts, and the second is the use of Hebrew lexicon in terms of implementing single lexical items or phrases in Judaeo-Arabic texts.[3] The Hebrew script has been used in two main ways: the first was to use Hebrew script to write original Arabic texts by Jewish authors; the second was to copy (or transliterate) some Arabic works written by Muslims into Hebrew script.

It is interesting to note that the varieties of use of Hebrew script have been extended to cover even sacred Arabic texts, e.g. the Quran was also written in Hebrew script in the Middle Ages (Blau 1971: 512; Vollandt 2015). Conversely, the Hebrew version of the Bible was written in Arabic script as well (Khan 2013; Reif 2000: 106–9). In addition, there were some Islamic texts embedded with Hebrew and Aramaic lexical items (Kraus 1930).

Hence, the cases in which Hebrew or Arabic scripts were used vary. It seems that using a certain type of script depended on the target audience. In other words, a Jewish copier or a Jewish author would use Hebrew script when targeting a Jewish audience and would logically use Arabic script if the targeted audience was non-Jewish (Blau 1981: 41). The interaction and the possible emergence of Hebrew/Arabic in one text, accordingly, is well represented in the Judaeo-Arabic texts – either in the Arabic texts that were copied into Judaeo-Arabic script or in the original Judaeo-Arabic texts that were embedded with Hebrew/Aramaic linguistic elements.

The question then arises: What are the main themes in the Judaeo-Arabic texts?

As to the geographical range of the use of Judaeo-Arabic texts, these were spread over most of the Islamic world centred on West Asia and the Mediterranean. This is due to the fact that Jews lived in every part of the Islamic world, including Spain, North Africa and the Middle East (Chetrit 2003: 128). These texts contain similar linguistic aspects owing to the fact that the Judaeo-Arabic texts were written in dialects that varied according to the influence of each vernacular on the Arabic language. For instance, there are even some linguistic features that are preserved in sub-groups in one country that are distinct from other vernaculars, e.g. the Arabic dialect spoken by Jews of ʻAqra and Arbīl (Jastrow 1990).

In general, the topics of Judaeo-Arabic texts in the Middle Ages were associated with religious elements. The most important literary variety in the history of written Judaeo-Arabic is the so-called *sharḥ* (pl. *shrūḥ*), which refers to the interpretation of sacred and liturgical texts by means of the Arabic language (in Judaeo-Arabic). These texts include the Bible, the Midrash, the Siddur and the Talmud. The term *sharḥ* used in Judaeo-Arabic literature was a sort of translation with a mode of interpretation for more straightforward understanding: *sharḥ* is a typical liturgical trait in Judaeo-Arabic literature, and it was used to introduce Judaic texts in Judaeo-Arabic form in a more simple for non-specialised scholars of Jewish religious studies. The fund of knowledge among Arab scholars during the Middle Ages, aside from religious and liturgical scholarship, was principally associated with philosophy and science. This was reflected in many Judaeo-Arabic texts which were written by Jews or copied from Islamic sources (Blau 1981: 36–7).

The emergence of the modern Judaeo-Arabic texts can be seen from the fifteenth century onwards. Judaeo-Arabic began to take on a new form of literary genre in the Jewish cycles during the late nineteenth and early twentieth centuries – for example, the appearance of Jewish newspapers and periodicals written in Judaeo-Arabic in North African lands and the Middle East (Stillman 2005: 49).[4] The activity of Judaeo-Arabic journalism spread over North African countries, Iraq and India. The subjects covered by these periodicals were varied, including Jewish life, the translation of European and modern Hebrew language and even entertainment (Chetrit 2003: 130).

As to fiction, these periodicals were the main source for publishing fiction in Judaeo-Arabic. The newspaper *Beth Israel* (the House of Israel) served as a channel which contributed to publishing diverse fictional works for a Judaeo-Arabic readership in Algiers during the 1890s, including Jewish and European novels (Chetrit 2003: 130). The activity of writing original literary works, mainly fiction, developed primarily in Tunisia. The development and the emergence of local secular literature written in Judaeo-Arabic in Tunisia, especially in northern Tunisia, resulted mainly from the influence of European literary works translated into Arabic (Tobi 2014). Writers such as Eliezer Farhi, Chalom Flah, Sameh Levi and Jacob Cohen contributed to Judaeo-Arabic literature by writing original fiction and poetry in Arabic written in Hebrew script.

The history of Judaeo-Arabic came dramatically to an end during the 1950s. This was because of the mass immigration of Jews from Arab lands shortly before and during the creation of the State of Israel. Arab Jews, accordingly, had to adopt modern Hebrew in Israel and to shift from other languages associated with the diaspora. Only a few groups in Tunisia and Morocco still use Judaeo-Arabic up to the present time (Hary 2009: 48).

1.3 Iraqi Judaeo-Arabic

The history of Judaeo-Arabic in Iraq cannot be studied in isolation from the map of Judaeo-Arabic in North African lands, Andalusia and old Babylon. What is essential for the present study is to focus in depth on the linguistic features of Iraqi Judaeo-Arabic as well as the literary contributions of Jews writing in Iraqi Judaeo-Arabic in modern times up until the mass emigration of the Iraqi Jews to Israel. In the following, the study presents a brief history of literary contributions written in Judaeo-Arabic in Iraq, followed by some general linguistic features of spoken Iraqi Judaeo-Arabic in modern times. Both Iraqi Jewish literature written in Judaeo-Arabic and the description of linguistic features of Iraqi Judaeo-Arabic are important for illuminating the literary, historical and linguistic aspects significant for the present investigation.

1.3.1 Literature Written in Iraqi Judaeo-Arabic

Iraq was one of the important rabbinic learning centres in the Middle Ages; an assertion that Arabic was totally adopted by the Jews living in Iraq in this period reveals the linguistic fact that the Jews shared Arabic with other inhabitants in Babylon (Ben-Shammai 1997: 16). Similar to other parts in the Middle East during the medieval period, the themes used in Iraqi Judaeo-Arabic texts at the time were mainly associated with religious topics, e.g. the translation and the interpretation of the Bible and other sacred texts using Judaeo-Arabic, as well as liturgical texts of Jewish events, such as the Passover *Haggada* (Avishur 1979: 84).

One significant contribution in the history of Iraqi Judaeo-Arabic is the literature of Sa'adya Ga'on[5] (882–942 CE), who is famous for the translation of the Pentateuch into Judaeo-Arabic. The works of Sa'adya Ga'on were diverse, although many of those known are incomplete, exist solely in fragments, or are non-extant but have been referred to through quotations in other works by later writers (Malter 1921: 137). His works also cover many fields of knowledge, including, as Malter (1921: 137) recounts: 'Hebrew philology, Liturgy, Halacha, Calendar and Chronology, Philosophy, and Polemics'.

As for the literary contributions of Iraqi Jews in modern times, the majority of Jewish writers, for instance, preferred to compose poetry and fiction in Modern Standard Arabic (Snir 2005a: 79–134). However, Jewish folklore writings flourished and were written in Iraqi Judaeo-Arabic from the mid-nineteenth century. The folklore literature of Judaeo-Arabic written by Iraqi Jews can be divided into three categories: (1) translations and copies from Jewish sources, (2) translations and copies from foreign sources, and (3) local folklore written by Iraqi Jews themselves (Avishur 1979: 84–6).

The Iraqi Judaeo-Arabic variety was also employed in literary works written in Arabic script by Iraqi Jews; the Arabic novels and short stories written in Israel by Samir Naqqāsh (b. Baghdad, 1938–2004), for instance, are full of complete paragraphs written in Judaeo-Arabic. Hebrew words are inserted here and there in the novels in Arabic script, and glossing in the footnotes for such words or/ and sentences is provided by Naqqāsh.[6]

Judaeo-Arabic periodicals which appeared in Iraq in the nineteenth century can be considered among the late literary contributions of Iraqi Jews to Judaeo-Arabic before their mass immigration to Israel during the 1950s. With the emergence of the printing industry in the nineteenth century there were more than fifteen printing presses in Iraq between 1850 and 1950 that offered publications on a range of various topics related to Jewish life in Iraq (Al-Maʿadīdi 2001: 31–7).

1.3.2 The Linguistic Features of Iraqi Judaeo-Arabic: General Remarks

In general, the Iraqi Judaeo-Arabic dialect was spoken mainly by Jews at home in Iraq. This vernacular was different, in terms of some phonological and lexical aspects, from other Arabic dialects spoken by both Muslims and Christians in Iraq (Blanc 1964). These distinctions are shaped mainly by the influence of classical Arabic on the vernacular spoken by Jews, as well as the use of Hebrew and Aramaic lexical items (Simon et al. 2003: 358–9). Blanc (1964) concluded with an important historical aspect of the three main dialects spoken in Iraq by Jews, Muslims and Christians. Comparing the two main dialects spoken in the Mesopotamian area – *qeltu* dialects and *gelet* dialects[7] – he pointed out that Muslims communicated in the newer, more rural *gelet* dialects, while Jewish-Christians spoke in the older, metropolitan *qeltu* dialects.

With reference to consonants, the Judaeo-Arabic spoken in Iraq shared almost the same consonants of Arabic dialects spoken by both Muslims and Christians (Blanc 1964: 17). Yet the way in which such consonants are connected to short vowels was not the same in the three main dialects spoken in Iraq by Muslims, Jews and Christians (Blanc 1964: 31). Blanc (1964: 31) claimed that: 'In M (Muslim dialect. MA) […] the /e/ has allophones clustering about a higher, more forward position than the /e/ of JC (Jewish and Christian Arabic dialects, M.A).' One should add here the different accent and pronunciation of Iraqi Judaeo-Arabic according to the geographical locations, e.g. Baghdadi Jews, Mosul, ʿAqra and Arbīl (Jastrow 1990).

From a phonological comparison between classical Arabic, the Arabic dialect of Iraqi Jews and the Arabic dialect of both Muslim and Christians, one can sum up by saying that the Arabic dialect spoken by Jews in Iraq was much closer to classical Arabic than the other two dialects spoken by Muslims and Christians (Blanc 1964: 20; Mansour 1991: 26–32).

Iraqi Judaeo-Arabic is famous for the pronunciation of the Arabic consonant /r/, which is pronounced as /ġ/, different from any other Arabic dialect spoken in Iraq (Mansour 1991: 29–32). Blanc (1964: 23–5) asserts that the use of /r/ and /ġ/ has a long history in the Iraqi Judaeo-Arabic paradigm and was associated with the way the *Tanakh* (Hebrew Bible) was read by Iraqi Jews; he noted that the /r/ sound, according to Saʿadya Ga'on, had two types of pronunciation (together with the b, g, d, k, p and t) – one is soft and the other is hard.

Another comparison between some Arabic consonants that were spoken by Jews in Baghdad is the pronunciation of /q/ *and* /k/. The Jewish pronunciation of these consonants is quite close to classical Arabic. On the other hand, they are not pronounced in the same way by Muslims and Christians (Blanc 1964: 26).

In the realm of syntax, Iraqi Judaeo-Arabic shares linguistic elements concerning syntactic structure from Mishnaic Hebrew. Linguistic elements not only from Aramaic and Hebrew are employed in Iraqi Judaeo-Arabic; there are also Persian and Turkish elements that contribute to the lexical and syntactic constructions of Iraqi Judaeo-Arabic (Mansour 1991: 25–50).

In respect to lexicography, the use of some Hebrew lexical items in the Iraqi Judaeo-Arabic is not determined exclusively by religious discourse; rather there are also secular uses of Hebrew elements: for instance, the use of *mazzal* [luck] and *sakkana* [danger], among others, in Judaeo-Arabic spoken by Iraqi Jews (Mansour 1991: 49).

After exploring the history and some linguistic and literary aspects of the phenomenon of Arabic/Hebrew in one text, which is associated with and relevant to the Judaeo-Arabic paradigm, it is necessary to look at another form of such phenomena in modern times, namely the use of Arabic or/and Judaeo-Arabic in modern Hebrew fiction written by Iraqi Jews who emigrated from Iraq to Israel.

1.4 Iraqi Jewish Novelists: From Arabic to Hebrew

> Among the Iraqi Jews who came to Israel were writers who had begun their literary careers in Iraq and had written in Arabic. Now, in Israel, they had to choose whether to continue to write in Arabic or to brave the transition to Hebrew [...] Those who decided to continue writing had to adapt the new language or remain in exile, using their native tongue in a 'foreign' environment. (Berg 1996: 43)

This quotation reflects the bitter fate the Iraqi Jewish authors may have faced after their emigration to Israel during the 1950s. One of the reasons underlying the decision to write in Hebrew or to continue writing in Arabic was, according to Berg (1996: 65–6), the socio-political backgrounds of those writers in Iraq before emigration to Israel. Berg claims that the authors who had a secular and communist background, for instance Sami Michael, Shimon Ballas and Nasim Fatal, adapted Hebrew as their literary and spoken language. On the other hand, authors from more traditional and isolated backgrounds preserved their Arabic mother tongue in Israel for literary contributions.

To discover more about the ensemble of motivations present beyond the transition to Hebrew, the study of the autobiographies of the three authors Sami Michael (b. Baghdad, 1926), Shimon Ballas (b. Baghdad, 1930) and Eli Amir (b. Baghdad, 1937) – focusing on issues such as language, emigration and their early engagements with Hebrew in Israel – is important.

These three Iraqi Jewish authors share some essential features. First, they all immigrated to Israel from Iraq, where Arabic was their mother tongue and they were a part of Arab life and culture, although Iraqi Jews of that generation also had some knowledge in Hebrew from Jewish schools in Baghdad. In Berg's words: 'The Iraqi Jews were traditionally well educated in Arabic and Arab culture, as reflected in their important contributions to the development of modern Iraqi literature before their exodus' (1996: xv). Second, they belong to the first generation of Jews who departed or were forced by political circumstance to emigrate from Iraq and find refuge in Israel. It may be easily claimed that the members of this generation had to reconstruct their life in a country that was new and in many quite essential ways foreign to them. Third, their writing is mainly autobiographical, and through it they try to come to terms with their past and their present, with Arabic and Hebrew, with the purpose of finding a bridge between the two.

In the aftermath of the mass migration of Jews from Arab lands to Israel after 1948, the Israeli regime decided to deal with new immigrants in two different ways: absorption and blending the exiles (Stahl 1979: 361). Regarding the former strategy, the government at the time took responsibility for providing all the necessities of life for the newly arrived immigrants, including housing, food supplies and work opportunities. The 'blending' process, on the other hand, was based on the model of the melting pot, in which the various cultural attachments of the new immigrants coming from different cultures and communities were united into one entity which would produce a new Israeli culture, albeit somewhat based on Ashkenazi European culture (Stahl 1979: 361–2). The general attitude among the Israelis in power at the time towards the *Mizrahim* (Oriental Jews) and other new immigrant Jews from different cultural backgrounds was to try to integrate them into their new Israeli lifestyle. The clash between the Mizrahi Jews who emigrated to Israel between the 1950s and 1960s and the local culture that had emerged in Israel by this time resulted in the Mizrahim being somewhat forced to join the new Israeli culture influenced by the elite Ashkenazi European stratum (Yaar and Shavit 2003: 873). This clash, accordingly, created a sort of struggle for identity and belonging among many first-generation Mizrahi Jews.

Despite the strong tendency to force the Mizrahim, including Iraqi Jews, to forget their cultural heritage and adopt the new Israeli cultural identity by means of a melting pot strategy, the plan did not entirely succeed; rather: 'Over the years, it gradually became clear that ethnic groups do not lose their identity in the span of a few years and that pressure to change often causes resistance' (Stahl 1979: 362). One such example can be seen in the protests of second-generation Mizrahi Jews against the Israeli discrimination policy in *Wādī Ṣalīb*, resulting in the establishment of the political movement *Ha-panterim ha-shehorim* (The Black Panthers) in 1971.

Indeed, many Mizrahi Jews have tried to maintain their oriental origins. During the 1980s, for instance, they started searching for their cultural heritage and began to consider their culture as equal, at the very least, to the Western culture adopted by the Ashkenazi Jews (Elazar 1989: 192).

According to Bensky et al. (1991: 40), the first generation of Iraqi Jews belongs to the generation that consists of all the immigrants to Israel during the period of mass migration (1948–51). As the three Iraqi Jewish authors belong to this first generation of Iraqi Jews in Israel, it is important to look at their socio-political background in Israel.

In general, Iraqi Jews preserved their cultural heritage in Iraq over the years and remained integrated within Iraqi society. They used the Arabic vernacular, followed Iraqi customs and traditions and even used Arabic in their religious rituals (Shiblak 2005: 34). Arabic, then, was a major factor in shaping the cultural identity of the Iraqi Jews, all of which would indicate that first-generation Iraqi Jews were greatly integrated into Arabic culture and its traditions greatly influenced them before migrating to Israel. As if to confirm the importance of the Arabic preserved by the first generation of the Mizrahim, their language continued to occupy a position, albeit not a great one, in the literature written after their emigration to Israel. Although Arabic was the 'language of the enemy' in the eyes of many Israelis, some first-generation Iraqi authors continued writing in Arabic after migrating to Israel until their death, including Samir Naqqāsh (1938–2004) and Ishac Bar Moshe (1927–2003) (Snir 2005a: 104).

The first generation of Iraqi Jews in Israel expressed their adherence to their cultural heritage. To give just one example, in the 1970s a group emerged among the intellectuals and elites of Iraqi Jews that laid the foundation of the Babylonian Jewry Heritage Centre.[8] One of the main goals of this centre was to gather and preserve the cultural heritage of Iraqi Jews. In addition, Mizrahi Jews in general (including Iraqis) managed to keep in touch with Arabic cultural ties. For example, they were keen to listen to Arab music and singers on the radio. Umm Kulthum, an Egyptian singer who gained widespread fame in the Middle East, was one of the favourite Arab singers for Mizrahi Jews. Moreover, with the spread of television in the early 1970s, Iraqi Jews were able to watch Arab movies and television at home (Shohat 1999: 16). Therefore, one can easily say that first-generation Iraqi Jews were greatly attached to their Arabic language and culture.

1.4.1 Shimon Ballas: *Adīb Al-Qaṣṣ*

Shimon Ballas was born on 6 March 1930 (Kressel 1965–7: 254) into a small Iraqi Jewish family in Baghdad and lived with two elder brothers and sisters (Hever et al. 2002: 298). From childhood, Ballas showed an interest in writing; he was keen on writing down every story he listened to at home (Alcalay 1996: 62–3). The first short story written by Ballas was in Arabic in Baghdad and has the title 'al-Qatl al-Ghāmiḍ"' ('The Mysterious Murder'), a kind of detective story. Unfortunately, this literary piece, among others, was burned by Ballas shortly before his emigration to Israel (Ballas 2005).

Ballas was brought up in a middle-class family that lived in the Christian quarter of Baghdad. Ballas studied at the Alliance Israélite Universelle school in Baghdad, which awakened dreams within him of studying in France. However, despite being included on the list of Iraqi students accepted by the Sorbonne for graduate studies, he did not go because, at the same time, Ballas had put his name on another list, that of the many Iraqi Jews who wanted to emigrate to Israel (Ballas 2009: 42). Some twenty years, Ballas received his PhD from the Sorbonne,[9] having gone to Paris from Israel (Alcalay 1996: 66–7).[10] Childhood and adolescence in Iraq, immigration to Israel and the years of studying and living in France all influenced Ballas's literature; Iraq, Israel and France are represented in his many characters of those nationalities in his literary works.[11]

During his early years in Israel, Ballas was very attached to his Iraqi identity, trying to keep up his belonging to cultural identity, including language: 'I have really kept my roots up, and in my early years in Israel there was no any doubt in my heart that Arabic will continue to be the language of my writings' (Ballas 2009: 43–4). As for the shift to Hebrew, the need for it was essential for Ballas to integrate into the Israeli community upon immigration. Ballas started to learn Hebrew through reading journals with the help of a dictionary as well as by means of language practice with the local Israeli speakers.[12] He even began to mimic the Ashkenazi pronunciation. But he regretted this and managed to use only the Mizrahi pronunciation later on (Ballas 2009: 43).

A Hebrew article written by '*Adīb al-Qaṣṣ*'[13] (The Novelist) appeared in the Hebrew communist journal *Kol ha-'am* in February 1955. This article, which introduced Jamāl al-Dīn al-Afghānī (1838–97) to an Israeli readership, was the first step taken by Ballas in his literary career in the new land. Using the pen name *Adīb al-Qaṣṣ*, Ballas introduced himself in Hebrew for the first time. At the time, discussions about writing in Hebrew were taking place in the 'Club of Friends of Arabic Literature in Israel', where debates about the decision to shift to writing in Hebrew were common. *Adīb al-Qaṣṣ*, or Shimon Ballas, was one of the members of this group, which also included Sasson Somekh (b. Baghdad, 1933) and David Semah (b. Baghdad, 1934–1997). The members of this group gathered regularly and discussed, among other things, the future and potential of Arabic language and literature versus Hebrew (Ballas 2009: 44–6).

The debate as to which language the new immigrants should adopt as their literary language developed during the meetings of the club members. Many members strongly believed that they should write only in Hebrew, while others, including Shimon Ballas and David Semah, opposed this idea, arguing on behalf of maintaining their mother tongue (Ballas 2009: 45).

1.4.2 Sami Michael: 'Saleh Menashe' or 'Samir Marid'?

Saleh Menashe (Sami Michael)[14] was born in Baghdad on 15 August 1926. Shortly After his arrival in Israel, he continued to write in Arabic under the Arabic name Samir Marid. Finally, Sami Michael was the name he used in publishing as a Hebrew writer in Israel. Michael uses all of these names, and every name represents a transitional stage in his life.

Under the Arabic title '*ḥarīq*' [fire], Samir Marid started his literary career in Arabic in Israel through the communist monthly journal *al-Jadīd*. The chapter appeared in December 1954 in Arabic and served as a starting point for writing his first Hebrew novel twenty years later as Samir Marid (the pen name of Sami Michael).[15] In this way, Michael continued his political activity as a communist in Israel. Michael was able to escape from Iraq to Iran in 1948 because of his activity against the Iraqi regime by joining an underground group in 1939 (Kerbel et al. 2003: 373). He was able to continue his political activity when he emigrated to Israel in 1949 by joining the Israeli Communist Party. As a native Arabic speaker, Michael worked on the editorial board responsible for the party journal *al-Jadīd* (Abramson 2005: 578–9).

Discussing his early years of acquiring Hebrew and adapting to the new culture, Michael (1984: 28) says: 'I shall never forget my first years in Israel when I continued to read the world's literature in English, spoke broken Hebrew on the street, and bemoaned my fate, silently, in Arabic'. The shift to speaking and thinking in another language, as well as his departure for a new country, constituted hardships for Michael. The first twenty years of Michael's life in Israel prevented him, as he claims, from investing his best years as a young man to becoming a famous writer. In the twenty years after his emigration to Israel, Michael worked in the Israel Hydrology Service in the Ministry of Agriculture.[16] However, he also praises these years of transition from Arabic to Hebrew, from Iraq to Israel: "As a writer, I think that the transition from one country to another and from one language to another has robbed me of a few good years of creativity. But it was worth it" (Michael 1984: 33).

The starting point for Michael as a writer, therefore, was to write in Arabic. In addition to his first chapter entitled *ḥarīq* [fire] published in *al-Jadīd*, Michael was preparing a novel in Arabic about the transit camp that was completed in 1950 under the title 'The city of dusters', but this manuscript has not been published.[17]

Michael preferred to study Arabic; he graduated from Haifa University where he chose to study Arabic literature. In the twenty years before publishing his first Hebrew novel *Shavim ṿe-shavim yoter* [All Men are Equal – But Some are More] (1974), Michael experienced a transition period marked by a situation of negotiations and reformation. This position led Michael, who knew very little Hebrew on his arrival in Israel (Berg 1996: 51), to choose Hebrew as his literary language (Snir 2005a: 318). For Michael, the decision to switch to Hebrew was the 'the real immigration to Israel' (Michael 1984: 50) after living for many years with the feeling of being a 'tourist who stays on for a while' (Michael 1984: 50) or a traveller who considers Israel as a 'temporary refuge that can be replaced by another refuge at any time' (Michael 1984: 50). Recently, the author declared that he is writing neither for Israeli nor for Haifa readers. Instead, he writes only for the humanity inside himself (Lachmanovitz 2011).

1.4.3 Eli Amir: *Ibn-'Arab*

> From time immemorial, even during my childhood in Baghdad, I have learnt from my parents and my family, from my teachers and my childhood's heroes that there is a possibility to create a synthesis between the two cultures where I grew up.' (Amir 2006: 109)

Iraq and Israel are the two cultures mentioned in the above quotation. For Amir, there should be an example of a potential co-existence between Arabic and Hebrew and between Iraq and Israel. *Ibn-'Arab* (or, the 'son of Arab culture'), is the first protagonist Amir introduced to modern Hebrew fiction as such an example. These two cultures constitute the background from which Amir developed his protagonist, Nuri, in his first Hebrew novel *Tarnegol kapparot* [Scapegoat] (1983). This is also the example to which Amir himself claimed to aspire (Amir 2006).

Ibn-'Arab is the reflection of using two languages and is also the attempt to find harmony between two different cultures. Amir, unlike Ballas and Michael, started to write only in Hebrew, even though he preferred to study Arabic language and literature at the Hebrew University in Jerusalem (Kerbel et al. 2003: 42).

Eli Amir is the youngest author among the three Iraqis. He was born in Baghdad in 1937, and he arrived in Israel when he was only thirteen years old (Kerbel et al. 2003: 42). About twenty years later,[18] Amir's own experience in the *ma'abara*[19] during the 1950s and his move to the kibbutz is tapped as experience in Amir's first and famous novel (1983). The motif of *Ibn-'Arab* is widely portrayed through the Iraqi-Israeli protagonist, Nuri.

Amir was able to integrate rapidly into Israeli society because of his Zionist activities; he was active, for instance, as a journalist writing in Hebrew for the journal *Bma'arakha*[20] during the 1970s in which he wrote about issues related to emigration to Israel and the question of the absorption of the new immigrants. During the mid-1970s, Amir served as the delegate of the Sephardic division in the US (Snir 2005a: 337). Amir was also employed in the ministry of absorption, where he was responsible for young people. Accordingly, the Zionist narrative is employed to a greater degree in Amir's literary works in comparison to those of both Ballas and Michael.[21]

1.5 The Novels

The following sections summarise the nine Hebrew novels selected for this study.

1.5.1 Scapegoat – Eli Amir (1983)

Tarnegol kapparot is the first published Hebrew novel by Eli Amir.[22] The novel describes the meeting between East and West as seen by Nuri, the fresh, new, Iraqi adult immigrant who experienced the absorption process during the period of mass immigration of Jews from Arab lands to Israel. Nuri is torn between his Iraqi cultural belonging and the new culture based on European model that he finds in Israel, especially in the kibbutz paradigm. In many places in the novel, Nuri asks questions about identity, belonging, secularism and religion. He is also portrayed by Ami as a model of successful absorption of new immigrant youth to Israel, despite all these conflicts between the world from which he came, i.e. Iraq, and the new Israeli lifestyle.

As a recent immigrant from Iraq, Nuri describes his experiences in the first person. He leaves the transit camp for a kibbutz for young people called 'Ahuza', where he meets Buzaglo, a Moroccan boy. Mothers from the *ma'abara* visit their children in the kibbutz. At the gate of the kibbutz, the doorman does not allow the mothers to enter, but Reuven, one of Nuri's colleagues, strikes the doorman. In response, the doorman calls him 'Asian dirt'. Olga, one of the members in the kibbutz and very beloved by Nuri and his friends, comes to see what the fuss is about. She is angry with the guard for not letting the mothers go inside the kibbutz to see their children; she allows them to enter the kibbutz and offers them coffee and cookies. Olga is an Auschwitz survivor, her entire family perished in the Holocaust. Nuri and his friends, Buzaglo, Reuven, Masul and Bar-Olam, were able to leave the kibbutz after passing an interview, moving to another kibbutz 'Kiryat Ornim'. The narrator describes the scene of leave-taking between Olga and the five friends with a sense of gloom.

Life in the new kibbutz was entirely different from life in the *ma'abara*. Nuri and his friends find it difficult to adopt the new lifestyle of the new place, and they must work. As the narrator puts it, they had no work in Iraq; rather, some servants did menial jobs for them. However, they start to work in farming. The narrator describes the first meeting of Nuri and his friends with the kibbutz; one of them asks where he can find a synagogue. The answer is: 'There is no synagogue here!' Ofer, the man responsible for Nuri and his friends as newcomers to the kibbutz, tries to change their names to Hebrew. However, when he wants to give Nuri the name *Nimrod*, Nuri refuses to change his name. Nuri also rejects the work in farming and decides to work in collecting garbage. Nuri lies to his father and sends him a letter, in which he writes that he works as a mechanic in the kibbutz. The first meeting between Nuri and his Mizrahi friends with the *tsabarim* (the locals) in the kibbutz ends in disappointment. Yet Nuri and his friends from Arab lands do seriously want to get closer to the local young men and women in the kibbutz as well as to adapt to the new community.

Nuri and his friends find another way to express their belonging to an oriental culture in the kibbutz – through oriental music, which is opposed by some of the locals. The conflict between East and West in this part of the novel reaches its peak of intensity. Nuri is lost between the two cultures and the two types of music. On the one hand, he wants to adopt the Western music in order to be like the Ashkenazi Jews, on the other hand he cannot stop listening to the oriental music *'ūd* played by Masul, one of Nuri's friends who is also of Iraqi origin. This confusion leads Nuri to think of leaving the kibbutz for the *ma'abara* and then for Baghdad.

Eli Amir wants to tell him that although there is a conflict between the Mizrahim and Ashkenazim, the relationships of love have created another dimension in the relations between the two sides, and Nuri falls in love with Nitza, an Ashkenazi girl. This is also what happened with Nilli and Masul. The relationship of love between Ashkenazi and Mizrahi Jews results in cultural conflict, as is the case with Nilli the Iraqi girl, in love with Zvika the Ashkenazi. Nilli is pregnant, and she shares with Nuri her feelings of fear if her parents learn about her relationship with Zvika outside of marriage. In order to save Nilli from being rejected by her parents, Nuri and Sonia go to Nilli's parents in the *ma'abara* and explain the situation. Nilli's parents, who were so angry at the beginning, accept the marriage at the end. Nilli marries Zvika and gives birth to a boy.

There is also another plot in the novel that expresses the conflict between oriental and Western culture: Nuri is sent by the kibbutz to teach in the *ma'abara*, where he meets Yehuda and Salima, his old neighbours in Iraq before his immigration to Israel. Nuri takes the initiative and starts talking to them in Arabic about their demands. The people in the transit camp are against girls dressed in shorts, and they demand separation between boys and girls. Nuri promises to respect their demands.

The novel ends with an open question. Nuri pays a visit to his family in the *ma'abara*, where his parents, brothers and sisters hug him when he arrives. His mother tells him that in two days it will be *Yom Kippur* and she does not know where she can get a chicken as a ritual scapegoat. Nuri tells her that he bought one with him. However, his mother and father refuse the chicken because it is from the kibbutz and they get rid of it. Nuri asks his mother to make him a cup of Iraqi tea, and he feels an intense longing for Iraq. At this point the narrator leaves the reader with the unanswered question that Nuri asks himself: will he go back to the kibbutz or stay with his religious family?

1.5.2 All Men are Equal – But Some are More – Sami Michael (1974)

The novel *Shavim ve-shavim yoter* includes two kind of narratives. The first provides for a short scene at the beginning of each chapter in the novel, which begins with a specific time and date covering four days during the June 1967 Six-Day War. The narrator tells the story of David (the main character and the narrator), an Israeli soldier participating in the war. David has been wounded and should shed his Israeli IDF uniform and speak Arabic in order not to be killed by the Egyptian soldiers. The other narrative strategy used in the novel is a flashback story, which extends over some sixteen years, telling the story of David, his brother, his family and the failure of his marriage, from his teenage years to the time of the war in 1967 and later.

The novel also describes the experience of new Iraqi Jews immigrants in Israel, the experience of the *ma'abara* and the hardships the new immigrants encountered on their arrival in Israel during the 1950s. The novel sheds light on the feelings of some new Iraqi immigrants of being underestimated by both the Israeli government and the broader Israeli community. Michael portrays this feeling in angry words:

> 'We thought that', he said, 'we will come here as people who return home. Jews among Jews. One people. But this is not true. Someone divides people here into two. You may remember, in Iraq they bothered us, but we were not less than them! Here in Israel they do not oppress us, thanks to God. But before we arrived, they had already determined a certain level for us, a second class.' (1974: 25)

The narrator tells the story of David, the Iraqi teenager, who is in a relationship with Madeleine, an Iraqi girl, in one of the transit camps in Israel. Madeleine had asked David before their emigration to Israel, accompanied by their families, whether it is true that the girls in Israel have more freedom than in Iraq. This question of freedom induced the young Iraqi woman to give up her virginity to David in the *ma'abara*, and to work later as a prostitute and to be murdered mysteriously in the *ma'abara*. The appearance of Margalit was the reason for the change in David's relationship with Madeleine. Margalit, the girl with green eyes, loves David; she agrees to marry him in spite of his poverty as well as the total refusal by her mother to accept the relationship. David is a self-made man, he insists on completing his education to enrol in the university. The young couple faces some difficulties at the beginning of their marriage; their lack of money, of course, is among the most significant obstacles they must face.

The *badon* (canvas hut) of David's family burns down and most of his family members die, only David and his brother Shaul survive. This accident brings the two brothers closer together.

One very important scene in the novel is when David as a soldier sees action in the war and is wounded. He needs to shed his IDF uniform and speak in Arabic so as not to be identified as an Israeli and be killed by the Egyptian soldiers. The two narratives come together at the end of the novel to complete the portrait of David's world and character. He returns as a hero, the Mizrahi who was able to rescue his Ashkenazi colleagues and himself. On this occasion, his use of Arabic is the trump card; by dint of his skin colour and knowledge of Arabic he manages to fool the Egyptian soldiers in Sinai and survive. But in a bad situation, his knowledge of

Hebrew serves as the basis of his new identity, and he manages to stay alive before finally being rescued by Israeli soldiers. David crawls back to the Israeli lines, where the Israeli soldiers think that he is an enemy. When he is asked a second time to get off the road, David replies in Hebrew. Now the Israeli soldiers start to listen, to think, perhaps to compare his accent and his Hebrew style with their own. He is one of them, David is successful in proving his identity for the second time, with neither papers nor clothes, and once again he survives. Yet this time it is thanks to his use of Hebrew.

David was wounded in the war, but he returned as a hero. On his return he finds his wife Margalit waiting for him in a small apartment. After a lengthy discussion between the two, David agrees to move with his wife to her mother's house. The mother, who was upset over her daughter's marriage to David, makes life difficult for David and Margalit in her house, and this sparks the start of a breakdown in their relationship. The distrust between David and his wife gradually increases every time Mr Zidovitch, the manager in the bank at which Margalit works, calls Margalit. This feeling leads David to divorce his beloved Margalit, leaving her and his son Shai.

1.5.3 The Transit Camp – Shimon Ballas (1964)

"מקהא אל-נצר לצחיביהי שלמה חמרה":

'Shlomo Hamra's Victory Bar'

With the above Arabic sentence written in Hebrew script, the narrator begins his novel. This is the way in which Ballas begins his first writings in Hebrew, with the use of Arabic in Hebrew orthography, a symbolic hybrid. The narrator describes the daily life of Iraqi Jews, a group of new immigrants in *Oriya*, one of the transit camps in Israel during the 1950s. Yousef Shabi is the main character in the novel. Shabi and his family (his mother and his brother Said) emigrate from Iraq to Israel in the 1950s and find themselves in a transit camp.

The café shop *al-Naṣr* is the place where most of the Iraqi immigrants in the transit camp spend their time, making decisions, listening to Iraqi music on the radio, drinking Iraqi tea and of course speaking Arabic, their L1. *Al-Naṣr* is not just a place; rather it is a transfer point in time at which two places co-exist, a kind of 'third space', Iraq and Israel.

Al-Naṣr became a place where the members of the Iraqi group share their problems and dreams. The decision to protest to the government about their situation was reached there. The misery of life in the transit camp *Oriya*, which reaches a peak with the failure of Na'īm al-Khabāz's wife to give birth because of the unpaved streets which prevent the doctor from entering the camp, led the group to think about a solution to their terrible situation. They decided to elect a delegate to represent their problems and demands. The members of the group gathered at a meeting, at which Shabi gives a speech about the importance of making their silenced voice heard by the authorities. During the speech, the Israeli police terminate the meeting and arrest Shabi and others. After the release of Shabi and his friends from jail, the group chooses Ḥaim Va'ad as their representative.

The narrator also includes the story of Esther, who works as a babysitter for an Ashkenazi family. The lady of the house, Mrs Zoherman, advises her to learn Hebrew and promises her a good job if she can speak Hebrew well. Hebrew, according to the narrator, is not a problem for Esther alone, other characters also have their difficulties with the language. For instance, Selim wants to send a message to the newspaper that can help solve his job problems. He asks his wife Meriam in which language he should write. He knows no Hebrew at that point. Ḥaim Va'ad advises Selim to learn Hebrew because he thinks that this is the only way to get a job in Israel.

As an axis locus in space for the events in the story, the novel also ends in the café al-Naṣr. Shabi is watching the people in the café playing *Shīsh Bīsh* (an Arab game), laughing and drinking Iraqi tea. He feels that he belongs to and among them, to the world from which they came, he belongs to Iraq.

1.5.4 Farewell Baghdad – Eli Amir (1992)

As a young boy, Kābī, the narrator in the novel, experiences the events as an observer and also as a kind of hero trying to rescue his arrested uncle in Baghdad, from the perspective of chronological time and biographical narrative. In this novel, the narrator tells his family's story in Iraq just before their emigration to Israel, and describes the feelings of fear in his family and of worry of being persecuted by Muslims because of the conflict between Arabs and Israel during and after 1948–51 spilling over into Iraq. The narrator tells not only his family story but rather an ensemble of stories about Iraqi Jews.[23]

The novel begins with the arrest of Hizkel, Kābī's uncle, by the Iraqi police. He is accused of hiding weapons and of supporting the Zionist movement in Iraq. The narrator follows the story of the efforts by the Jewish family to have Hizkel released from prison.

Ms Silvia, the British Jewish teacher, has come to Baghdad to teach English language. Kābī is one of her students. In a tour around the city, the narrator describes the Baghdadi streets, people and foods through the eyes of the new teacher, accompanied by the communist Jew Sālim Imari

(Sālim Afandi). Sālim Afandi was also a teacher at the same school. He loved the dancer Bahia and was keen on attending all of her parties. At one party, at which the famous Egyptian singer Abdulmuttaleb is singing, Sheikh Gasem, one of Bahia's fans, knows that Sālim is a Jew. The Sheikh is about to kill Sālim Afandi, but the singer and the dancer entreat him not to.

The narrator tells his autobiographical story and goes back in time to his childhood. The co-existence between Jews and Muslims in Iraq during the *Farhud*, the outbreak of mob violence against Baghdad Jewry in early June 1941, is also represented in the novel that describes Kābī's childhood. Kābī remembers his old house in the Muslim quarter before leaving for another house in the Jewish quarter; he tells the story of Farha, the Muslim neighbour who protected and supported the Jewish family during the Farhud attacks against the Jews. The narrator also illustrates how this warm relationship between the two families changed after 1948. Ismail, the son of Farha and the close friend of Kābī and his half-brother for ten years, has a fight with Kābī. In a short, unplanned visit to the area around the house of his childhood, Kābī describes his feelings of disappointment about what happened between Jews and Muslims: both sides were driven to madness, he claimed.

The main event in the novel is the rescue of Hizkel from prison. Rachel, Hizkel's wife, does her best to find a solution in order to obtain news about her imprisoned husband, but to no avail, until the Muslim lawyer Karīm ʻAbd al-Ḥaq tells her that Hizkel is still alive in the main prison in Baghdad. Kābī is the hero in this scene; he endangers himself by going to the prison to see his uncle, and by working as an intermediary and messenger between him and the family later on. Kābī's father goes to see Amari, his cousin, who is a wealthy man and has close contacts with the Iraqi power structure at the time. He asks him to help his cousin, Hizkel, who is rescued from being sentenced to death, not because of Amari, but rather because of the singer Salma Basha, who loves his brother – who is Kābī's father.

Edward, *Mafriaḥ ha-yonim* ('the dove flyer'), does not support the idea of emigration to Israel, he wants to become a rich man, and to send his daughter Amira to study in the US. Sālim Afandi becomes depressed after the murder of the communist leader in Baghdad, and also is upset because his beloved Bahia travels to Egypt with the Egyptian singer Abdulmuttaleb. These circumstances open the door for Ms Silvia, who falls in love with Sālim Afandi.

Salman Amari (Abu Kābī) dreams of emigrating to Israel. The Iraqi government announces a law whereupon Iraqi Jews are allowed to leave

Iraq for Israel on the condition of renouncing their Iraqi citizenship forever. Abu Kābī discusses the emigration issue with his wife, who is against the idea of going to Israel. After a period of waiting for some news from Israel, Kābī and his father celebrate the arrival of the first plane to transfer Jews from Iraq to Israel. Sālim Afandi, the communist, manages to escape from the Iraqi police. He is smuggled first to Iran, and then, with the help of the Zionist movement, on to Israel.

Amira, *Mafriaḥ ha-yonim*'s daughter, escapes to Israel instead of to the US, her father is angry and intends to kill the Zionist Abu Saleh, as Abu Edward thinks that the Zionist helped his daughter to leave for Israel. The narrator describes the immigration process of the Iraqi Jews to Israel, and how the new inhabitants bought their houses, which once belonged to the Arab refugees. Rachel refuses to go to Israel with Abu Kābī; she wants to wait for her imprisoned husband to be released. Abu Saleh is hanged instead of Hizkel, after a great store of weapons is discovered in the basement of his house, and he is revealed to be a Zionist activist in Iraq.

The narrator then tells the story of the first meeting of Kābī's family with Israel in the transit camp. Abed, who was their servant in Baghdad, welcomes them and provides them with a tent, beds and food. Abed was one of those smuggled together with Sālim Afandi from Iraq to Israel via Iran. Sālim Afandi joins the Communist Party in Israel and becomes one of its magazine's writers.

The novel's conclusion is open-ended. Abu Kābī goes to ask the man in charge of the transit camp to help get his brother Hizkel out of prison in Iraq. The man in charge tells him that he has no way to help Hizkel. Abu Kābī asks him to think about a project of cultivating rice in Israel, but the man in charge disappoints Abu Kābī, informing him that the swamp where Abu Kābī wishes to cultivate rice is to be used to build Jewish settlements. The next day, Abu Kābī goes to the swamp and the workers there save his live. On his return home, his wife gives birth to a boy.

1.5.5 Victoria – Sami Michael (1993)

Victoria is the main character of this novel, and the novel takes her name as its title. She is the central character through whose eyes we see the events. The narrator adopts a point of view that almost matches the first-person narration. The reader borrows the eyes of Victoria, her feelings and thoughts, in order to have insight into the extended history of an Iraqi Jewish family, including the grandmother (Michal), her three sons (Azury, Yehuda and Elyahu), and dozens of grandchildren who all live in an old mansion in the Jewish neighbourhood of Baghdad at the beginning of the last century.

The narrator starts the novel describing an interesting scene with Victoria, a woman dressed in a traditional black ‘*abāye* long gown, who is thinking of jumping down into the river when walking on the bridge over the Tigris in Baghdad. This is used as a point of departure to narrate the story sequences that have brought Victoria to this point in time and place, using flashback narrative. The narrator then tries to tell us her story, or the story of the house she left a few hours before. He also provides us with the story of the characters and their lives, in which the events slowly unfold to complete the story.

The narrator tells the love story of Victoria and Rafael, who grew up together in the mansion in Baghdad. Miriam, Victoria and Toya are relatives. Toya is a young girl married to the older man Ehud. Rafael is the son of Eliyahu and Hanina. Miriam wants to marry Rafael, whom Victoria also loves. The narrator tries to illustrate how Miriam and Victoria both desire to win Rafael as their husband, and how the circumstances play out in favour of Victoria.

The narrator also relates how nine men from the Jewish family were hiding from the Turkmen in a hole in the house in order to escape from military service during the war. During the war, Rafael decided to move to Basra; he took his family in a horse-drawn carriage despite Najiya’s opposition to that decision. The narrator continues to describe the sad situation of the men in hiding; the ceiling of the house was about to collapse upon them and kill them. The sadness in the novel’s tale peaks with the death of the grandmother, Michal.

Rafael promises to become engaged to Miriam when he returns from Basra, but she is preparing to get engaged to someone else. During a visit from the family’s groom, Azury announces that the child, Barukh, is dying, so he asks the visitors to leave the house. Despite enormous efforts to save the baby, he dies. Then the neighbour Abd Allah Nonoh arrives to announce the defeat of the Turkmen and that the British are now taking control over the country. Miriam gets engaged. After the end of the war, Rafael returns to the Jewish house in Baghdad. Miriam is now married to Gorgy the locksmith. The way was then set for Victoria to win Rafael’s heart. The narrator compares the marriage of Miriam and Gorgy to that of Victoria and Rafael. Miriam was whipped by her husband, whereas Victoria was happy with Rafael. Gorgy then breaks Miriam’s leg. Rafael does not wait to finish his shower in the evening when told by his wife what has happened to Miriam; he goes to Miriam’s room to find her lying on her bed, with her parents sitting beside her. The conversation between the three is a shock to Rafael. Miriam’s father sends a message to Rafael in Basra telling him that he wants Rafael to marry his daughter. However, the message does not reach Rafael. He marries Victoria on his return, after which he finds out that Miriam is already married. Rafael and Victoria move to another apartment, where Rafael is struggling with his illness – tubercolosis – and he decides to leave Iraq for Lebanon to receive treatment there. Victoria returns to the big house once again with her two children Suzan and Calementine. Her mother does not welcome her and blames her for her choice of husband. Rafael leaves Victoria pregnant; she seeks an abortion but is unsuccessful in her attempts to arrange one. This depressing life – living with her hate-filled mother who wants Victoria to leave the house and refuses to help her with money in order to feed her children and to buy them warm winter clothing – brings Victoria to the point where she goes to jump into the Tigris to take her own life. The novel has come full circle. On her way back from the Bridge of Death, Victoria meets Ma'tuq Nono, who offers her a job in a small tobacco factory. He knows about her suffering in her mother's house so he advises her to rent a small room to get away from the family home. The next morning Suzan, Victoria's small daughter, dies. Victoria's mother Najiya is also pregnant. She visits her daughter at her newly rented room and asks her to return to the family home in order to serve her and the father, and she promises Victoria to give her money to take care of the baby soon to be born.

A messenger visited Victoria's house with news from Lebanon: Rafael is still alive and making progress, but still needs money to complete his treatment. The messenger is a guest of the family for two weeks. Victoria does her best to send money to her ill husband as Ezra, Rafael's brother, did. He gave Victoria all the money he had, and then asked people for more money to save his brother's life. With the help of Ezra, Victoria writes a message to her husband telling him that their baby Alber has been born. At this time, a messenger from the Zionist movement visits the family and discusses with them the idea of emigration to Israel.

Rafael comes back to Victoria. All the family members move to another house. Uncle Nissan rapes Calementine, a child of eight years, and threatens to kill her if she tells anyone. Calementine falls ill for many days and subsequently dies. After her death, only Alber and the little Linda are left for Victoria and Rafael.

The narrator continues to tell the story of Rafael at the age of ninety-two in a hospital in Israel, holding his wife's hand and looking silently through the window; when Victoria asks him why he is doing this, he answers after a while: 'I am afraid.' He then dies.

1.5.6 The Other One – Shimon Ballas (1991)

Ṿe-hu aḥer is based on the autobiography of Dr Aḥmad Nasīm Soussa (1900–82),[24] who was an Iraqi Jew who converted to Islam. Aharon Sawsan, the main character in the novel, is an Iraqi Jew born in 1902, the youngest of his three sisters and one brother. His father, Moshe Sawsan, sends him to a 'Talmud Torah' at the age of four to receive a religious education. One year later, he switches to the Alliance School where he learns French, Hebrew and Arabic. His mother loves him more than his brother and sisters. Many times his mother calms him down after his father has punished him for something. The elder brother, Robin, was close to his father. The father gives Robin significant responsibility at work as well as at home when the father is absent. Robin does not allow his little brother Aharon to play outside the house after school. The relationship between the two brothers is strained at the time, and after their father's death it becomes worse.

Aharon's father encourages him to get a good education, and sends him to Baghdad to learn at the Alliance School, and then to Beirut. The father dies in India while undergoing treatment. In Beirut, Aharon meets Jean, an American student who is studying there, and he falls in love with her. Now he thinks for the first time about converting to Islam; he wants to marry Jean, but Judaism does not allow him to do so. Therefore, he wishes to convert to Islam in order to marry her. But this is not what Aharon did. Instead, he finds a solution to his problem with the help of money.

Aharon, the narrator, marries Jean, and they move to the US together, but he is unable to live happily in the States. He decides to return to Iraq, and he convinces his wife to go with him. Jean is unable to adjust to the lifestyle in Baghdad and returns to the US. The relationship between the two continues; they stay in touch through correspondence. Later, Jean and Aharon divorce. Jean marries an American pilot. In a tragic accident, she and her husband are killed.

On 28 August 1930, Aharon publishes an article in an Arabic magazine calling on the Jewish people in Iraq to stand together with their Muslim and Christian friends against Zionism. Aharon is upset about the attitude of ʿAzīz Laḥḥām to him, who decries his call to encourage a holy war (jihad) against the Jews in Iraq. This is not the sole opposition expressed against Aharon. His close friend Asʿad Nasim visits him after the appearance of his article and tells him that he too disapproves of what Aharon wrote, claiming that Aharon has damaged and insulted the honour of Iraqi Jews.

The relationship between the two brothers, Aharon and Robin, continues to be strained. After the death of Jean, Robin sends many messages to his brother seeking reconciliation. Robin believes Jean's death might help to bring Aharon back to the family. However, Aharon does not wish for any reconciliation, given Robin's negative behaviour towards him.

After the death of Aharon's mother, the last hindrance between Aharon and conversion to Islam is removed. He travels to Cairo in 1936, where he announces his conversion to Islam on 7 November, and then takes a new Muslim name, Aḥmad Hārūn Sawsan.

After converting to Islam, the narrator feels that no one is paying any attention to his decision. Even his close friends, Kāzim and As'ad, have not read his book, *My Path to Islam*, which he wrote in Cairo after his conversion.

The narrator describes the meeting of the Academy of Arabic Language representatives, of which Aḥmad Hārūn is a member, with the new Iraqi president. He describes his attempts to get Zohair (a relative of Kāzim) out of prison. Zohair has been arrested by the Iraqi police because of his Uncle Kāzim's communist activities in Iraq against the new government. Kāzim, one of Aḥmad Hārūn's closest friends, was arrested more than once because of his political opposition until he went into exile abroad. He left Iraq for Europe before the war, travelling on to the Soviet Union. Zohair goes down the same path his Uncle Kāzim took; he studies law and is arrested several times because of his communist activities. The narrator remembers his feelings after the birth of his daughter Bothaina, the outcome of his Islamic marriage to Ḥamīda, and continues to talk about his satisfaction and happiness with Jean.

The narrator closes the novel with a conversation between him and his friend Kāzim. Kāzim did not condemn his friend who converted to Islam, but rather felt sorrow for him. The narrator compares the position of Aḥmad Hārūn to the religious mystery of the 'Other One',[25] where Aḥmad Hārūn is that Other One, that heretic.

1.5.7 What's Left – Eli Amir (2010a)

Ma she-nish'ar is the story of Daniel, fifty-six years old and a businessman receiving treatment in a cardiac hospital in Israel. Daniel, the narrator and the protagonist, relates his love story that occurred thirty years ago, narrating the tale in the first-person singular while lying in bed at the hospital. The narrator briefly points out his Iraqi origin. His father had to leave his Jewish education and find work to help ease his family's poverty. His father met his mother in one of the Iraqi markets, and they got married.

Daniel, who has been married to Nitza for twenty-eight years with no children, takes the opportunity of being alone almost all the time in the hospital to remember his first exciting love story. When Daniel was in his twenties, he met Abigail, a dentist who was in a relationship with an officer. Daniel was attracted to Abigail from the first look; she invited him to her house for dinner, and from that night on Daniel was unable to stop loving Abigail, despite her repeated attempts to put an end to the relationship. Daniel asks Abigail many times to end her relationship with the officer, Dobi, and to marry him. Abigail hesitates; having to decide between Dobi and Daniel is not easy for her. In the end, Abigail chooses Dobi.

Daniel marries Nitza, a social worker and the daughter of a man on the left in politics. Their life together is not harmonious. After Daniel recovers and returns home, the relationship between them becomes worse. Nitza leaves the house and asks for a lawyer, as does Daniel. Their relationship comes to an end, and they seek a divorce.

At the end of the novel, Daniel decides to see Abigail one last time. He searches for her and finds her private clinic. He waits for her until her clients have left. Abigail appears, looking much older. She invites him for lunch, and he agrees. She tells him about her daughters and grandchildren. Her husband Dobi is ill in hospital. Daniel asks only one question: 'Why did you leave me?' He does not get a direct answer to his question.

1.5.8 End of the Visit – Shimon Ballas (2008)

In *Tom ha-biḳur*, Jacob Sālim is an Iraqi Jew who did not emigrate to Israel in the period of the mass emigration of Iraqi Jews during the 1950s. He preferred to stay in Iraq. After ten years, he went to Israel as a political refugee, arriving via Iran. In Iraq, Sālim was behind bars for six years. During his imprisonment, he gets to know some communists from whom he learns a great deal. Afterwards, Sālim manages to escape to Iran. His stay there is brief. He is forced to travel to Israel via the Jewish Agency. During his stay in Iran, Sālim tries to arrange a visa and emigrate to the UK, but without success. Yet after his arrival in Israel he manages to achieve this goal. In the UK, he completes his studies in the field of Semitic languages, which he had begun in Israel, and becomes a professor in the field of Arabic dialects.

The novel is about Sālim's short visit to Israel during the first days of the US-led attack on Iraq in March 2003. During this visit, Sālim meets with a small number of friends with whom he has been in touch during his stay in the UK. The narrator, Sālim, chooses to live in exile, he chooses to live apart from his family and to live alone away from the political conflicts. He finds refuge in the autobiographies of authors and intellectuals who have spent their lives in exile and who have experienced loneliness and confusion, strung between two worlds.

During his short stay in Israel, Sālim visits his sister Adna, and he celebrates her son's birthday. Sālim's mother phones him while he is a guest in his sister Adna's home. His ageing mother hates farewells, she wishes that her son Sālim would stay and take care of Adna, and not go off somewhere far away again. The visit ends with a farewell party for Sālim.

1.5.9 Diamond from the Wilderness – Sami Michael (2011)

Yahalom min ha-yeshimon tells of a love story that occurred during the 1930s between Kamāl and Elmāsa. In a wealthy Jewish family, Kamāl, the novel's protagonist, is living with his mother Regina and his father, Moshe Irani. Elmāsa (the diamond in English), is the name that Regina gave to the poor orphan girl. Elmāsa served the family after the death of her mother. Kamāl falls in love with Elmāsa, and she shared his feelings, although she was intelligent enough to understand that their relationship would not last for long. Michael cleverly describes Elmāsa inner conflict. She was illiterate, orphaned and poor. On the other hand, her beloved Kamāl is intellectual and belongs to a higher strata. Moreover, he was the only son of Moshe Irani, a prominent Baghdadi merchant.

Elmāsa fears were proved right. After Kamāl 's school marks did not satisfy the father, Moshe Irani expelled Elmāsa from the house, accusing her of distracting his son. Kamāl tried to help her; he secured another place for her in his aunt's house. His aunt found a job for Elmāsa as an assistant for Iraqi businesswomen, where she worked as a babysitter for wealthy Iraqi families. That place opened her eyes to a different world, and she was gradually able to learn some foreign languages. Elmāsa and Kamāl decided to get married secretly, they also had a baby boy called ʿAbūd. The novel's ending is unexpected. Elmāsa leaves Kamāl and departs Iraq for the US with an American businessman.

Sami Michael manages to give the reader a detailed portrait of life in Iraq/Baghdad at the time. The novel travels in time and place to Baghdad during the 1930s, illustrating its streets, markets, quarters, river and people.

2

Exophonic Writing, Stylistics and the Study of Iraqi Jewish Fiction

'Exophony' is a term that has gained currency to designate authors who write literature in an adopted language. Due to the author's bilingualism or multilingualism, the linguistic choices available for her/him go beyond one language system. Therefore, exophonic texts have distinct linguistic and stylistic features. Although code-switching constitutes a considerable feature of exophonic texts, it seems that such texts may contain other linguistic aspects that do not belong to code-switching; for instance: paradigmatic deviations, syntagmatic deviations and syntactic interference/transference. Yet, these aspects occur mostly because of the author's bilingualism. Although exophonic texts may contain elements of non-code-switching, mainstream academic studies follow the sociolinguistic trends in terms of comparing literary written code-switching to conversational code-switching. Accordingly, the majority of approaches developed to analyse literary texts written by bilingual authors are mainly driven by research on bilingualism and languages in contact.

This chapter is divided into two main parts. The first part constitutes the theoretical framework of the book and introduces an approach to the study of exophonic texts. The second part applies that suggested model to this study's selected Hebrew novels.

The first part of the chapter explores the possibilities of and the motivations for using stylistics as a theoretical framework in approaching exophonic texts. The first section is divided into three main parts. The first part constitutes a brief review of the literature concerning research on exophonic texts. The second part points out to what extent stylistics could be employed as a prism for the analysis of such texts. In its conclusion, the chapter suggests a stylistic analytical model in which the possibilities of relating the style as a choice to the analysis of such texts are introduced.

2.1 Stylistics: An Approach to Exophonic Texts

The research approach of the book is derived mainly from the early attempts to approach bilingual literary texts by means of stylistics. It was Keller's study of Spanish-English bilingual literary texts (Keller 1976) which stimulated the present study to embark on the use of a stylistic approach to literary works written by bilingual authors. Commenting on the literary style of using Spanish in English writing by Eduardo Rivera and Gary El Huitlacoche, Keller claims that both authors use Spanish with 'highly charged emotional' lexical items. According to Keller (1976: 139–40), the equal language representation of each language involved in the bilingual literary text is not the scale by which such texts should be measured; rather, with very minimum use of embedded language we can expect the emergence of a bilingual continuum.

Keller's use of the stylistic approach to investigate such linguistic and literary aspects in some bilingual literary texts is a pioneering step towards a better understanding of such kinds of texts. Unfortunately, the paths Keller pursued have not been well explored nor followed by subsequent studies. The present study seeks to delve into the possibility of using stylistics as an approach to exophonic texts. It discusses the possibilities and the motivations of using stylistics as a theoretical framework approaching literary texts written by bilingual/multilingual authors. It provides a relevant review of the literature regarding the different methods to approach such literary texts and, further, it delivers an interpretation of the possibilities of linking style as choice to the analysis of literary texts written by bilingual authors.

2.1.1 Exophonic Texts

Living in a world with more than 5,000 languages across more than 150 countries creates an apt environment for multilingualism. With all of these different languages and cultures in a mobile world, it is not surprising to learn that three decades ago Grosjean (1982: 24) claimed that: 'bilingualism is present throughout all nations in varying patterns of distribution'. This can tell us more about the possibility of multilingualism and multiculturalism in the present-day's more globalised world.

Bilingualism and multilingualism have a long history of research and investigation. The determination of who counts as bilingual constitutes an immense debate. This is due to the various branches of knowledge associated with the bi-/multilingualism phenomenon by which the bilingual is seen, including: literary studies, linguistics, sociolinguistics, literacy and second-language acquisition. Back in the 1950s, Haugen (1953: 7) viewed a bilingual as a person who has the ability to 'produce complete meaningful utterances in the other language'. According to the *Linguistic Encyclopaedia*: 'A bilingual (or multilingual) person is one whose linguistic ability in two (or more) languages is similar to that of a native speaker' (Malmkjaer 1991: 76). The world *similar* here is in contradiction with Bloomfield's definition of the term; he claimed that being bilingual means: 'native-like control of two languages' (1933: 56). On the other hand, there are some scholars who see that bilingualism does not necessarily mean mastering the second language like a native; a more recent definition of bilingualism suggested by Myers-Scotton (2006: 44), for instance, asserts bilingualism to be 'the ability to use two or more languages sufficiently to carry on a limited casual conversation'. The statement by Baetens Beardsmore (1986: 1) about the different definitions of bilingualism remains to my mind valid and insightful: 'Bilingualism as a concept has open-ended semantics.'

Yet the debate on defining bilingualism continues.[1] The present study will not pursue in depth an appropriate definition of bilingualism; rather, it focuses on the exophonic text as a result of bilingual and bicultural contexts and does not seek to engage with the phenomenon itself. Accordingly, the question arises: What is an exophonic text?

Before answering the above question, it is worth drawing on the typology of bilingual literary writers. This can shed light on the producers of exophonic texts, and can make a solid base in order to define it within the context of bilingual settings. Grosjean (2010) divides bilingual authors into three main types: (1) authors who write only in their mother tongue, (2) authors who write in their second or third language, and (3) those who write literature in two languages. Grosjean (2010: 134–44) adds that the last type of writer may use two languages in one literary piece of work. One of the better attempts to describe the term is the interpretation by Grosjean of the description of the bilingual who has experiences in two cultures as a 'bicultural bilingual'. He claims that in most cases bilingual people are not bicultural. On the other hand, there are some cases of bilinguals who are bicultural, such as immigrants: i.e. they often acquire the language alongside the culture of the new land. So they have two different cultural experiences and two different languages: one belongs to the homeland, and the other is adopted in the new land. Grosjean (2013: 21–4) also touches on the influence of biculturalism on the bilingual's ability to comprehend words in two languages, particularly the words that hold cultural patterns, which requires cultural experience alongside language competence so as to be comprehended. He situates this ability of bicultural-bilingual in comparison to 'monoculture bilingual' as a confirmation of the difference between the two, the 'monoculture bilingual' does not have the cultural background in order to differentiate between some lexical items associated with cultural patterns.[2]

Few attempts have been made to describe the phenomenon of writing literature in a language other than one's mother tongue. One of the earliest observations of bilingual authors was 'mixing' (Haugen 1953). Kellman (2000) describes authors who 'write in more than one language or at least in a language other than their primary one' as translingual authors (Kellman 2000: ix). According to Kellman, the term translingualism entails a combination of 'colonialism, war, increased mobility, and the aesthetics of alienation' (2000: 7).

Exophonic literature as a concept derived from research on several African writers who write in adopted European languages, mainly French (Heinrichs 1992). The notion was used later by Wright (2010) as a tool through which the translator should approach such texts.

Exophonic writers are those who write literature in a non-mother tongue, and this is associated with authors who live in bilingual/multilingual communities, or immigrant authors who adopt a new language in a voluntary or mandatory exile. In English literature, Conrad is an iconic example of such a writer; in contemporary German, works by Emine S. Özdamar are a superb example, such as her stories in the collection *Mutterzunge* (1990).

Exophonic writing is potentially a focus to be investigated by stylistics because of the strong connection between the linguistic and stylistic features of exophonic texts that results from writing with and from a bicultural background (Wright 2008: 40). Wright also suggests that the understanding of the term exophonic might contribute to a better interpretation of literary works by those writers who write in a language other than their mother tongue (2008: 40).

Exophonic texts are probably more foregrounded than others in terms of stylistic distinctions in language that present some unique aspects of cross-cultural practices by which the use of particular linguistic elements foregrounds not only the texts, but also the style of their authors. The use of non-translated words, for instance, may be perceived as an unexpected literary practice by the author in the canon's discourse of a given literature. It is true that this practice may bring the text into a kind of zone of 'otherness', a hybrid space in which some cultural concepts might not be readily perceived. Yet the salient phenomenon of using two languages in one text encourages and maintains modes of intercultural discourse:

> The use of untranslated words as interface signs seems a successful way to foreground cultural distinctions, so it would appear even more profitable to attempt to generate an 'interculture' by the fusion of the linguistic structures of two languages. (Ashcroft et al. 2003: 65)

The uniqueness of such exophonic texts also derives from the fusion of syntactic structures between two language systems. The dominant language of the text, in fact, is one of these languages, to which the author should adapt the linguistic and the literary norms to be perceived as an 'authentic' writer. The 'ungrammatical' practices of the exophonic author might be regarded as incompetence in mastering the adopted language. This is because of the influence of the mother tongue on some of the author's writing in terms of syntactic structures. According to Wright (2010: 27–30), however, that should be seen as a foregrounding aspect of such texts. Although some editors regard the unexpected and the non-appropriate forms of linguistic aspects in such literary texts as mistakes that should be corrected, Wright sees them as a foregrounding stylistic feature of that text:

> I would argue that if a stylistic feature in an exophonic text is foregrounded, if it calls attention to itself, particularly if it exceeds the limits of what appears to be grammatical [...] then its presence should be considered deliberate rather than evidence that the writer has an inadequate grasp of his or her adopted language. (2010: 28)

Living in a mobile world, particularly in the period of post-colonialism, constitutes an appropriate atmosphere for exophonic authors who write *in between* languages and countries to express their cultural experiences (Sarkonak and Hodgson 1993: 48). The language negotiation via exophonic authors results in the quest for establishing connections to cultural backgrounds from which the exophonic authors stem. This attitude is likely to be regarded as one of the salient aspects of post-colonial literature, where the conflict between adaptation and refusal of some linguistic norms characterises the nature of such writings (Ashcroft et al. 2003: 38).

The motivations for writing in the exophonic zone impact on the bilingual author in terms both of her/his creativity and isolation at the same time. The isolation derives from the fact that the texts, similar to the situation of their authors, might be viewed as situated in a space outside the existing canon of literature.

Authorial creativity is likewise covered by the unique practices of bilingualism within bilingual literary texts. For example, giving the characters of one novel distinctive names that make overly explicit the bicultural and bilingual belonging of its protagonists is one distinctive marker. Another is a productive use of bilingualism, which reflects the community in which the characters of a realistic fictional text are presented through the dialogue in which they participate. Not only does bilingualism have to do with word and sentence level, rather its influence spreads throughout the literary work in a way that points up its uniqueness (Sarkonak and Hodgson 1993: 17). Moreover, writing by means of two or more linguistic backgrounds offers the author possibilities and chances to broaden her/his readership; the author is expected to have the linguistic repertoire by which the literary work is to some extent different from other monolingual authors in terms of linguistic, metaphoric and stylistic qualities (Wright 2010: 24).

Regardless of the different motivations and reasons underlying the exophonic texts, they embody certain unique features. These are focal points of interest for analysts looking at stylistic, linguistic and literary aspects; features that draw on some common and general linguistics and stylistic aspects by which the exophonic texts are distinguished from other monolingual literary texts.

2.1.2 Approaches to Exophonic Texts

Although the use of two or more languages in a literary text constitutes a significant literary and linguistic aspect, it is marked by two dissimilar approaches – one literary and the other more linguistic. Linguists look at the embedded foreign elements in literary texts as a mere case of linguistic code-switching. Whereas scholars of literature are much more concerned about a 'hybrid text', in which the involved languages constitute the 'verbal fabric' of this text (Sarkonak and Hodgson 1993: 17).

In the following, this book tries to illustrate the different approaches concerning exophonic texts. The main argument is guided by the consistent relationship between language-contact phenomena and exophonic texts. Language contact and code-switching will be defined briefly. Code-switching, in general, and written code-switching, in particular, are reviewed in connection with exophonic texts.

2.1.2.1 CONVERSATIONAL CODE-SWITCHING

Before embarking on the notion of code-switching (CS), the language contact phenomenon as a macro context within which CS may occur should be introduced briefly. Answering the question 'what is language contact?', Thomason (2001) touches on the simplicity of defining the term, putting it very simply: 'language contact is the use of more than one language in the same place at the same time' (2001: 1). According to Thomason, the simplicity of the definition, however, does not omit some other complicated aspects associated with language in general and dialects in particular. In addition, Thomason asserts some complicity regarding the place and time; she points to the use of sacred texts, mainly Christian and Islamic, as instances of language contact in many places at different periods of history where the two participants of two or more languages might not share the same geographical zone.

Languages are considered to be in contact when they are in use interchangeably by one person; as Weinreich defines it (1968), the result of the contact is the interference between the two language systems involved, the interference is asserted by Weinreich to be the deviation from the norms of one language of the two.

CS is one of the most common phenomena in connection with languages in contact zones; it springs from the bilingual/multilingual context when people communicate by means of more than one language/dialect due to their linguistic background. Jakobson developed the early investigation of the term code in his research on language contact (Jakobson and Halle 1956). Poplack's (1980: 583) early investigation of the term suggested defining CS as: 'the alternation of two languages within a single discourse, sentence or constituent'. She also touched on the possibility of employing CS as a tool for indicating the language competence of the bilingual (1980: 615–16). Many recent studies take a closer look at the idea of CS. Myers-Scotton (1993b) defines CS as: 'the term used to identify the alternations of linguistic varieties within the same conversation'. The *Cambridge Handbook of Linguistic Code-Switching* defines it more generally as: 'the ability on the part of bilinguals to alternate effortlessly between their two languages' (Bullock and Toribio 2009: 1).

The search for CS phenomena makes a distinction between three main types of CS: (1) 'inter-sentential', (2) 'intra-sentential' and (3) 'tag-switching' (Poplack 1980: 589). Starting from the last type, according to Poplack (1980), tag-switching refers to the use of tags that are repeated mostly by the bilingual particularly in ethnic contexts. She adds, since it can take any order in the utterance of the sentence, that this kind of switch is frequently used compared to the other two types: 'Tags are freely moveable constituents which may be inserted almost anywhere in the sentence without fear of violating any grammatical rule.' Examples of such tags are words like the interjections/exclamations that come before the sentence or before the whole text (Appel and Muysken 2005: 118).

Inter-sentential CS is switching the codes between the sentences and clauses, or 'at a sentence boundary' as Thomason (2001: 132) puts it.

The intra-sentential CS (or code-mixing) occurs within one sentence itself. It is more complicated than the other two types because of the high possibility of the linguistic interference that may be involved during the process of CS. The interference settings in this type of switching may touch on the morphological, syntactic and phonological levels.

The research on CS at the spoken level is based on quantitatively and qualitatively solid research studies. In other words, at the level of interactive language contact (spoken/conversational), there are well-studied and well-categorised phenomena such as CS, borrowing, code-mixing, pidgin, creole, etc. Although the exophonic text is produced within the context of bi-/multilingualism, the investigations of such kinds of texts are mainly linked to the aspects of CS. The question arises: Are there special attributes of the exophonic texts concerning the contact phenomena? In the following section, the growing research on exophonic texts as well as the motivation for using stylistics as a theoretical framework in approaching the suggested corpora will be discussed.

2.1.2.2 CODE-SWITCHING IN WRITTEN DISCOURSE

The phenomenon of CS at a conversational level has been widely investigated in recent decades; this was done through linguistic studies, for instance (Lipski 1977, 1985; Muysken 2000; Pfaff 1976, 1979; Poplack 1980, 1981; Timm 1975). Other studies were conducted concerning the functional and social aspects of CS, such as (Auer 1998; Blom and Gumperz 1972; Gumperz 1977; McClure 1981).

Due to the extensive studies concerning the conversational level, the approaches to exophonic texts mostly focus on CS phenomenon when approaching literary texts (Callahan 2004; Ibhawaegbele and Edokpayi 2012; Jonsson 2005, 2010; Montes-Alcala 2000, 2012; Torres 2007). These studies, although an important contribution to the study of written CS, follow the strand of treating the linguistic and literary nature of the texts mainly as CS/code-mixing. Some of them applied models designed for investigating conversational CS in their texts. Callahan (2004), for instance, used the Matrix Language Frame model developed by Myers-Scotton (1993a, 2002) in her analysis of some fictional works of Spanish/English bilingual authors. Jonsson (2005) studied the function of using CS in Chicano theatre from two perspectives: local and global functions as developed by Auer (1998, 1999). Jonsson lists five main local functions of CS in her suggested corpora: quotations, interjections, reiterations, gaps, and word/language play. Montes-Alcala (2012) compared the socio-pragmatic functions in oral CS as contrasted with written CS. Based on corpora of some Latino novels in the US, she claimed that the socio-pragmatic functions also occur in written CS. Moreover, in the study of three African writers from Nigeria, Ibhawaegbele and Edokpayi (2012) treated the presence of two of the most familiar phenomena of language in contact (CS and code-mixing) as stylistic devices employed by the three authors. The use of such strategies in Nigerian prose serves as a representation of the local linguistic environment:

> Various situational variables or extra-linguistic factors impose constraints on the language and styles of Nigerian novelists in their literary works. Code-switching and code-mixing are some of the stylistic strategies devised to tackle the problems of language in Nigerian prose fiction, thereby catering adequately for the varying Nigerian local situations, culture and environment. (2012: 18)

In all, in most studies concerning bilingual/multilingual texts the scope of conversational/spoken CS is generally the dominant term for comparison. In other words, the focus on investigating CS at the written level (written CS) derived mainly from research on spoken CS. This explains the reason for the paucity of studies looking at exophonic texts as an independent sub-field of research. In addition, approaches to exophonic texts might also be influenced by considerations of CS in written literary works as supposedly 'non-authentic' literary practice, a hybrid practice as a result of which the author and her/his work might be deemed to be beyond the bounds of the accepted literary canon.

On the other hand, there is an important study pointing out that the special nature of such (bilingual/multilingual) texts requires other approaches than those employed in analysing CS: 'There are genres of written text that are multilingual (i.e. contain elements drawn from more than one language) but that cannot be analysed insightfully using the tools developed for spoken code-switching' (Sebba 2013: 98).

Sebba touches on the uniqueness of bilingual texts and developed a multimodal approach based on the following: units of analysis, language-spatial relationships, language-content relationships, and types of linguistic mixing. The last category is of particular interest in the present study. Sebba (2013: 107) sees such linguistic mixing as:

> Mixed units are units that contain elements from two or more languages. These elements may be of different types, for example, they may be smaller visual units [...] or they may be textual units such as paragraphs or grammatical units such as sentences.

CS at the written level, according to Sebba (2013: 108), might be studied as a prototype of mixed textual units. At the same time, Sebba claims that the CS should not be applied entirely to all mixed units. He gives examples of visual units containing mixed units that still do not constitute CS.

The multimodal developed by Sebba (2013) seems to be a praiseworthy attempt to make the under-researched field of bilingual/multilingual texts more independent. The broadening of linguistic mixing types so as to include CS and other related bilingual practices at the written level opens the door to other studies and interpretations as regards the distinctive types of such texts, and creates other possibilities for placing the linguistic phenomena of exophonic texts at a distance from the boundaries of sociolinguistic approaches to CS. However, the model accords greater importance to the visual bilingual/multilingual texts in the given headings of the multimodal.[3] The question arises: What about other genres, like fiction and poetry, that seek to combine literary and linguistic approaches in fruitful analysis?

2.1.3 Aspects of Non-Code-Switching in Exophonic Texts

After exploring written CS, this study aims in the following to introduce other linguistic aspects that exophonic texts may contain. There are but few studies to date examining non-CS in literary works by bilingual writers. The study of bilingual word-play strategies in several literary works by the Chicana writer Sandra Cisneros deserves attention. The study asserts that non-CS linguistic phenomena used by Cisneros constitute a form of word-play in her literary works. Such word-play includes games with names, loan-shifting, games with syntax and loan translation (Cortés-Conde and Boxer 2002). In looking at post-colonial literature, some studies assert that there are certain common strategies used in the 'cross-cultural texts' in addition to CS. These include glossing, untranslated words, interlanguage and syntactic fusion (Ashcroft et al. 2003: 58–76). To merge the two studies, one can sum up with the following main linguistic aspects noticed in exophonic texts outside the sphere of CS: lexicon choices, syntactic structure, interference and translation, e.g. direct translation and loan translation.

One should also consider the deviation from paradigmatic or syntagmatic norms that are likely to be frequent when there is some interference between two languages. This is because of the number of language systems involved in addition to the mother tongue.

It is essential for the present analysis to investigate not only CS but also non-CS aspects in the exophonic texts, employing stylistic analysis.

The variations and the alternatives which exist in the dominant text language come into question when the bilingual author sets out her or his linguistic choices. The working hypothesis here derives from the assumption that the analysis of exophonic texts would be based on the stylistic theory of 'the style as choice'. The understanding of the term 'choice' here goes beyond the variations and the alternatives existing in one language system, where the author can set out her/his preferences. In the suggested approach, however, this sphere is located in two or more language systems, and accordingly the possibilities for choice are more likely to be more compared within only one language system.

To better examine the correlation between stylistics and exophonic texts, this study attempts in the following to discuss certain aspects of stylistics in general, and style as choice in particular.

Style, in general, is: 'the way in which language is used', and usually 'consists in choices made from the repertoire of the language' (Leech and Short 1981: 38). It is thus understood within this area of study as 'the selection of certain linguistic forms or features over other possible ones' (Thornborrow and Wareing 1998: 2). Stylistics is: 'the study of style' (Wales 1994: 347), and stylistic analysis is the linguistic tool by which the literary texts are analysed.

According to Spillner (1974: 15–16), stylistic analysis constitutes three components: (1) the linguistic component, (2) the pragmatic component, in which some categories such as the author, the reader, the historical situation, etc., are involved, and (3) the literary-aesthetic component. In this regard, Leech and Short (1981) stress the importance of two main questions in studying stylistics: Why and how? 'Why' enquires into the reasons beyond the linguistic choices made by an author in the text, while 'how' interrogates the artistic aspects achieved by means of such linguistic choices. Stylistics then, according to Leech and Short, should follow a pathway between the two questions to find a complementing answer for both dimensions, *why* and *how*. The stylistic task according to Leech and Short (1981: 13) is thus 'to relate the critic's concern of aesthetic appreciation with the linguist's concern of linguistic description'. Hence, stylistic analysis identifies and examines the basic linguistic levels of a language when approaching stylistic phenomena in texts, e.g. phonology, graphology, morphology, syntax, lexicology and semantics (Jeffries and McIntyre 2010: 34–61; Simpson 2004: 5–8).

The writer's choice of some linguistic forms as favoured over others has a deep-rooted conceptual basis in stylistic theory. An author's selection and arrangement of lexical items and other linguistic levels may be studied stylistically as the authors' linguistic choices drawn from variations and alternatives extant in one language system. The importance of the term choice for creativity as well as the distinctive style of a literary work is key: 'What makes styles distinctive is the *choice* of items, and their distribution and pattering. A definition of style in terms of choice is very popular, the selection of features partly determined by the demands of genre, form, theme, etc.' (Wales 1994: 436).

Concerning the term *choice*, Short and Leech define style as: 'the selection from a total linguistic repertoire that constitutes a style' (Leech and Short 1981: 11). They touch here on selection or the practice of choice by the author to stylise her/his literary work. The connection of the style with the term choice is very applicable in approaching literary texts, because 'in a text we can study style in more detail, and with more attention to what words or structures are chosen in preference to others. We can exhibit our material on the page, and examine the interrelations between one choice of language and another' (Leech and Short 1981: 12). In addition, the choices made by an author constitute an important element in the production of the literary work: 'Choices in style are motivated, even if unconsciously, and these choices have a profound impact on the way texts are structured and interpreted' (Simpson 2004: 22).

In view of that, the possibility of varieties an author can use is likely to be increased according to how many language systems she or he can access. In other words, the more languages an author knows, the more she or he has a possible variety of language choices, not only within one language system but in two or more (Myers-Scotton 1998: 18). This claim is particularly relevant to the study at hand, as it touches on the possibilities for choices available to the exophonic author as compared to monolingual authors. In many cases, the author's bilingualism/multilingualism results in creating a bicultural mode that may also influence the author's choices. Mackey gives examples of French-English bilingualism, concluding that 'literary biculturalism can exert a subtle influence upon a writer's choice of words, including those borrowed from the other languages' (Mackey 1993: 58).

The author's choice could also be influenced by social and physiological elements. In her Markedness Model (MM), Myers-Scotton (1998: 6) connects the switches between two languages or more in different genres to the social and physiological terms that influence the speaker's/writer's choices when she/he tends to switch codes between two or more languages.

Unlike possibilities of choice available to the bilingual speaker on the spoken level, as illustrated above, the act of choice constitutes a conscious performance when it comes to the exophonic author. Moreover, when an exophonic author selects lexical items from another language outside the dominant text language of a literary work, she/he may use two different strategies: glossing and inserting. The first term refers to an author's attempt to translate and explain selected word(s) to be understood by an audience that does not share the same linguistic and cultural background with the author. The second term, 'inserting', derives from the intentional behaviour of the author towards certain words and sentences employed in the text. The author brings such inserted items for cultural and identity representations that belong to the author her-/himself and portray the author's individual experience of otherness (Ashcroft et al. 2003: 62).

In this regard, it is worth noting that 'code choice' or '*Wahl des sprachlichen Codes*' as a concept first appeared in the study by Spillner (1974: 47) in his attempt to categorise the possible choices that could be available for the speaker. Spillner points out the importance of choosing codes from other languages when writing literary texts. Based on Spillner's idea, the present analysis seeks to examine in depth the linguistic, literary and stylistic features resulting from the practice of code choice between two or more language systems. The study argues that there are deliberate linguistic features that the exophonic text contains, in which 'code choice' plays an essential role in the way that literary structure and style of the exophonic text are shaped.

Answering the question of why stylistic analysis, the nature of the present study involves literary, linguistic and sociolinguistic aspects, so stylistics is germane. Therefore, the choice of stylistic analysis as a tool in approaching exophonic texts also constitutes a fundamental motivation for the present study because of the interdisciplinary approaches associated with it.

In his study of the relationship between stylistics and the theory of literature, Bloomfield (1976) counts eight fields in which stylistic analysis could be applied. Bloomfield (1976: 273–5) adds to his argument other critical categorisation settings; these are the author, the text and the audience/reader. These three basic elements mentioned here are significant for the present study. These terms are discussed in detail in section 2.1.4.1.

Stylistics is more likely to be associated with other disciplinary approaches in terms of analysis (Stockwell 2006: 749). In addition, Stockwell (2012: 152) asserts that 'stylistics uses linguistic models that have been generated by linguistics to account for the language system in general'. This study, in view of that, involves a multidisciplinary approach based on stylistics to investigate exophonic texts. In the following section of this chapter, the study discusses the suggested approach to exophonic texts.

2.1.4 Towards a New Approach to Exophonic Texts

2.1.4.1 LITERARY CODE-SWITCHING: NEW PERSPECTIVES

The attempts to describe the strategies for employing codes in a literary text that are outside the dominant text language include an insightful study by Torres (2007) on CS strategies used by Latino/a writers. Torres sees the strategies of using Spanish in English Latino/a texts as: (1) easily accessible codes, i.e. the use of Spanish lexical items with a clear meaning that is comprehensible from the context; and (2) the translation of Spanish words and phrases into English. In this vein, the categorisation of the cases of CS in the three Hebrew novels that are the subject of this study relies on the mutual relationship between three main elements: the author, the text and the reader. The following section discusses these categories in connection with those three elements.

With regard to the author, CS in interactive modes (spoken CS) is likely to be more spur of the moment, where the participants in the bilingual conversation are only slightly aware of it (Gardner-Chloros 2009; Shanon 1991), although the use of register or code variation may undergo a 'stylisation' during the time of the conversation (Coupland 2001a, 2001b). The same perhaps does not hold true for the literary text, where less time is spent choosing the codes in the conversations than when the bilingual author is writing the manuscript (Lipski 1982: 192). The author has both the time and opportunity to edit and review what she/he has written. One should also consider the role of the editor. Her or his task is essentially to maintain the general canon and repertoire of a given literary form of expression. In general, the act of written CS in literary genres is more subject to conscious practices and less dependent on accidental and more spontaneous linguistic behaviour.

Concerning the text and audience, this study draws on Jakobson's model for the factors involved in verbal communication (1960: 353). In this context, the 'addresser' is the author/writer of the text, while the 'addressee' is the reader. The text acts as the contact or physical channel by which the message (which is structured via codes that are familiar to both author and reader) is transmitted. The code, according to Jakobson (1960: 353), must be 'fully, or at least partially, common to the addressee'.

Given that an author's decisions and intentions are both involved in the process of inserting codes from outside the dominant text language as well as interpreting the text as a message that requires a decoding process, as discussed above, this study divides literary CS into two main types: hard-access code-switching (HA-CS) and easy-access code-switching (EA-CS). The former refers to any code added by the author that does not belong to the dominant text language and may be expected to create difficulties for any reader who does not share the author's bilingual and bicultural linguistic background, an outsider reader (Out.R). On the other hand, EA-CS is the insertion of foreign codes in the literary text by the author, who tries to elucidate these codes so as to make them decodable to the Out.R. The strategies available to the bilingual author, in this case, are varied and include direct translation, footnotes and glossing the foreign codes using the dominant language of the text.

2.1.4.2 NOTES ON CATEGORIES

a- Since tag-switching largely involves words (like the interjections/exclamations that come before the sentence), the author does not need to work as hard to interpret them to make them decodable as with the other two types of CS (inter-/intra-sentential CS). Additionally, tag-switching is much more popular in bilingual communities when compared to inter-/intra-sentential CS. In view of this, tag-switching may be easy and/or difficult to access, depending on the sociolinguistic aspects of the reader's community. Therefore, this study suggests the term ambiguous-access code-switching (AA-CS) to replace the term tag-switching.

b- The accessibility of code-switches in exophonic texts is relative. It depends on the individual reader and/or the community of readers in which one reader's linguistic background is not identical to another's and the bilingualism in one community is not as strong as in another.

c- In view of the mutual relationship between the reader and the author via the text, the study divides the readers into insider reader (In.R) and outsider reader (Out.R). The term In.R refers to the reader who shares the same linguistic and cultural background as the author regarding all the codes employed in the text. The Out.R, accordingly, is the reader who cannot comprehend, to some extent, the codes of the embedded language in the text as the In.R does. The categories of foreign codes employed by the author are, then, applied to the Out.R because the In.R has full access to all of the text's languages.

d- The Matrix Text Language (MTL) refers here to the dominant language in which the text is written. Although the term is similar to the term used in the Matrix Language Frame model (MFL) developed by Myers-Scotton (1998) in her research on conversational CS, this study does not use the concept of matrix and embedded language in view of the MFL. The MTL and the embedded language terms used in the present study, however, are connected to the linguistic background of the author and the reader, as explained above in (c).

e- The Iraqi Jewish authors and the texts selected for this study constitute a case of exophonic authors and the way in which they employ codes from their mother tongue in the exophonic texts. In general, the model developed by this study could be applied to investigate CS phenomena in any exophonic texts regardless of the languages involved.

2.1.4.3 NON-CODE-SWITCHING ASPECTS: SYNTAGMATIC AND PARADIGMATIC CHOICES

Foregrounding, a term borrowed from the field of art, was later developed to serve as an essential theory in stylistic analysis (Leech and Short 1981; Mukařovský 1964). One mission of this type of analysis, which approaches literary texts using linguistic tools, is to compare the text to a norm, which may take several forms. In Enkvist et al.'s words:

> All stylistic analysis is ultimately based on the matching of a text against a contextually related norm. Such norms may be explicitly circumscribed, or they may remain implicitly embedded in the past experience of a speaker, writer, or literary critic. (1964: 54–5)

Regarding Enkvist's interpretation of the term 'contextually related norm', Leech and Short (1981: 53) discussed the issue of the 'relative norm', in which the anticipation of participant elements (e.g. speakers, hearers, writers and readers) shows a discrepancy due to the sets of language situations. They define the term deviance as 'the difference between the normal frequency of a feature and its frequency in the text or a corpus' (1981: 48). In addition to the 'circumscribed and gained norm through experiences' established by Enkvist et al. (1964), McMenamin and Choi (2002: 133) have also discussed related norms pertinent to this study (e.g. prestige norms, norms of social convention or necessity, norms governing use of registers, varieties and other languages, class norms, regional norms, circumstantial norms, appropriate-language norms and correct-language norms).

Although deviation may be considered an undesirable behaviour within a linguistic repertoire, it can be perceived as Leech (2008: 59) asserts: 'Deviation provides us with a working criterion (though not an exclusive criterion) for the selection of those linguistic features which are of literary significance.' In this context, the difference between syntagmatic and paradigmatic needs to be established. According to the *Oxford English Dictionary*, a 'syntagm' is defined as 'a set of linguistic forms in a sequential relationship', while the term 'paradigm' is 'a set of units which are linguistically substitutable in a given context'. De Saussure (1986) was one of the scholars who suggested that syntagmatic/associative [paradigmatic] relations are represented by means of vertical/horizontal axes.[4] Example 2-1 elucidates the syntagmatic/paradigmatic difference:

Example 2-1

a- Adam drinks water.
b- Adam drinks juice.
c- Drinks Adam water.
d- Adam drinks sorrow.

If the cause of the deviations in (2-1-c) and (2-1-d) is the interference between English and Arabic, the results are as follows:

1. The syntagmatic relationship between the units of one sentence is due to the *combination* of its units in a horizontal axis (Adam+drinks+water). The paradigmatic settings, on the other hand, stand for the *selection/replacing* of units in the vertical axis (water/juice).
2. Syntagmatic deviation, accordingly, is supposed to be the form of the word order (the combination) in which this combination does not follow the rules of one linguistic norm; see (2-1-c).
3. Paradigmatic deviation, on the other hand, is a selection of unexpected or infrequent units instead of the available or expected choices in one context; see (2-1-d).

The deviation from paradigmatic or syntagmatic norms is likely to be frequent when there is an interference between two languages. The deviation from a norm can be demonstrated by the author's choice, making it also somehow connected to the author's writing style (McMenamin and Choi 2002: 132).

Since Hebrew novels contain Hebrew/Arabic interference in many places, the likelihood of deviating from the Hebrew norm is expected. These Hebrew paradigmatic/syntagmatic deviations are discussed in the second section of this chapter.

2.1.4.4 THE SUGGESTED MODEL

The attempt to regard the linguistic phenomena associated with exophonic texts as the stylistic term 'choice' might serve as a reassessment tool in approaching these phenomena. CS, for instance, will be perceived in connection with the author's readiness to choose codes from another language system (embedded language). Loan translation is to be interpreted as semantic choices of other linguistic phenomena discussed below. The midpoint in the approach is that the embedded language system has a significant influence on a bilingual author's choices; not only in terms of using linguistic elements outside the MTL but also on some linguistic elements that belong to the MTL itself. In view of that, the present study deals with the embedded language use in the MTL as: first, the author's choices within the MTL; this comprising lexical, semantic, phonological and morphological choices in a way where embedded language has a significant influence on the author's choices. Second, deviation from the norm (e.g. paradigmatic and syntagmatic deviations). Third, CS by the author. In view of that, the present study deals with the embedded language use in the MTL as:

1. The author's choices within the MTL.
2. Deviation from the norm (paradigmatic and syntagmatic deviations).
3. Code-switching.

Since the bilingual author, as noted, writes her/his literary work consciously, the term 'choice' should be extensively adhered to in the analysis of exophonic texts. The following linguistic patterns are suggested by the present study to approach exophonic texts:

Code choices: Selecting different codes from two language systems, this takes account of HA-CS, EA-CS and AA-CS:

- HA-CS includes: Inter- and intra-sentential CS.
- EA-CS includes: Direct translation, glossing.
- AA-CS occurs probably in the cases of: interjection, place and character names and word-for-word translation from the embedded language into the MTL.

Syntagmatic choices: Syntactic interference in MTL influenced by the syntactic structure of the embedded language, i.e. word order.

Paradigmatic choices: **Lexicon choices:** Lexical item choices from MTL influenced by the embedded language.
Loan translation: Semantic choices in MTL influenced by the embedded language.

As discussed in section 2.1.4.1, the present study divides written CS into three main types: hard-access code-switching (HA-CS), easy-access code-switching (EA-CS) and ambiguous-access code-switching (AA-CS).

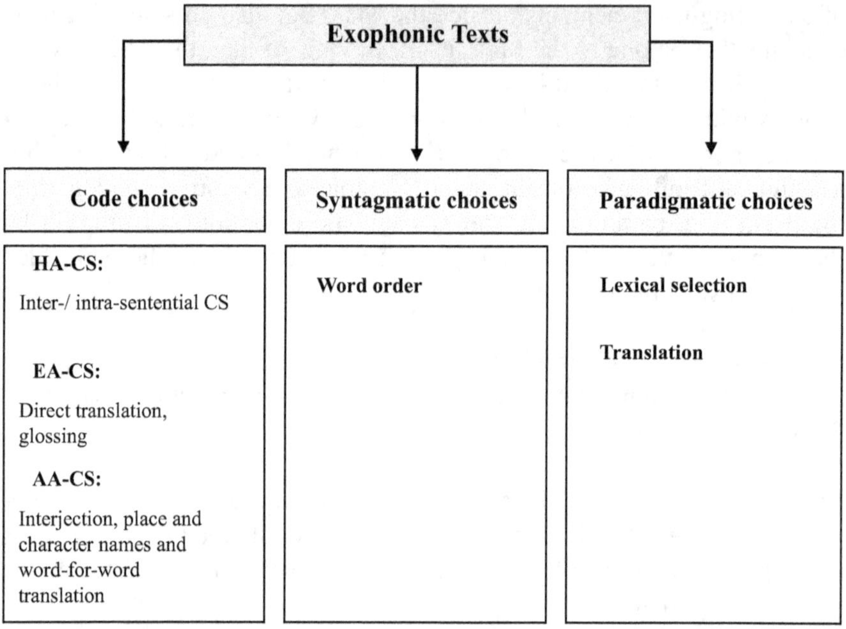

Figure 2.1 Suggested approach to exophonic texts

Linguistic behaviour towards the non-CS aspects of exophonic texts which resulted in an author's linguistic choices from the varieties in MTL can be primarily categorised along two axes: syntagmatic and paradigmatic. The first category involves the word order of some MTL's lexical items structured in a way that violates the norm of the dominant language of the text, on the one hand, and imitates the syntactic structure of the embedded language, on the other. The second category (paradigmatic deviations) includes the lexical selection of varieties existing in the lexicon of MTL in which the influence of the embedded language lexicon has great impact. Paradigmatic deviations are highly expected in cases of translation from embedded language into the MTL as well.

The above three main linguistic features found in exophonic texts are connected directly to the authors' ability to access two or more language systems. The choices here are associated with two main terms: the first embodies the choices available to a bilingual author between the two language systems (the dominant and the embedded languages in the text), which is CS. The second constitutes the selecting of some linguistic varieties within the MTL system in a way that the embedded language influences the choices. The relationship between these three main elements of the exophonic text is presented in Figure 2.2.

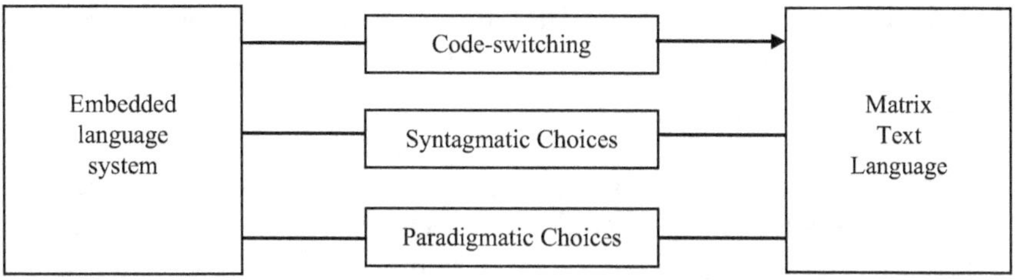

Figure 2.2 The relationship between the three main elements of the suggested approach

In sum then, the study of exophonic texts is under-researched. In addition, it tends to follow the sociolinguistic trend in terms of comparing conversational CS/code-mixing to written CS in literary works. The majority of approaches developed to analyse the exophonic text have been driven mainly by research on bilingualism and/or languages in contact. However, the exophonic text has deliberate linguistic and literary features including CS and non-CS aspects that stylise them. Because of the author's bilingualism or multilingualism, the choices available to her/him go beyond one language system. For that reason, the study of the style as choice is more appropriate for investigating linguistic, literary and pragmatic features of exophonic texts.

Moreover, the ability of stylistic analysis as a linguistic tool to investigate aspects on more than one linguistic level in the text is necessary for a better understanding of the linguistic features in exophonic texts. In order to analyse the embedded language uses in the exophonic text, the linguistic levels will be investigated (linguistic component). In addition, and this adds to the importance of using stylistic analysis to approach the exophonic texts, stylistic analysis pays attention not only to the linguistic features in the literary work; instead, it tries to find an objective answer for the question of '*why?*' (pragmatic component), and '*how?*' (literary-aesthetic component).

2.2 The Analysis of Arabic Use in the Iraqi Hebrew Novels

In this section the model suggested for analysing exophonic texts (section 2.1.4.4) is applied to the selected Hebrew texts in this study.[5] The study considers the first-generation Iraqi Jewish novelists as exophonic authors who write literature in their non-mother tongue. The three authors selected for this study are originally from Iraq, their mother tongue is Arabic, and they immigrated to Israel where they decided to choose to write in Hebrew and not in Arabic; i.e. they write fiction in Hebrew, and not in Arabic – their L1.[6] Therefore, the study at hand argues that these three Iraqi Jewish authors should be considered as exophonic writers.

To apply the suggested model discussed early in this chapter to the present study, there are some notions used in the model that should be linked to the corpora of the study. The MTL in all the selected Hebrew texts of this study is the modern Hebrew language in Israel. The embedded language is Arabic.

The Out.R for this study is the reader of modern Hebrew literature who has neither an Arabic linguistic background nor Iraqi Jewish culture. The In.R, on the other hand, is: first, an Iraqi Jew who reads Hebrew novels; second, a Mizrahi Jew whose mother tongue is Arabic (regardless of dialect); or, third, a reader of Hebrew literature with advanced knowledge of Arabic. It is important to point out that the third type of In.R may not be able to access all Arabic codes embedded in the texts, in particular the codes that involve cultural translations and require a cultural background in Iraqi Jewish traditions.

In view of the Insider/Outsider types of reader, the HA-CS and the EA-CS are the embedded Arabic codes employed by Iraqi Jewish authors in their Hebrew texts, in which Hebrew is the MTL.

2.2.1 Data

The study data are taken from nine Hebrew novels written by three Iraqi Jewish authors: Eli Amir (1983, 1992, 2010a), Shimon Ballas (1964, 1991, 2008) and Sami Michael (1974, 1993, 2015). The study constitutes an annotation to and explanation of the data. All Arabic uses employed by the authors in their books were extracted and analysed linguistically. The study relies on the manual annotation to the data. All Arabic uses employed by the authors in the selected corpora are extracted and analysed linguistically.

Since the study at hand deals with Arabic use in the suggested corpora as a stylistic device, any Arabic use, despite repetition or its pre-existence in the Hebrew lexicon at the time of writing process, is to be considered in the analysis.

The study traces all Arabic uses in the Hebrew texts at all language levels according to the linguistic levels under the three main banners of the suggested model in section 2.1.4.4.

All Arabic extracts in the study are written according to the Mizrahi pronunciation. In addition, the typography of the extracts exploited in the study is identical to its appearance in the original Hebrew texts.

2.2.1.1 NUMERICAL RESULTS

In order to show to what extent Arabic is used in the suggested Hebrew novels, every instance of Arabic use is extracted from the Hebrew texts under consideration. This includes visible Arabic uses. i.e. CS, direct translation, glossing and syntactic interference, as well as invisible uses, i.e. paradigmatic deviations and AA-CS. The numerical findings are divided into categories and sub-categories according to the suggested model developed in (2.1.4.4). Invisible Arabic uses are not included in the statistics, yet they are discussed in this chapter. This study deals with the nine Hebrew novels in this chapter as a single unit. The discussion of the chronological Arabic use in a period of about five decades will be introduced in Chapter 3. Accordingly, in Chapter 3, the nine Hebrew novels are to be divided into three corpora, each covering a period of time.

2.2.1.2 COUNTING METHOD

All Arabic lexical items and sentences have been incorporated in the counting. However, the study counts every Arabic code used in the Hebrew text as a separate unit, regardless of its position either in an Arabic sentence or in a Hebrew sentence. Arabic interjections, such as יא *yā* (used for calling someone), יאללה *yalla* (let's go) or אינשאללה *inshālla* (God willing), have been counted as single items, although a considerable number of them constitute complete Arabic sentences, as in *inshāllā* which constitutes an Arabic sentence of three items (*in* + *sha'*+*Allā*). Arabic proper names, i.e. place names and character names, are not considered in the counting, even though for the most part they contain Arabic cultural and linguistic features associated with the literary style of the three Iraqi Jewish authors. Visible Arabic uses – i.e. HA-CS, EA-CS, direct translation and glossing – are counted. For precise statistical reasons, AA-CS, loan translation and paradigmatic deviations are not included in the counting. Yet, examples of such cases are discussed. A general classification of Arabic use according to part of speech has been numerically represented as well.

The study shows that the noun is used primarily in all novels compared to other parts of speech. In all nine Hebrew novels in the analysis, approximately 60 per cent of Arabic uses are nouns. Verbs and adjectives are identical and constitute only about 5 per cent of embedded codes in the Hebrew texts. They rank in fourth place after particles and interjections, which comprise about 11 per cent and 14 per cent of Arabic use respectively. It is important to point out that Arabic interjections used in the Hebrew texts are not only single lexical items; in many cases, a complete Arabic sentence is used as an interjection, for instance, *ahlan wa sahlan* (welcome), *inshāllā* (God willing).

2.2.2 Code-Switching in the Hebrew Novels

The use of Arabic codes instead of Hebrew codes constitutes the dominant aspect in the corpora. The study investigates all Arabic codes employed by the three Iraqi Jewish authors in their Hebrew texts. This was done in keeping with the insider/outsider reader concept suggested by the study in section 2.1.4.1. In view of this, the study divides the types of embedded Arabic codes in the Hebrew texts into two main groups: HA-CS and EA-CS. In Table 2.1, the counts of the two groups of codes are presented according to each novel. The third group, AA-CS, will not be counted in the study, as it applied to the ambiguity mode and cannot be precisely verified.

Looking at the Arabic codes used in the Hebrew novels in Table 2.1, the sum of HA-CS overall is 1,454, whereas the total number of EA-CS is only 156. This means that of the total number of Arabic codes implemented in the nine Hebrew novels, 90 per cent are HA-CS, and about 10 per cent are EA-CS. In all novels, HA-CS stands for the dominant type of codes used. This shows to what extent the Arabic codes, which are combined into sentences or stand alone in lexical items, could hardly be accessed or are sometimes non-decodable for a reader who is not familiar with the Arabic language (the Out.R). The attitude of the three authors towards some Arabic codes – making them decodable solely to an Israeli readership with an Arabic background – has two functions: literary and sociologic. The literary is derived from the stylistic effects that are brought to Hebrew texts by means of hard-access Arabic codes. The second function of using such codes is to

Table 2.1 Code-switching in the novels

Novel	Hard-access code-switching	Easy-access code-switching
(Ballas 1964)	44	31
(Michael 1974)	217	–
(Amir 1983)	108	29
(Ballas 1991)	19	7
(Michael 1993)	103	3
(Amir 1992)	837	66
(Ballas 2008)	3	3
(Michael 2015)	101	13
(Amir 2010a)	22	4
Sub-total	1454	156
Total	1610	

confirm the linguistic and ethnic belonging of the authors to Arabic and Iraqi culture.

2.2.2.1 EASY-ACCESS CODE-SWITCHING

This type of CS has been highlighted in the study by Torres (2007) on CS strategies by Latino/a writers. Torres examines the strategies of using Spanish in English Latino/a texts relating to: (1) direct translation of Spanish words and phrases, as well as (2) the use of Spanish lexical items that have a clear meaning, comprehensible from the context.

The above two strategies are both used by the three authors in this study so as to make the Arabic codes accessible for more readers. In the following, examples from the Hebrew texts concerning EA-CS are discussed.

The strategy of direct translation of Arabic lexical items and phrases is often used in the Hebrew texts. Arabic lexical items, including nouns, names, verbs, adjectives, pronouns and interjections, as well as Arabic phrases (verbal/noun) are translated into Hebrew. The translation comes in the text sometimes directly after Arabic, or it is footnoted. The wide range of translated Arabic lexical items and phrases points to the way Arabic is widely used in the Hebrew texts.

Example 2-2

מחטופה [קלת-דעת]

makhṭūfa [*qallat-da'at*]
[flighty]
(Amir 1983: 176)

In Example 2-2, the author inserted an unexpected Arabic code *makhṭūfa* (flighty) in the Hebrew conversation held between Elna, Nilli and Avner in the kibbutz. Yet, the Hebrew equivalent comes in a form of direct translation in brackets.

The same holds true for the next example. Sami Michael puts the direct translation after the Arabic code employed in his late Hebrew novel *Yahalom min ha-yeshimon* (2015), he translates some Arabic words into Hebrew in the main text:

אלמאסה, יהלום

el-māsa, *yahalom*
[a diamond]
(Michael 2015: 8)

In some cases, the author puts the Arabic codes between quotation marks followed by a glossing of the inserted term in Hebrew:

אתה תיבחר ב "תַזכִּיה", כלומר ללא הצבעה של ממש
*atah tebbāḥēr be "**tazkiyah**", kelomar lelo hatsba'a shel mammash*
[you will be elected by means of "***tazkiyah***", i.e. without a real voting]
(Ballas 1991: 130)

The strategy of direct translation is also applied to both noun and verb phrases in the below examples:

Example 2-3: Noun phrase

"**עַלַא כֵּיפַכּ, אִבְּנִי**, לאט-לאט, בני"

***'alā kēfak, 'ibnī**, le'aṭ-le'aṭ, beni*
[Slow down son]
(Amir 1992: 18)

Here Eli Amir uses the translation strategy to make the Arabic sentence *'alā kēfak 'ibnī* (slow down son) accessible. He puts the Hebrew translation directly after the Arabic sentence. This holds true for the next example:

Example 2-4

אַל-חִזְבּ אל-וַטַנִי אל-דִימוּקְרַטִי, המפלגה הלאומית הדמוקרטית
***Al-ḥizb al-waṭanī al-dīmūqrāṭī**, ha-mmiflagah ha-le'umit ha-demoqratit*
[The Democratic National Party]
(Amir 1992: 63)

In the next example, Shimon Ballas puts the Hebrew translation in the footnote:

Example 2-5

" ראית את הכתובת? א-נאצר... באיזן אללה אינתצרנא*
*"ra'ita et ha-ktovet?**annaṣr … be'izne-llah intaṣarna**"*
[Did you see the placard? (it says) Victory, we win with the help of God]
(Ballas 1964: 9)

* בעזרת השם ניצחנו

Unlike Example 2-5, in which Ballas puts the translation in the footnote, Eli Amir uses direct translation and puts the translation between brackets directly after the Arabic codes:

Example 2-6: Verbal phrase

אוסכות וחליהא [שתוק ותניח לה]

***'uskut w-khalīhā** [shtoḳ ve taniaḥ lah]*
[Shut up and leave me alone]
(Amir 1983: 125)

This holds true also for the next example of translating a verbal phrase:

Example 2-7

עאשת אידיק [תבורכנה ידיך] (עמ' 153)

'āshat 'ēdēk *[teburakhna yadekha]*
[May your hands will be blessed]
(Amir 1983: 153)

Sami Michael also uses this strategy of employing EA-CS in his Hebrew novel (1974: 245):

Example 2-8

"תפאדאל, תיכנס"

tfaḍḍal*, tekkanes*
[come in]

Along with the use of direct translation strategies as discussed above, the Iraqi authors use other strategies to make some inserted Arabic codes accessible for the Out.R, for which the direct translation seemed to be insufficient. By means of glossing strategy, the author attempts to explain embedded Arabic codes using the context in the novel scene in which the Arabic code is employed. This can also be achieved when the author clarifies the embedded Arabic code through the dialogues between the characters. This technique makes Arabic more integrated into the Hebrew text, and not so isolated. See for instance the cases of EA-CS in the following examples.

Example 2-9

"היא יודעת שחזרת?"
"לא".
"היא תישתגע משמחה, הילדה. יא-וואילי, כמה בכתה...אשכנזיה-אבל בחורה זהב".
לגבי נאג'יה היה הזהב לא רק רכוש, מתכת וקישוט אלא גם ערך.

"hi yoda'at she-ḥazarta?"
"lo".
"hi teshtagga' mi-simḥa, hayyalda. ***yā-wāylī****, kammā bakhtā... ashkenaziyya-aval baḥora zahav". legabe* ***Najiyyah*** *haya ha-zahav lo raḳ rekhush, mattekhet ve-ḳishut 'ela gam 'erekh.*
["Does she know that you have turned back?
"no"
"She will get crazy cause of happiness, the girl. Oh God, she cries so much … she is Ashkenazi. Yet, a girl of gold". According to Najya, the Gold was not just property, metal or adornment; rather a value as well.]
(Michael 1974: 195)

In this example, the author did not translate the Arabic connotation of *baḥora zahav* into Hebrew. Although there is the existence of the lexical item *zahav* in the Hebrew lexicon, the term *baḥora zahav* has another semantic denotation associated with an Arabic cultural expression used to praise someone. The Arabic word *dhahab* (gold) is used in the Iraqi Judaeo-Arabic to refer to someone who has good manners (Yona-Swery 1995: 97). This is what Michael pointed out concerning the Arabic meaning of using the term *baḥora zahav* by Najiyya. The act of glossing here adds another connotation influenced by Iraqi spoken Arabic to the Hebrew lexical item *zahav*. Michael might also have made use of the lexical phonological semantic similarity between the two Semitic languages of the word *zahav*.

This also holds true for the way in which Shimon Ballas explains an Arabic term he employed in his literary work:

Example 2-10

מַג'מַע אל-בַּחְרין, הוא המקום בו מתחבר הפרת עם החידקל

(Ballas 1991: 123)

majma' al-baḥrayn*, hu hamaqom bo mitḥabber haperat 'im ḥiddeqel*

[***Majma' Bahrain***], the confluence of the Tigris and the Euphrates

(Ballas 2007: 154)

Glossing also can be done through the dialogue between the characters. Mrs Zebora, an Ashkenazi lady, asks Abū Ḥalāwa, an Iraqi Jew, to elucidate the Arabic code *khazūq* during their conversation:

Example 2-11

"גברת ציפורה", נהם אבו-חלאווה בבטחה, "מי שלא יבוא יקבל חאַזוק!"

"יקבל... יקבל מה, אדון-חלאווה ?"

אבו-חלאווה נעץ מרפק בצלעותיו של ניסים.

"לתרגם !" פקד לאקונית.

"חאזוק זה יתד בתחת". ציית ניסים.

"geveret Tsepora, naham ***Abū-Ḥalāwah*** *be-veṭḥa, mi she-lo yavo yeḳabbel* ***khazūq***

"yeḳabbel ... yeḳabbel ma, adon Ḥalāwah?

Abū-Ḥalāwah *na'ats marpeḳ be-tsal'otav shel Nisim*

"letargem!" paḳad laḳonit.

*"**khazūq** ze yeted ba-ttaḥat" tsyyet Nisim.*

["Mrs. Zeborah", raged *Abu Ḥalāwa* certainly, "who will not come will get **khazūq**!"[7]

"Will get … will get what, Mr. Ḥalāwah?"

Abū-Ḥalāwah stabbed Nisim's rib with an elbow.

"Translation!" gave (**Abū-Ḥalāwah**) an order laconically.
"**khazūq** is a stake in (inserted in) the bottom". Obeyed Nisim.]
(Michael 1974: 78)

In the above example, the translation of the Arabic lexical item goes through glossing for low register Arabic use, which is inherited in the dialogue between two Iraqi Jews and an Ashkenazi woman.

2.2.2.2 HARD-ACCESS CODE-SWITCHING

The use of some Arabic codes in the Hebrew texts without the authors' interpretation to make them easily accessed by the Out.R is also employed by the three authors alike. Playing with hard-access Arabic uses has a significant stylistic function for the Hebrew texts. On the one hand, this type of Arabic use brings the reader only to Arabic and Iraqi bilingual speakers/characters at the dialogue level, in which the interference between Arabic and Hebrew can be expected. On the other hand, these codes reflect the linguistic background of the author. Since the hard access codes require an In.R, it can be easily said that the more HA-CS is used in the text, the more bilingual is the text. The two main types of HA-CS – inter-/intra-sentential CS[8] – are used in the Hebrew texts as it appears in the following examples.

Example 2-12

In the following dialogue, Sami Michael uses the so-called inter-sentential CS. In order to bring the conversation to the reality mode, Michael uses complete Arabic sentences and clauses along with Hebrew sentences. Arabic sentences here are more isolated from the Hebrew text. Although CS here interrupts the message, in which only an addressee with Arabic/Hebrew linguistic background can encode it (the In.R), the use of such codes distinguishes the work of Michael as they foreground the scene through the use of foreign codes.

"מאייה... מאייה..." אני מילל אליהם בערבית, "אנא מגרוח!"
"מאפיש מאייה", עונה לי ברנש עצום-מידות.
"מאייה... מאייה..." אני מתחנן בקול.
היחיד בהם שנשק בידו מצמיד את לוע-הקנה אל רקתי:
"פין אל-קואת?" הוא שואל.
"מאייה... מאייה..."
"פין ?" מתעקש הלה ומצמיד בכוח את ראשי אל החול.
"הונאַכּ !" אני מצביע בידי כלפי הבהקי-התותחים.

A- *"**mayya** ... **mayya** ... " ani miyallel elehem ba'aravit, "**ana magrūḥ**!"*
B- *"**mafīsh mayya**", 'one li barnash 'atsum-medot.*
C- *"**mayya** ... **mayya** ... " ani mitḥannen b-ḳol.*

D- *ha-yyaḥid ba-hem she-neshek̦ be-yado matsmid 'et lua'-hak̦ane 'el rak̦ati:*
E- *"**fēn el-quwwāt**?" hu sho'el.*
F- *"**mayya** ... **mayya** ...".*
J- *"**fēn**?" met'ak̦k̦esh hella u-matsmid be-khuaḥ 'et rashi 'el ha-ḥol.*
H- *"**hūnāk**" ani matsbiyya' biyde kelabe hevhak̦e-ha-totaḥim.*

[A- "Water ... water" I cry to them in Arabic, "I am injured".
B- "No water", answered me a huge guy.
C- "Water ... Water". I am begging loudly.[9]
D- The only one of them who was carrying a gun sticks the barrel of a gun to my temple.
E- "Where are the forces?" he asks.
F- "Water ... Water ..."
J- "Where? He insists while pressing my head firmly down into the sand.
H- "Out there!" I point to the flare of the field guns.]
(Michael 1974: 191)

Unlike inter-sentential CS, intra-sentential CS (or code-mixing) is likely to be more integrated within the dominant language of the text (here Hebrew). This kind of CS is much more difficult for the Out.R to access, because the embedded codes take a position in the syntactic structure of the sentence. Therefore, these codes cannot be as easily identified as in the case of inter-sentential CS. These codes can be any figure of speech, as is illustrated in the examples below.

Example 2-13

"מה אתה אומר, יא תאופיק, הרי אתה ראש־הממשלה, ובלעדיך לא יכון דבר, אמר הפאשה.

(Amir 1992: 246)
*ma atta 'omer, **yā Tawfīk**, hare atta rosh-ha-memshala, u-vil'adekha lo **yekūn** davar, amr ha-pasha*
["what do you say to that, Tewfik? You're the prime minister. It cannot be done without you, said the pasha[10]]
(Amir 2010b: 300)

The Arabic code *yekūn* is well integrated into the Hebrew sentence; it is an Arabic verb meaning 'to be', which comes in the middle of the Hebrew clause. This might also be a word-for-word translation of the Arabic *we bedūnak lā yekūn she'*.

Example 2-14

"הָרון," טפח בעוז על השולחן, "אולי תגיד לי מה הביא אותך לכתוב את המאמר הזה?"

"בוא נדבר גליות," ביקשתיו כשאני מושך כסא לשבת לידו.
"זה בדיוק משאני רוצה, שתדבר גליות ותגיד לי מדוע עכשיו ש'אל־עאלם אל־ערבי'
מפרסם בתרועה גדולה את 'מאיין קמפף', ש'אל־יקד'ה' אינו יורד מהנושא היהודי,
שמאשימים את היהודים בתעמולה ציונית, מדוע עכשיו החלטת לצרף את קולך
לקולם?"

(Ballas 1991: 72)
"Harun," ṭafaḥ be-'oz 'al ha-shulḥan, "'ulay tagid li ma hevi 'otkha li-khtov 'et ha-ma'mar haze?"
"bo nedaber galiyut," biḳashtav ki-she-ani moshekh kisse la-shevet li-yado.
"ze be-diyuk ma she-ani rotse, she-tedabber galiyut ve-tagid li madua' 'akhshav she ***al-'ālamu al-'arabī*** *mefarsem bi-tru'a gedola 'et Mein Kampf, she* ***al-yaqaẓa*** *'eno yored me-ha-nośe ha-yhudi, she-ma'shimim 'et ha-yhudim be-ta'mula tsiyonit, madua' 'akhshav heḥlaṭta le-tsaref 'et ḳolkha le-ḳullam?*

["Haroun!" He slapped his hand on the table. "Why don't you tell me what made you write this article?"
"Let's be frank," I said, pulling a chair to sit next to him.
"That is precisely what I want, for you to be frank and tell me why now when *al-'alālamu-l-'arabī* publishes *Mein Kampf* with great pomp and circumstance when *al-Yaqda* will not leave the Jewish question alone]
(Ballas 2007: 87)

In the scene, in a conversation between Haron (the narrator) and his friend, Nasim blames Aharon after his article has been published. In the article, Aharon calls for the integration of the Iraqi Jews into the Iraqi National Army as well as for struggling against the activities of the Zionist movement in Iraq. The author uses the so-called intra-sentential CS within the Hebrew sentences. This type of Arabic use is very complicated, because of the great possibility of interference between the involved languages. Here the Arabic code constitutes a noun sentence *al-'ālam al-'arabī,* which takes the position of the subject in the Hebrew sentence. In addition, the use of the Hebrew conjunction "ש" renders the Arabic codes more integrated into the utterance of the Hebrew sentence.

Example 2-15

"יַא עְיוּנִי, יַא כַּאבְּי, איחרת הבוקר, אבל שמרתי לך את הקֶמַר,"
"מַאשַלְלַהּ על הקֶמַר היום, משהו מיוחד," אמרה כבכל יום ועור פניה, כמו הקֶמַר שלה,
חלק, רך, מֶשְיִי.

(Amir 1992: 23)

a- *"**ya 'yūnī**, **ya Kābī**, 'ekharta ha-boker, aval shamarti lekha 'et ha-**qemar**,"*
b- *"**mashālla** 'al ha-**qemar** ha-yom, mashehu meyuḥad," amra ke vekhol yom ye-'or paneha, kemo ha-**qemar** she-lah, ḥalak, rakh, meshi.*

a- ["Ya ayuni, ya Kābī," she said to me. "You are late this morning, I've kept some *kemar* (butter) for you.] (Amir 2010b: 20)
b- [*Mashallah* the *kemar* came out extra good today," she said as she did each morning. Her complexion was like the *kemar*, smooth, soft and silky.] (Amir 2010b: 21)

The intra-sentential code-switching is very obvious in this sentence. In 2-15-a, the Hebrew sentence begins with Arabic codes and ends with Arabic codes too. In 2-15-b, the Arabic/Hebrew codes are more of an intervention; the sequence of Arabic/Hebrew codes in this sentence reads:

"מַאשַׁלְלַה + על + ה(קֶמַר) + היום, משהו מיוחד"
Ar. (*Interjection*) + Heb. (*Particle*) + Heb. Particle (Ar. *Sing. Lexical*) + Heb. (*Sing. lexical*)

Another example of intra-sentential CS is also found in the late Hebrew novel by Sami Michael.

Example 2-16

"אני עולה מיד להביא את **הדשדאשה**."
*ane 'oleh meyyad le-havi et ha-**dishdāsha.***
[I will just go upstairs and get the ***dishdāsha*** (long robe).]
(Michael 2015: 131)

2.2.2.3 AMBIGUOUS-ACCESS CODE-SWITCHING

The study uses the term 'ambiguous access' to reflect the use of such Arabic codes that are difficult to translate into Hebrew on the one hand, and that could be comprehended within the Hebrew context in the novel on the other. This type of code cannot be considered as HA-CS, as might be elucidated within the context of the novel. Conversely, such codes cannot be seen as EA-CS, since for the most part they are not translated within the utterance of the Hebrew text. The study counts three main cases in which AA-CS is likely to occur: *interjection*, employing some *characters and place names* and *word-for-word translation*.

The use of Arabic interjections in the Hebrew texts is frequent. Sometimes the use of such codes is followed by translation, and sometimes not. In Example 2-17, Ballas inserts an Iraqi code in the dialogue between Nazima, an Iraqi Jewish woman, and Yusuf Shabi. The code is not translated into Hebrew. Yet the context of the scene guides the reader to the mode in which this code is most likely used, which constitutes sadness, anger and feelings of sorrow:

Example 2-17

נזימה התיפחה וטפחה על חזה. משראתה אותו פתחה בצעקה:
"הכל בגללך, יוסף! הכל בגללך... אתם הרסתם אותנו ! יאבוי'..."

Nazima hityafḥa ve-ṭapḥa ʻal ḥazah. Me-she-r'ata 'oto patḥa be-tse'aḳa: "ha-kol be-glalkha, Yusuf! ha-kol be-glalkha ... atem harastem 'otanu! ***yābūy ...***"

[Nazima weeps and strikes her chest. When she saw him she began to cry:
"The whole matter is because of you, Yousef! All because of you ... you have destroyed us! **yābūy** ..."]
(Ballas 1964: 29)

The Arabic code here **yābūy** يابوي [word-for-word translation: Oh my father] is not highlighted by the author to mark it as Arabic code. Neither is the Arabic code translated into Hebrew in the footnote nor in the text. Yet the scene of an Iraqi woman Nazima crying makes it clear to the outsider reader that the Arabic code here is associated with modes of anger and sorrow. The use of Arabic interjection adds to the reality of representing the characters' voices, which are mainly Iraqi Jewish characters, in the novel. It is important to point out that Arabic interjections constitute about 14 per cent of Arabic used in the Hebrew novels selected for this study, where most of them are not translated into Hebrew.

Another example also touches on this case of non-translated Arabic terms in the Hebrew texts. However, due to the context, the reader can expect a word that is associated with anger and violent. Sālim Afandi, one of the characters in the novel *Mafriaḥ ha-yonim* (Amir 1992: 55), was about to be banished from the theatre in which the Egyptian singer Abdul-Muṭaleb was singing because of a misunderstanding between him and one of the attendees. The Iraqi *shaykh* was angry and was shouting with an Iraqi Arabic dialectical term *welak* (oh idiot):

Example 2-18

וְלַכְ, תסתלק מפה! זעם השיח'

welak, *testaleḳ mepo! za'am hashekh.*
[Oh idiot, get out! the *shaykh* was angry.]

Some characters who have Arabic names used in the novels also can be counted as AA-CS. As pointed out above, Arabic names employed by the three Iraqi Jewish authors reveal the cultural and historical patterns associated with Iraq and the Arabic language. This connection between names and cultural background renders Arabic names as codes that constitute marked choices. Although names can hardly be translated, the context might help to maintain the meaning and the value of using such names. However, in many cases neither the translation, if any, nor the context can preserve the meaning of this type of codes.

Example 2-19

אחר־כך אמרתי שלא הייתי רוצה שיהיה קצר רואי כמוני, ובתוך כך סיפרתי על המצוקה שהיתה לי בבית־הספר כשלא הייתי מסוגל לקרוא מה שכתוב על הלוח עד שציידו אותי במשקפיים שהחמירו עוד יותר את מצבי. "אבּו־עְוֵינאת",קראו לי הילדים, והכינוי הנלעג הזה דבק בי עד שסיימתי את העממי.

(Ballas 1991: 23)

*"aḥar-kakh amarti she-lo hayyiti rotse she-yihye ḳetsar ro'i ke-moni, ove-tokh kakh sipparti 'al ha-matsoḳa she-hayta li be-bet ha-ssefer ke-she-lo hayyiti mesugal li-ḳro ma she-katuv 'al ha-luaḥ 'ad she-tsiydu 'oti be-mishḳafaym she-heḥmiru 'od 'et matsevi. "**Abū-'wēnāt**", ḳar'u li ha-yeladim, ṿe-ha-kennuy ha-nel'ag ha-ze davaḳ bi 'ad she-siyyamti 'et ha-'amami.*

["Then I said I wouldn't want him to be short-sighted like me, and told her of my distress at school when I was unable to read from the board until I got fitted with glasses, which only worsened my condition. The kids called my Abu-'Awynat, and this nickname stuck to me throughout primary school".]

(Ballas 2007: 23)

The narrator wishes that his son Jimmy should not weaken his eyesight like that of his father. Within this plot in the novel, the narrator recalls memories from his childhood, he remembered how he was called **Abū-'wēnāt** (the man in glasses) among his classmates because he was not able to see what was written on the blackboard. The glasses he wore made his situation more embarrassing. **Abū-'wēnāt** here is neither HA-CS nor EA-CS. On the one hand, the author did not elucidate precisely the Arabic embedded code in the paragraph using strategies discussed above. On the other hand, the context in which the code is employed is associated with childhood memories of his father, when he was repeatedly humiliated and bullied by his classmates because of his weak eyesight.

The same holds true for some Arabic place names which have historical and cultural symbols, in which only the first degree of the In.R (an Iraqi Jewish reader) can recall and taste the value of such places. The significance of such places as well as the local colour they have is apparently not only inaccessible for the Out.R but also for some groups among In.R, who belong to the second and the third classes:

Example 2-20

"הרון," אמר בטלטלו אותי, "אם תעלה לצריח שוק אל־ע'זל ותצעק יומם ולילה שרק מאהבת אומת מוחמד התאסלמת, גם זה לא יעזור לך!".

(Ballas 1991: 94)

*"**Harūn**," amar be-ṭaltlo 'oti, "'im ta'aleh le-tsariyaḥ **Sūq Al-ghazl** ye-tits'aḳ yomam va-layla she-raq me-ahavat 'ummat Moḥammad hitaslamta, gam ze lo ya'zor le-kha!".*

["Haroun," he shook me and said, "if you climb to the top of the minaret in the Souk al-Ghazl and yell out day and night that you became a Muslim for no other reason than love of Muhammad's nation, that wouldn't help you either".]
(Ballas 2007: 116)

In this conversation, Kāzim is not convinced that Harūn has converted to Islam motivated by love for Islam and its people. In order to convey this opinion about the situation of his friend Harūn, Kāzim uses an Arabic Iraqi metaphor. The metaphor he uses depends mainly on a famous marketplace in Baghdad at the time, Sūq al-Ghazl.[11] This code constitutes the chief factor in the metaphor, yet the historical and cultural value it holds could not be translated into Hebrew. Thus, it also belongs to the in-between Arabic codes in the Hebrew text.

When the author translates an idiom or folk saying, she/he wants to make the employed codes in this idiom more accessible to the reader. The translation, however, might not transfer the metaphoric sense of the original idiom. This is highly expected in the case of word-for-word translation of an embedded Arabic idiom or folk saying in the Hebrew texts. Although the self-translation of the embedded codes contributes to making them easy access, at least at the utterance level of the text, the complicity of perceiving the denotations they hold might make them inaccessible. Therefore, the term AA-CS may be applied to some of them:

Example 2-21

אבוס עינק [אנשק את עיניך]

abūs 'ēnak [*'enashēq 'et 'enekha*]
[***abūs 'ēnak,*** I am kissing your eyes]
(Amir 1983: 201)

The author uses Arabic in the most convenient way for the reader who does not know Arabic. He puts the Arabic term in his Hebrew text in Hebrew letters followed by a direct translation. In this case, even if the word-for-word translation was not to some extent successful in transmitting the exact meaning of the Arabic Iraqi dialect term (أبوس عينك), the context serves as an assistant.

Example 2-22

"תסאות אל גרעה ואום אל שער (הקירחת ומקורזלת השיער אותו דבר),"

"tsāwat al-gar'a we 'um al-sha'er. *(ha-ḳeraḥat u-meḳurzelet ha-śe'ar 'oto davar,)"*

[Both bald women and women with hair bacame the same]

(Amir 1983: 79)

In reference to the translation, the metaphor the above idiom holds is not clear enough. The metaphoric connotation here is to wonder how two things, one of which is precious and valuable and one which is not that valuable, come together in one scale and are seen as one equal thing. The *Arabic-Hebrew Dictionary of the Babylon Jewish Dialect* presents a more enriched translation of this item:

"תסאות אל גרעה ואום-אל-שעע' (אימרה) – (בעלת הקרחת ובעלת השיער נהיו שוות): העשיר והעני נראו זהים"

*"**tsāwat al-gar'a we'um al-shagher ('imra)** – (ba'lat ha-ḳeraḥat u-va'lat ha-śe'ar nehiyu shavot): he'ashir ṿe-he'oni ner'u zahim.*

(Yona-Swery 1995: 109)

Here the authors of the dictionary thought that the word-for-word translation was not enough to transfer the Arabic code into Hebrew.[12] Accordingly, they were keen on adding another gloss to help in understanding the Arabic message conveyed by the idiom: העשיר והעני נראו זהים.

The same holds true for some other Arabic idioms employed by Amir (1983: 19, 66, 87, 201). Unlike what he uses in the same novel, Amir adds a gloss after the word-for-word translation:

Example 2-23

דולק נכנס למקלחת וקטע את השיחה. רוַח לי. "מה שלומך?"
"פוג־אלנח'ל," אמרתי לו בערבית.
"מה זה פוג־אלנח'ל ? חייך. ביטויו העילג דיגדג, מצול ואני פרצנו בצחוק.
"מעל צמרות הדקלים, או, כמו שאתם אומרים, מעל המגדל סביב אשקיפה."

(Amir 1983: 173)

Doleḳ nekhnas la-miḳlaḥat ṿe-ḳata' 'et ha-śiḥa. rivvaḥ li. "ma shlomkha?"
*"**fōg al-nakhl,**" amarti lo ba'aravit.*

"ma ze ***Fōg al-nakhl****? ḥiyyekh. biṭuiyav ha-'illeg digdeg, Matsul ya-ani paratsnu be-tsḥoḳ.*
me'al tsammrot ha-deḳalim, 'o kemo she-atem 'omrim, me'al ha-migdal saviv ashkifa.

[To my relief Dolek came into my showers and cut the conversation short. 'How are you?' he boomed in his hollow voice.
'*foq-alnahal*' I said in Arabic.
"What does *foq-alnahal* mean? He smiled. Tickled by his accent Masul and I burst into infectious laughter.
"At the top of palm trees", or, as you might say, looking down from the top of the water-tower.]
(Amir 1987: 186)
Or like what Ballas wrote (1964: 52, 86, 125).

2.2.3 Syntagmatic/Paradigmatic Deviations

In the above section 2.2.2, the study discussed the first banner of the suggested model to approach exophonic texts, which is CS. This was done by means of a new perspective on the typology of CS as discussed in section 2.1.4. In this section, the second and the third banners suggested by the model are discussed. The two banners investigate the syntagmatic/paradigmatic relations that occur because of the Arabic/Hebrew interactions in the Hebrew novels selected for this study.

2.2.3.1 SYNTAGMATIC DEVIATION

The syntagmatic deviations in some Hebrew sentences within the novels highlight the way in which Arabic/Hebrew interference influences the author style. It is most important to refer to the norm of standard word order in modern Hebrew. Modern Hebrew is considered one of the SVO languages (subject–verb–object) (Shlonsky 1997: 7). Shlonsky asserts that there are two cases in which the verb might come before the subject; the first is 'triggered inversion', while the second case does not require a trigger and is termed 'free inversion' (1997: 145). He enumerates nine types of triggers: 'Triggers can be sentential adverbs, PPs (Prepositional Phrase) and preoposed clauses, direct and indirect objects of the verb, clausal complements, certain negative phrases, wh-expressions and (null) relative operators' (1997: 146).

The free inversion, according to Shlonsky (1997: 163), is likely to occur in the passive voice. We expect deviation, then, when there is no trigger and the sentence is not in the passive mode. This is what is discussed in the following lines.

Example 2-24

"חנן אלוהים את כאזֶם וחסך ממנו מפח־נפש כזה"

(Ballas 1991: 117)

"ḥanan 'elohim 'et ***Kāẓim*** *ve-ḥasakh me-mennu mappaḥ-nefesh kaze"*

["God has graced Kazem by saving him such bitter disappointment"]

(Ballas 2007: 146)

The word order in Example 2-24 does not follow the word order in modern Hebrew. The example shows that the writer's knowledge of Arabic has influenced his syntagmatic choices; the word order in the Modern Hebrew Norm (MHN), as has been pointed out above, is subject (1) + verb (2) + object (3) = (SVO). However, the word order in Example 2-24 is VOS, which is closer to standard Arabic, and in which the verb precedes the subject. When we reorder the sentence according to the MHN, it is like in Example 2-24-b:

(a) ḥanan + 'elohim + 'et **Kāẓim**
V + S + O

(b) 'elohim + ḥanan + 'et **Kāẓim**.
S + V + O

If we assume that the verb > subject in the above example is by no means a triggered inversion, then it seems that the main reason for syntagmatic deviation here might be regarded to the influence of standard Arabic which prefers to raise verb before subject. The same holds true for these examples:

"ירחם האל עליה"

(Ballas 1964: 36)

"חרב עלי עולמי."

(Amir 1983: 144)

"יתן לך אלוהים בריאות, אמא."

(Michael 1993: 105)

"אלוהים ימחל לנו," אמרה עזיזה. "ימחל לנו אלוהים."

(Michael 1993: 154)

2.2.3.2 PARADIGMATIC DEVIATIONS

As two Semitic languages, Hebrew and Arabic share a lot of phonological and morphological aspects. The paradigmatic deviations are expected in the Hebrew texts written by the three authors of the study. This is because of the influence of Arabic on the authors' selection of certain Hebrew lexical items in favour of others. This study asserts that the authors' choices from the alternatives and variations in the Hebrew lexicon are sometimes influenced by Arabic lexis or loan translation from Arabic.

2.2.3.3 LEXICAL CHOICES

Example 2-25

"...ירימו תרומה להגשמת החלום הכביר"

(Amir 1992: 197)

"... yarimu teruma le-hagshamat ha-ḥalom ha-kabir"

["... would fulfil our share of the great dream"]

(Amir 2010b: 239)

The Hebrew lexicon item *kabīr* has a long history in the Hebrew lexicon, an adjective that has two meanings: it refers to 'much' in the sense of quantity or quality, and also describes something with greatness (Ben-Yehuda 1980: 2242–3; Kena'ani 1998: 1997; Sagiv 2008: 652). The item also shares the Arabic use of the term as one of God's attributes (Kena'ani 1998: 1998). The alternative replaceable units available for the author might be (*'atsum, gadol*) which mean *great, big* respectively. However, the author selects *kabīr*, which is rare in modern Hebrew. The choice of *kabīr* is likely to be motivated by the Arabic lexical item, which phonologically and semantically is identical to the Hebrew lexical item.

This lexical item is also employed in Michael's novel (2011: 18, 59, 114, 223); as well as by Ballas (1991: 82).

Example 2-26

"טבע נפסד הוא באדם שאינו יכול לומר לא"

(Ballas 1991: 8)

"ṭeva' nifsad hu ba'adam she-'eno yakhol lomar lo"

["Of what worth is the character of a man who can't say no"]

(Ballas 2007: 3)

The word *ṭeva'* (nature) is phonetically closer to the Arabic lexical item *ṭab'*. Although one of the meanings of *ṭeva'* is 'essence' or 'personality', using this lexeme is not common in modern Hebrew when it comes to references to human beings.[13] Moreover, the Iraqi Judaeo–Arabic lexicon also uses the term *ṭeva'* (Yona-Swery 1995: 151). Here, the author selects a Hebrew lexical item which shows the influence of Arabic on his lexical choices, instead of using other Hebrew lexical items such as *'ofi, tekhuna*. It is important to point out here that this use of Arabic appears in a non-dialogue narrative. Moreover, this reflects Ballas's stylistic intention, as indicated through his lexical choices. The same holds true for the next example:

Example 2-27

כבר היה בן שש־עשרה, עלם יפה וגבוה.

(Ballas 1991: 67)

"kevar haya ben shesh-'eśreh, 'elem yafe ve-gavoah"
["He already was sixteen and a tall, handsome youth"]
(Ballas 2007: 81)

The author again chooses a Hebrew lexical item closer to Arabic: *'elem.* The Arabic equivalent lexical item is *ghulām/ghulum*, which is semantically identical to the Hebrew *'elem*, which refers to *youth, adolescent*; (Ben-Yehuda 1980: 4526; Kena'ani 1998: 4344).

The similar phonological lexical aspects between Arabic and Hebrew are employed by the author when he wants to make his Hebrew close to Arabic. Example 2-28 can also support this hypothesis:

Example 2-28

The use of *avi* and *'emmi*, which are phonologically close to *abi* and *'umi* respectively, in favour of אבא שלי *'aba sheli* and אימא שלי *'emma sheli.* See for instance Ballas (1991: 54, 55).

According to the *Linguistic Encyclopaedia*, there is a loan translation when 'the meaning of a foreign word or expression is borrowed, and the word or words are translated in the borrowing' (Malmkjaer 1991: 284). Backus and Dorleijn (2009: 77) define 'loan translation' as follows: 'any usage of morphemes in Language A that is the result of the literal translation of one or more elements in a semantically equivalent expression in Language B'. Loan translation may constitute a deviation from the paradigmatic norm in the target language; this is because of the semantic and the lexical interference that may occur as a result during the translation.

Since the Hebrew novels have a lot of translated Arabic codes and expressions into Hebrew, the paradigmatic deviation is highly expected, especially when a context or a narrative in one novel represents an element of Arabic culture. The examples below discuss this phenomenon in the Hebrew texts.

Example 2-29

"אם הבנים אינה בבית."

"'em ha-banim 'enah ba-bayt."
(Ballas 1964: 33)
[The mother of the *boys* is not at home.]: word-for-word translation.
[The children's mother is not at home.]: free translation.

In the above Hebrew sentence, the author seemed to use a merely Arabic dialectic expression: *ūm lewlād*, which refers to a mother, a wife in the Arabic cultural context. Yet, there is no such use of *'em ha-banim* (the mother of boys) in modern Hebrew. On the other hand, modern Hebrew uses *'em*, and *'ema* to refer to mother. The interference might happen here with the use of the Hebrew lexical item *banim*[14] (boys) in association with *'em* to provide the connotation of 'mother of children', the mother. However, the loan translation employed by Ballas here may be understood as implying that the mother has only boys and not girls: 'the mother of the boys'. But in fact this term is widely used in Arabic dialect to refer to the: (mother of children, both boys and girls). This approximation between Arabic/Hebrew semantic terms may be seen as a style feature in Ballas's writing. Moreover, by means of loan translation of an Arabic expression, the author adds a new connotation to the lexical item *banim*, to refer to *yeladim* when it is connected to *'em*.

It is important to point out here that Amir uses a word-for-word translation of the above expression used by Ballas, and Amir chooses to use the word *yeladim*: [15]

Example 2-30

"התהיי לי לאישה, רעיה, מאהבת, חברה, אם ילדַי?"

"hatihyyi li l'isha, ra'ya, me'ahevet, ḥavera, 'em yeladay?"

["Would you accept to be my wife, friend, beloved, comrade, friend, mother of my children?"]

(Amir 2010a: 186)

Daniel, the narrator, asks his beloved Abigail to be his wife. Among the attributes the author mentions is *'em yeladay* (the mother of my children), which is likely to be closer to dialect Arabic *'ūm lewlād*.

See also the next example:

Example 2-31

"ועם הזמן נעשיתי כמוהו עבד לכסף."

"ye-'em ha-zman ne'śeti kemohu 'eved la-kesef."

["And eventually I became like him, a slave to money."]

(Amir 2010a: 95)

The selecting of the expression *'eved la-kesef* (a slave to money) shows the influence of Arabic on the author's style concerning the loan translation into Hebrew. The Arabic expression *'abdū-lmāl* associated with a dire personal attribute of greed, was transmitted into Hebrew. It constitutes a deviation from the Hebrew norm concerning the common use to express the same denotation in Hebrew lexicon, which is, for instance *petsa' kesef*, or *rodef petsa'* (Sagiv 2008: 470). In the same novel, interestingly, Amir (2010a: 347) uses the term "רודפי דינרים" *rodfe-denarim*. Ballas (1991: 66) also uses the Hebrew lexical term *rodfe petsa'*. It is important to say that there are some other idioms which are used to express similar denotations of the term (greedy) in the Arabic dialect spoken by Jews in Iraq, for instance, *ṭemmāʿ* (Yona-Swery 1995: 156) and *bani ʾādam ṭemmāʿ* (a greedy person), *ʿenū gawʿānah* (his eye is hungry – a greedy person) and *nefsu deneyyē* (someone despised) (Me'iri 2006: 171–2). However, *ʿabdun lelmāl* was not included in the Iraqi Judaeo-Arabic dictionaries.

2.2.3.4 ARABIC IN HEBREW: FOREGROUNDING OR DEVIANCE?

As has been discussed in section 2.1.4, the term foregrounding and its relation to some deviations from the norm are examined in the novels. The following example briefly looks at this issue in relation to Iraqi Jewish fiction.

Example 2-32

"אלוהים ימחל לנו," אמרה עזיזה. "ימחל לנו אלוהים"

(Michael 1993: 154)

ʾelohim yemaḥel lanu, amra ʿaziza. yemaḥel lanu ʾelohim.

[God forgives us, said ʿAziza, forgives us God.]

This example demonstrates an interesting literary and linguistic aspect in Michael's novel *Viḳṭoryah.* The author presents the linguistic variety of the word order in two forms: SVO and VOS, the former of which represents the norm, while the latter shows the deviation from this norm. In this way, Michael wants to show that the way in which the words are ordered is intentional and conscious. It is clear from this example, therefore, that not all deviations occur because of interference between two language systems. Rather, sometimes deviation should be perceived as a literary device by which the author wants to foreground his work.

The paradigmatic deviation is also expected when it functions to transfer folk sayings into Hebrew texts. The following example demonstrates the same type of stylistic manoeuvre within the paradigmatic range. Once again, in the example below the phonological similarity between Arabic and Hebrew plays an essential role in the selection of Hebrew paradigms:

Example 2-33

"ואללה עשיתי אוכל יערב לחכך. שאַל את מונירה"

*"**walla** ʿaśeti ʾokhel yaʿarav le-ḥakekha. sheʾal ʾet Monira."*

[I swear to God that I cooked food for you that is pleasant to your palate, ask Monira.] (Ballas 1964: 33)

The use of loan translation here echoes the style used by Ballas. On the one hand, the choice of the lexical item *ḥek* (palate) makes the dialogue language sound like high classical Hebrew with regard to the choice of biblical lexical items. Yet the use of such lexical items might reflect the influence of the Iraqi Arabic dialect. The Arabic sentence used in the same context would be *walla sawwēt akel yestāhel ḥanakak.* A reader may regard Ballas's use of such codes as a high use of language, although it is most likely a loan translation of an Iraqi folk saying used in the context of expressing hospitality in Arabic culture. Indeed, the image used to describe the food and the way in which the guest is offered the food are uniquely Arab cultural images.

2.3 Conclusion

Applying the suggested model of the study to approaching literary texts written in the non-mother tongue reveals that a rich diversity marks the use of Arabic in the novels examined. The Arabic codes employed in the Hebrew texts can be divided into three main types hard-access code-switching (HA-CS), easy-access code-switching (EA-CS) and ambiguous-access code-switching (AA-CS). Each type adds to the style of Arabic used in the Hebrew novels due to the distinct linguistic feature that each type of the three embodies.

Not only is CS employed in the suggested corpora. The texts also contain a considerable number of cases where Arabic/Hebrew interference is evident, which resulted in some syntagmatic and paradigmatic deviations from the modern Hebrew norm. The deviations were categorised mainly in two axes: syntagmatic and paradigmatic. The first category rearranges the word order of Hebrew lexical items in some sentences in a way that violates the Hebrew norm on the one hand, and imitates the Arabic norm on the other. The second category (paradigmatic deviation) includes a lexical selection of varieties in the Hebrew lexicon that are likely to be closer phonologically to the Arabic lexicon. Paradigmatic deviations are also expected in cases of loan translation from Arabic into the Hebrew text. Deviations do not derive entirely from interference and/or unconscious desire. Rather, the author's choices in the literary paradigm are more likely to be intentional. Therefore, deviations in Iraqi Jewish prose can arguably be seen to be an example of foregrounding.

3

The Use of Arabic Between Authors and Novels

This chapter discusses the style of Arabic use and each corpus of each of the three authors. It is divided into three main parts: the first investigates the diachronic analysis of Arabic use in the nine Hebrew novels over some fifty years. The second part discusses the distinctive style of each author regarding Arabic use. This will be achieved by means of a comparison between each author and each novel. The third part looks at the Arabic dialects and Judaeo-Arabic varieties in the selected novels.

As to the choice of the corpora, it is essential to recall the main research questions of the study: (1) How did Iraqi Jewish novelists use Arabic in their early Hebrew novels? (2) In what ways has the style of Iraqi Jewish novelists regarding Arabic use changed? (3) Why did Iraqi Jews use Arabic in the suggested corpora?

As to question (1), Chapter 3 gave a general overview regarding the use of Arabic in the suggested nine Hebrew novels. In order to trace the style changes in the use of Arabic of the three Iraqi Jewish authors answering (2) a diachronic study is required. The diachronic analysis is structured on the basis of three periods. The first period represents the early novels written in Hebrew by the three authors. Three novels chosen from the 1990s represent the second period and the last period comprises the three late Hebrew novels. In this way, the study seeks to span approximately fifty years.

Question (3) is discussed in Chapter 4, in which the concept of belonging regarding language shifting, language conflicts, migration and homeland versus new land is examined.

3.1 A Diachronic Analysis of Arabic Use in the Selected Hebrew Novels

In order to highlight the historical implications of the issue, the study suggests a diachronic analysis based on three periods in which each period signifies a corpus, as pointed out above. The three early novels written in Hebrew by the Iraqi authors at the beginning of their literary career are Ballas (1964), Michael (1974) and Amir (1983). The middle period that follows is assigned to three Hebrew novels published in the 1990s – Ballas (1991), Michael (1993) and Amir (1992) – while the late literary works of the three authors designate the third period: Ballas (2008), Michael (2015) and Amir (2010a). These three periods are termed three corpora, and each corpus represents a period: the early Hebrew novels (corpus 1), the middle period of the 1990s (corpus 2) and the three late Hebrew novels (corpus 3).

It was essential for this study to trace all Arabic uses in the suggested corpora. The tables below illustrate the use of Arabic in connection with the three suggested corpora. It is important to mention that all the data are extracted manually from the texts as the texts are not digitalised.

3.1.1 Early Hebrew Novels, Corpus 1

Table 3.1 shows that Amir's novel (1983) has more use of Arabic than the other two Hebrew novels, although it was published twenty years after Ballas's novel (1964) and about ten years after Michael's novel (1974). It is interesting to note that the first Hebrew novel written by an Iraqi author (Ballas 1964) ranks last among the three with regard to the use of Arabic.

Table 3.1 Use of Arabic according to parts of speech, corpus 1

Novel/Figures of speech	(Ballas 1964)	(Michael 1974)	(Amir 1983)	Total according to figures of speech
Noun	45	34	110	189
Verb	12	11	17	40
Adverb	5	5	9	19
Adjective	9	6	19	34
Pronoun	0	1	13	14
Conjunction	0	0	1	1
Interjection	10	70	69	149
Particle	7	103	31	141
Total	88	230	269	587

Looking at the use of Arabic in connection with parts of speech in corpus 1, we can see that of a list of 587 uses, 32 per cent are nouns, verbs make up only 7 per cent, interjections comprise 26 per cent, particles make up 24 per cent, adverbs and pronouns comprise almost the same proportion with 3 per cent and 2 per cent respectively, adjectives account for 6 per cent, and there are no Arabic conjunctions used. It is clear from the pie chart in Figure 3.1 that the three authors favour the use of nouns over Arabic verbs. Particles and interjections together comprise 50 per cent of the total Arabic uses. In all three early Hebrew novels, the use of Arabic nouns is dominant, with only one exception in one novel: the use of the Arabic particle */yā/* used extensively by Michael (1974), along with the number of interjections, is higher than the use of Arabic nouns in the same novel.

Regarding semantic fields in corpus 1, the use of nouns varies. This includes foods: פאצ'ה *pāñeh*[1] (Ballas 1964: 28, 77), במיה *bamiya* [okra dish][2] (Amir 1983: 199), קובה-בורגול *kubba-burghul* [crushed meat with bourghul wheat] (Michael 1974: 188); music: חפלה *ḥafla* [party] (Amir 1983: 106, 129), תקאסים *taqāsīm*[3] (Amir 1983: 107); sex: טיז *ṭīẓ* [buttock] (Amir 1983: 24, 25, 51), כרכאנה *karakhāna*[4] (Amir 1983: 58), שארמוטה *sharmūṭa* [bitch] (Michael 1974: 24); and Arabic games: ג'האר יאק *jehār yak* (Ballas 1964: 145).[5]

The interjection constitutes about one-quarter of Arabic uses in corpus 1. These interjections, which are used in the dialogue mode, are

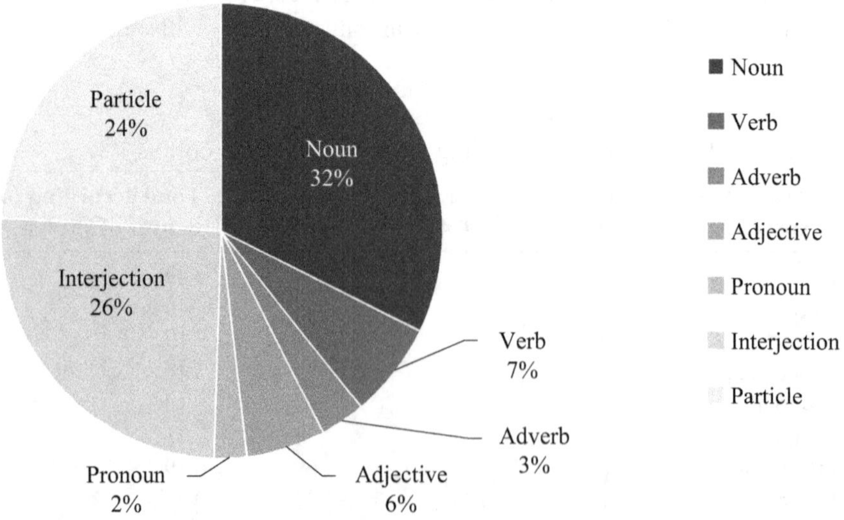

Figure 3.1 Parts of speech, corpus 1

Table 3.2 Arabic use strategies, corpus 1

Novel/strategy	(Ballas 1964)	(Michael 1974)	(Amir 1983)	Sub-total
HA-CS	44	217	108	369
EA-CS	31	–	29	60
Total	75	217	137	429

present mainly in Arabic Iraqi vernacular, e.g. יא עיני *yā ʻēnī* [hey my eye – cool] (Amir 1983: 174), וואללה *wallah* [I swear to God] (Michael 1974: 14), יאבוי *yābūy* [My father – Oh God] (Ballas 1964: 29). The use of such lexical items serves likewise as a stylistic device reflecting the use of many Iraqi characters employed in the novels of the corpus. In addition, such uses of vernacular items, interjections and particles, imbue the conversations in the three early Hebrew novels with the local colour of Iraq/Baghdad.

To draw a general and comprehensive picture about the style of Arabic use in corpus 1, the comparison of strategies of employing Arabic embedded codes used by the authors in their Hebrew texts is useful. Table 3.2 illustrates the strategies of using Arabic in corpus 1.

The main three strategies of using Arabic in Hebrew texts – hard-access code-switching (HA-CS), easy-access code-switching (EA-CS) and glossing – highlight the varieties of employing Arabic. The portion of each strategy sheds light on the style of each novel, each author and each corpus. The strategy of using CS in the three early Hebrew novels serves, accordingly, as a literary device. HA-CS strategy is most used in corpus 1 with 86 per cent, followed by 14 per cent of EA-CS. In view of these results, the stylistic features of corpus 1 can be associated generally with the use of Arabic as hard-access codes, which involve using embedded Arabic codes without translation, footnotes or glossing. Employing the majority of these codes in early Hebrew texts, this may be encountered by an Israeli reader who has neither an Iraqi nor Arabic linguistic background (the outsider reader), giving these literary works a unique style in the canon of modern Hebrew literature.

3.1.2 Hebrew Novels Written in the Middle Period, Corpus 2

According to Table 3.3, the noun is the dominant part of speech in corpus 2, with almost 70 per cent, followed by interjections at 10 per cent and particles at 8 per cent. The verb in corpus 2 constitutes only 4 per cent of the total parts of speech used in the Hebrew novels (see Figure 3.2). It is important to point out that in corpus 2, the significant increase in the use of

Table 3.3 Arabic uses according to parts of speech, corpus 2

The novel/Parts of speech	(Ballas 1991)	(Michael 1993)	(Amir 1992)	Total parts of speech
Noun	42	113	855	1010
Verb	–	19	42	61
Adverb	–	3	6	9
Adjective	7	3	53	63
Pronoun	–	13	29	42
Conjunction	–	2	6	8
Interjection	1	14	136	151
Particle	–	12	100	112
Sub-total	50	179	1227	1456

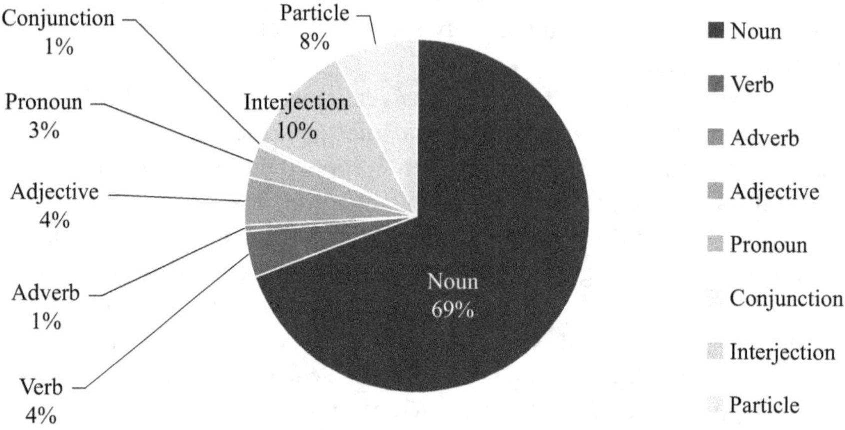

Figure 3.2 Parts of speech, corpus 2

Arabic is concentrated in the novel *Mafriaḥ ha-yonim* (Amir 1992). This novel alone contains *c.* 85 per cent of the Arabic parts of speech used in corpus 2.

In comparison to corpus 1, the use of noun is the most preferred part of speech in the two corpora. One should add that the novel *Mafriaḥ ha-yonim* (Amir 1992) was actually written *before* the first Hebrew novel by Amir, published in 1983. This fact can answer the question as to why Amir employed Arabic codes in *Mafriaḥ ha-yonim* more than in his first Hebrew manuscript published in 1983. Thus, the period in which the manuscript was written, and not the date of publication, is important for understanding and answering the question of why Arabic is used in one text more than in another.

Table 3.4 Arabic use strategies, corpus 2

Novel/strategy	(Ballas 1991)	(Michael 1993)	(Amir 1992)	Sub-total
HA-CS	19	103	837	959
EA-CS	7	3	66	76
Total	26	106	903	1035

Table 3.4 illustrates the strategies used in employing Arabic in the selected Hebrew texts. HA-CS is once again the dominant strategy among the three. The use of non-translated and non-glossed Arabic codes constitutes slightly more than 92 per cent, while EA-CS strategy is only about 7 per cent.

In comparison to corpus 1, the strategy of employing HA-CS in both corpus 1 and corpus 2 exceeds EA-CS strategy. One further important note about corpus 2 is the fact that Arabic use in general in corpus 2 is higher than Arabic use in corpus 1; the Arabic parts of speech and the strategies used in corpus 2 are twice those used in corpus 1. Here again, the significant increase in the use of Arabic is associated solely with one novel, Amir (1992). Amir's style with regard to Arabic use is discussed in detail in this chapter.

3.1.3 The Late Hebrew Novels, Corpus 3

Corpus 3, which consists of the three late Hebrew novels written in the 2010s, shows that the style of Arabic – although the use of Arabic, in general, decreased in the recent Hebrew works – still employs a preference for the noun instead of the verb. Of a total of 194 Arabic parts of speech employed in corpus 3, the noun constitutes the majority of Arabic use, and only three verbs are used. These ratios are similar to those of corpus 1 and corpus 2.

In corpus 3, HA-CS is the most used strategy with 86 per cent in connection with Arabic codes, as compared with 14 per cent for EA-CS. In corpus 3, unlike the other two corpora, glossing strategy is given no preference by the three authors.

3.1.4 General Remarks on the Diachronic Analysis of Arabic Use

To sum up with general remarks on the development of the style of Arabic use over some fifty years, it is clear from the corpora that Arabic is employed in the Hebrew texts in several ways. This finding is based on the wide range of Arabic parts of speech found in the texts, as well as the variety of strategies employed by the authors.

Table 3.5 Arabic uses according to parts of speech, corpus 3

The novel/ parts of speech	(Ballas 2008)	(Michael 2015)	(Amir 2010a)	Total according to parts of speech
Noun	5	131	25	161
Verb	–	2	1	3
Adverb	–	1	–	1
Adjective	1	3	4	8
Pronoun	–	–	1	1
Conjunction	–	–	–	–
Interjection	–	19	–	19
Particle	–	1	–	1
Sub-total	6	157	31	194

Table 3.6 Arabic use strategies, corpus 3

Novel/strategies	(Ballas 2008)	(Michael 2015)	(Amir 2010a)	Sub-total
HA-CS	3	101	22	126
EA-CS	3	13	4	20
Total	6	114	26	146

The noun is the first favoured term used by the Iraqi authors, with the noun phrase favoured over the verb phrase. The use of noun as the most favoured part of speech has the same ratio throughout the three corpora.[6]

As to interjections, there is a considerable decrease in the employment of such parts of speech: from 25 per cent in corpus 1, to 10 per cent in corpus 2, ending with 9.7 per cent in corpus 3. The decrease in the use of interjections, associated mostly with the Arabic Iraqi vernacular, indicates how the use of Arabic in the literary works by the Iraqi writers was gradually diminished. Although the protagonists of the three late Hebrew novels (Amir 2010a; Ballas 2008; Michael 2015) are of Iraqi origin,[7] the use of interjections in these novels is minimised compared to Hebrew novels published in the 1990s or earlier, where interjections are used even more widely.

The use of Arabic particle, mainly */yā/*, which is associated with the act of calling someone, is also unique in the Hebrew texts. It occupies the second position after the use of interjections. Indeed, the use of this particle reflects the Iraqi vernacular used by some characters in the novels. Some novels used the Arabic particle extensively in almost every dialogue between the characters that involves calling someone by their name.[8]

In addition to the fact that the Arabic lexical items used in the Hebrew novels reveal the variety and multiplicity of borrowing from the Arabic lexicon in the Hebrew texts, exemplifying internal borrowing and occurring at the micro level, there are some cases of external borrowing that were employed by the authors in their early Hebrew manuscripts. These cases of external borrowing show the diachronic process of inserting some lexical items into the Hebrew lexicon, mainly slang, that are borrowed from Arabic, such as when a lexical item like מסטול *mastūl* [drunk, on drugs] was used in Ballas's first Hebrew novel (Ballas 1964: 181). The author added a Hebrew glossing of the Arabic code in the footnote. Yet, presently, the Hebrew lexicon includes this word (Sagiv 2008: 764), which occurs mainly in Israeli spoken language. This attitude towards such a word from Arabic would not exist if the lexical item *mastūl* had already been a borrowed lexical item in Hebrew in the 1960s. In other words, if the Hebrew speakers in Israel at the time the novel *Ha-maʿabara* (Ballas 1964) appeared had been familiar with this lexeme, Ballas would not have had to add a footnote glossing the term.

CS continued to be the most used strategy of employing Arabic codes over the three corpora. This fact proves that even in the late Hebrew novels, the tendency towards using hard-access Arabic codes is the most central trait in the style of the novels. In all the nine novels, HA-CS is used more than the other two strategies, EA-CS and glossing.

To conclude at this point, it is obvious from the data analysed through the corpora that the use of Arabic in the nine Hebrew novels discussed was gradually decreasing. This fact, however, does suggest a conclusion about the employment of Arabic in modern Israeli literature. Arabic was also employed in other Hebrew works by the Iraqi authors as well as by other Palestinian writers (Levy 2014). Therefore, this study does not generalise about the diachronic decrease of Arabic in Iraqi, or in Israeli literature in general, based on the given results. This study, rather, gives an example of a specific group of Israeli authors concerning Arabic use in selected Hebrew novels of their writing. Further, as the next chapter argues, the use of Arabic is mostly associated with the geographic location of the narrative setting in each novel.

3.2 Arabic Use as Compared Between Novels and Authors

In order to examine the style of each author regarding Arabic use, the study conducted an analysis of a sample of the first fifty pages from each novel of the three writers. Bearing in mind the diverse range of pages in each novel – some have fewer than 200 pages while others exceed 450 pages – a decision was made to investigate only the first fifty pages of each novel as a sample. In addition, taking a sample of fixed page numbers assures the precision of the statistical calculations and percentages applied to the novels. In this way, the representative sample can make grounded statements about the style of Arabic use with regard to the following aspects: Arabic parts of speech; the strategies of Arabic use; the comparison between dialogue and narrative cases in which Arabic is used; and the investigation of Arabic semantic fields employed by each author. The representative samples total 450 pages taken from the nine Hebrew novels – 150 pages for each author.

3.2.1 Shimon Ballas

According to Table 3.7, the sample collected from the three novels (Ballas 1964, 1991, 2008) indicates that the style of using Arabic in Ballas's literary works over some fifty years tends to decrease. The noun was the dominant part of speech in his use of Arabic, with 62 per cent. The last Hebrew novel by Ballas has no Arabic uses in the first fifty pages.

To add colloquial taste to his literary works, Ballas uses Iraqi folk sayings in different ways in his novels. These kinds of idioms and folk sayings appear mostly in Hebrew script in the form of EA-CS. The direct translation or the glossing are used by the author to make the metaphor of idioms or folk sayings more understandable for the outsider reader.

Take, for example, the extract "אִח'תלַט אל־חאבל באַל־נאבל", *ikhtalaṭa al-ḥābil bi-lnābil* [The valuable and the invaluable have been merged] (Ballas 1964: 52). Ballas adds the meaning of the Arabic idiom in the

Table 3.7 Arabic parts of speech in Ballas's sample

The novel/parts of speech	(Ballas 1964: 7–56)	(Ballas 1991: 7–56)	(Ballas 2008: 8–57)	Total according to parts of speech
Noun	20	3	–	23
Verb	1	–	–	1
Adverb	2	–	–	2
Adjective	2	1	–	3
Pronoun	–	–	–	–
Conjunction	–	–	–	–
Interjection	4	–	–	4
Particle	4	–	–	4
Sub-total	33	4	–	37

footnote – which means that the valuable and the less valuable things have been merged; referring to the loss of value and respect in general.

Another means which stylises Ballas's use of such Arabic items is the manipulation of folk sayings by translation into Hebrew. In most cases, the word-for-word translation cannot help but illustrate better the denotation of the metaphoric language of an idiom or folk saying. Thus, Ballas sometimes adds glossing of the translated idiom in the context of the plot or in the footnote, as in this the example (1964: 92):

"הן כל אחד הארי אוכל בו שנה.*"

hen kol eḥad ha-arye okhel bo shana
[Each one the lion eats him over the course of a year]

In the novel's footnote, glossing of the Hebrew translation was given by Ballas:

* פתגם ערבי: אדם חזק ואחסון שהארי, לאחר שטרף ממנו לשׂבעו, ישוב אליו ויטרוף ממנו שנה שלמה.

(An Arabic folk saying: That describes a fat and huge person, the lion eats him over the course of a year after he has hunted him).[9]

What distinguishes Ballas's style is not the quantity of Arabic used in the sample from the texts. Rather, the structure of many Hebrew sentences deviates from the modern Hebrew norm. This is indeed intentional. In an interview with Ammiel Alcalay, Ballas said that he is trying to make the Hebrew in his writings closer to Arabic in terms of structure and the way in which he approaches things and issues in his literary works (Alcalay 1996: 68). At several points, Ballas applies Arabic structure, mainly in the dialogue mode, to Hebrew, e.g. (1964: 36): ירחם האל עליה *yeraḥem ha'el 'aleha* [Blesses God her]. Or he employs metaphors borrowed from vernacular Arabic: הקערה נהפכה על פיה *ha-ḳe'ara nehfekha 'al peha* [The basin has been turned upside down], which refers to disorder and illogic. Or, לא איש רוצה לשתות את דם אחיו *lo 'ish rotse leshtot 'et dam aḥiv* [No one wants to drink the blood of his brother] (1964: 51). And also in the example in *Ṿe hu-aḥer* (Ballas 1991: 19): השינה נסה מעיני *hashina nasa me'eni* [the sleep fled my eyes], referring to the inability to sleep.

Ballas also uses a unique syntactic structure associated with biblical Hebrew in which the V(S)O can be condensed into a single word. This structure is used widely in his first novel (1964) as well as in the second novel (1991), e.g.: שהביאוה *she-hevi'oha* [who they brought her] (1964: 19); השכיבתו *heshkivato* [(she) put him down] and העבירתו *he'verato* [(she) moved him to] (1964: 20); שמעתיה *shma'teha* [(I) heard her] (1991: 40).

The use of אבו /*abū*/ as a prefix before Arabic names is also a key phenomenon in Ballas's novels. This item, although it is excluded from the statistics of the study, functions to stylise Ballas's use of Arabic in terms of referring to characters. *Abū*, which means in Arabic the 'father of', is used for both standard and metaphoric contexts. The standard, non-metaphorical uses give many characters in Ballas's novels two proper names, e.g. *Sālim* is called *Abū-Suhayl* (1964: 41). Metaphoric purposes are revealed in the use of *Abū* as well: *Abū-ghāyeb* (the father of the absent) (1964: 23) is the name that *Shlomo Ḥamra* used to call Shaul, *Abū-ghāyeb* used in Iraqi vernacular to refer to the person who has no children. *Abū* is used for humorous effect as well: *Abū-'wenāt* (The person with glasses) (1991: 23) is a nickname that stuck to Aharon Sussan through all his school years until high school. This nickname reveals the vernacular denotation associated with people who used to wear glasses.

Ballas uses Arabic in both dialogues and narrative modes. According to the sample of 150 pages in which the first fifty pages of each novel is analysed, the uses of Arabic in the dialogue mode are 26, compared to 13 Arabic uses in the narrative. This means that the ratio of Arabic in dialogue to the narrative is (2:1). This result points to the variety in using Arabic in Ballas's style, not only in the dialogue mode when the characters are expected to reflect on their cultural and linguistic background, but also in the narrative mode.

The strategies used by Ballas concerning Arabic use in the sample, as shown in Table 3.8, suggest that the use of Arabic regarding employing HA-CS and EA-CS in Ballas's style is quite balanced; in the sample there are twelve cases of HA-CS and ten cases of EA-CS. The majority of these cases appear in the first Hebrew novel (Ballas 1964). This fact reflects the diachronic decrease of Arabic use in Ballas's literary works. Yet one should add that in the late Hebrew novel (Ballas 2008), the use of EA-CS and glossing strategies are still in keeping with Ballas's style. To show how Ballas has employed Arabic in his late Hebrew novel, the following example is appropriate: תקופת ההריון, אל-חמל בערבית *teḳufat ha-herayon, al-ḥaml ba-'aravit* [the period of pregnancy, *al-ḥaml* in Arabic] (2008: 57). This example reveals the development in Ballas's style regarding Arabic, unlike his early Hebrew works in which EA-CS has been employed in using Hebrew direct translation, footnote translation or glossing. In this example, Ballas uses the Hebrew lexical item *ha-herayon* (the pregnancy), after that he inserts the Arabic equivalent *al-ḥaml* in the next clause with an indication as to the source of the foreign code *ba-'aravit* (in Arabic).

Table 3.8 Arabic use strategies in Ballas's sample

Novel/strategy	**(Ballas 1964: 7–56)**	**(Ballas 1991: 7–56)**	**(Ballas 2008: 8–57)**	**Sub-total**
HA-CS	8	4	–	12
EA-CS	9	–	1	10
Glossing	3	–	1	4
Total	20	4	2	26

As to the analysis of Arabic semantic fields in Ballas's sample, Figure 3.3 reveals that the lexical sets used by Ballas in the sample of 150 pages taken from the three Hebrew novels are to some extent variable, although some lexical sets are not used in Ballas's sample compared with the two other authors Sami Michael and Eli Amir, as is shown later in this chapter. In the sample covering the first novel (Ballas 1964), Ballas uses Arabic interjection lexical sets widely, e.g.: *'ahlan be-Abū Ṣabbāḥ* [welcome Abu-Sabah] (1964: 9); *'ahlan be-Yūsuf* [welcome Yousuf] (1964: 33); *wallā* [I swear of God](1964: 33); *yābūy* [*Oh my father*, My God] (1964: 29); and *al-quwwa* [To be strong] (1964: 30). The use of lexical sets related to religion ranks among the most commonly used lexical sets after the interjection; Ballas uses Arabic words like *Alla* [God] (1964: 8, 9, 35) to express both the vernacular and religious belonging of some Iraqi characters in the novels.

Regarding the contextual settings in which Arabic is frequently used in the sample gathered from the three Hebrew novels written by Ballas, it is clear from Figure 3.4 that Arabic use in Ballas's style is associated largely with the normal mode, in which the author uses mainly the narrative or the non-dialogue technique. The use of Arabic is also associated with emotional contexts, e.g. in connection with excitement, happiness and sadness. By contrast, Arabic use is quite sparse in connection with contexts of anger and humour. The figure also shows that the contextual settings in the first Hebrew novel written by Ballas (1964) are diverse and higher in quantity than in the other two later novels (1991, 2008). This fact also reveals the diachronic decrease in the use of Arabic in Ballas's literary works.

3.2.2 Sami Michael

Looking at Table 3.9, Michael's style with regard to inclusion of Arabic evinced a tendency to variation over his three selected novels in this study. The late Hebrew novel (Michael 2015) also contains a considerable amount of Arabic use in the first fifty pages. It is interesting that

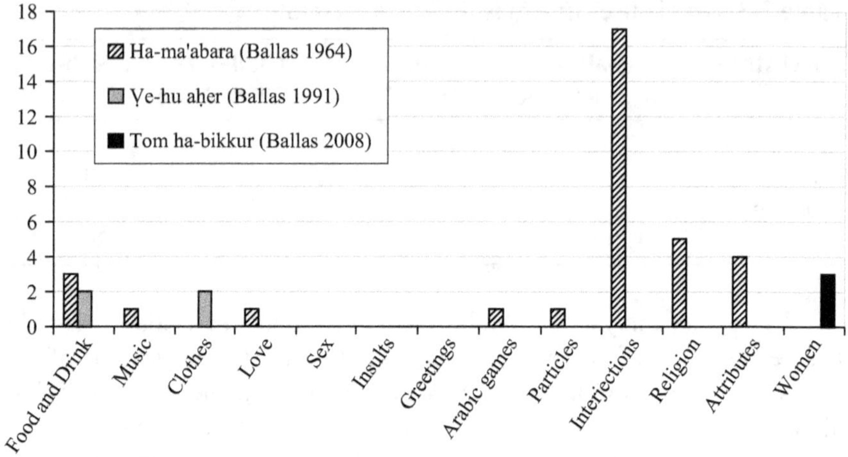

Figure 3.3 Semantic field analysis of Ballas's sample

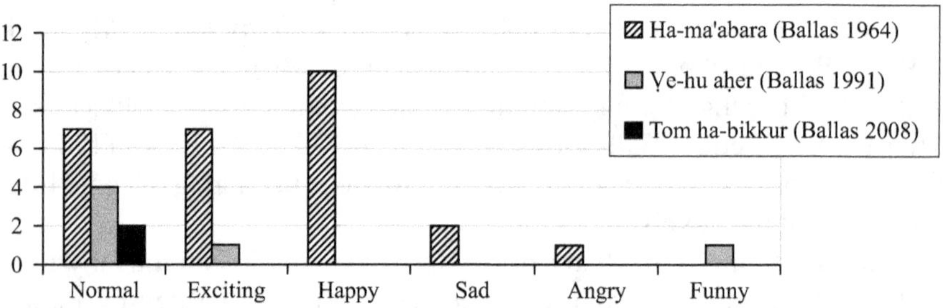

Figure 3.4 Contextual settings of Ballas's sample

Table 3.9 Arabic parts of speech in Michael's sample

Novel/parts of speech	(Michael 1974: 9–58)	(Michael 1993: 5–54)	(Michael 2015: 5–54)	Total according to parts of speech
Noun	7	35	34	76
Verb	6	–	2	8
Adverb	1	–	1	2
Adjective	1	–	3	4
Pronoun	–	–	–	–
Conjunction	–	–	–	–
Interjection	27	1	19	47
Particle	45	–	1	46
Sub-total	87	36	60	183

the particle, mainly the use of יא/yā/, is the most commonly used item in Michael's style. The use of this Arabic particle is in excess of the use of noun, the former with 36.5 per cent, the latter with 34 per cent.

Indeed, the /yā/ particle is employed in various ways in Michael's novel. The main purpose of inserting such a particle is to call somebody by using /yā/ as a prefix before the name. e.g. *yā Abū sha'ul* [hey Abū-Shaul] (1974: 13). In addition, /yā/ has other uses that call attention to the Arabic Iraqi vernacular, for instance the use of /yā/ in combination with *Alla* is associated with expressing the feelings of anger and sorrow; Abū-Shaul, the father of David, the protagonist in the novel *Shavim ṿe-shavim yoter*, expresses his annoyance and anger with the bitter life in the *Ma'abara*. He says: ***yallah*** *isha – lekhol ha-paḥot leṭbol leḥem be-mashehu* [Oh God, woman – at least to dip some bread in anything] (1974: 13). Another use of /yā/ is added to Hebrew lexical items/adjectives giving different denotations, e.g. to express humour, as in the dialogue between David and his colleague from Yemen during their military service in the 1967 War. The 'Yemenite' offers David a cigarette: קח יא ממזר *kaḥ* ***yā****-memazer* [take it bastard] (1974: 14). /yā/ is also used for reference to non-human objects: לא כל כך מהר יא רכבת *lo kol kakh maher* ***yā****-rakkevet* [hey train, do not go so speedy] (1974: 23) said Shaul while he was trying to catch and spring aboard the moving train in which all his family were riding.

Michael's style with regard to Arabic favours employing nouns and interjections, for instance the use of merely Arabic interjection associated with angry: תפו *tfo* (1974: 28); *tfo, tfo, tfo*[10] (1993: 47); טוז *toz*[11] (1974: 29).

The extensive use of particles and interjections in Michael's style may spring in part from the author's tendency to favour employing dialogues rather than narrative. Of a total of 183 uses of Arabic (this also includes proper names) in the sample collected from the three novels by Michael, 128 Arabic uses are associated with the dialogue mode, and only fifty-five appear in a narrative mode. The ratio of dialogue to narrative in Michael's style with respect to the use of Arabic can be calculated as (2.3:1). According to this ratio, one can easily say that Michael's style of using Arabic is associated with the conversational mode much more than the narrative mode.

Michael's style often involves spoken dialogue in the Hebrew texts, insertion of some Arabic particle, interjection and vernacular idioms in limited ways, as in עביה *'abāye*[12] in the novel *Ṿikṭoryah* (1993), or the particle /yā/ in *Shavim ṿe-shavim yoter* (1974). The Hebrew syntactic structures in Michael's texts, however, are not influenced by Arabic structure as much as in Ballas's style.

Table 3.10 Arabic use strategies in Michael's sample

Novel/ strategies	**(Michael 1974: 9–58)**	**(Michael 1993: 5–54)**	**(Michael 2011: 7–56)**	**Sub-total**
HA-CS	98	31	32	161
EA-CS	–	1	2	3
Glossing	–	–	–	–
Total	98	32	34	164

Another phenomenon notable in Michael's style is his avoidance of the use of EA-CS and glossing strategies. Table 3.10 indicates that almost all Arabic codes in the sample from the three Hebrew novels are HA-CS. Moreover, Michael uses Arabic particles extensively, such as /yā/ and /Abū/ in the first Hebrew novel (1974). In addition, the Arabic lexical item *'abāye* is repeatedly employed in his second novel (1993). It is interesting to note that, as Table 3.10 indicates, Michael's use of such strategies is the same in his novel from the 1990s and his late Hebrew novel.

In the sample gathered from the three novels, looking at Figure 3.5 shows that in connection with semantic fields, Michael makes principal use of the *particle* and *interjection* lexical sets. These two lexical sets are used extensively, but only in the sample gathered from the novel *Shavim ve-shavim yoter*, the first Hebrew novel written by Michael (1974). This may reflect the extensive use of these two lexical sets closely associated with vernacular Baghdadi Arabic dialect: for example, *yā-Alla* [Oh my

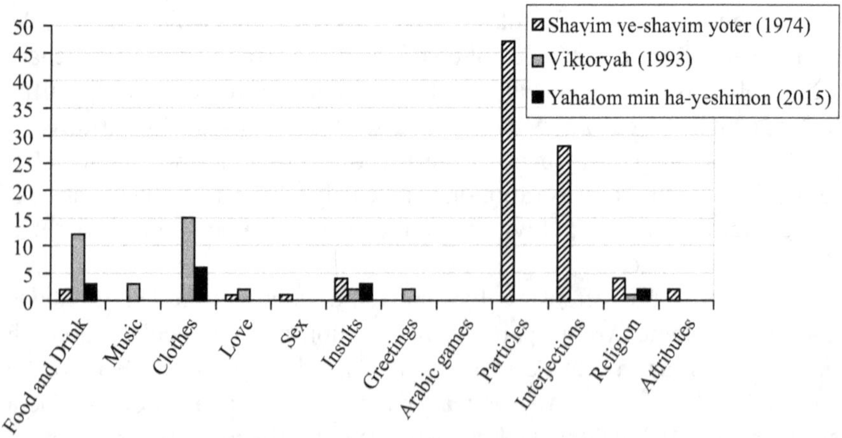

Figure 3.5 Semantic field analysis of Michael's sample

God] (1974: 13); and the use of the particle /yā/ in the novel, as has been pointed out above.

The lexical set *Clothes* ranks after the Arabic *particle* with 21 instances and appears in the second and last novel (1993, 2015). The repeated use of *'abāye* in Michael's sample has it is own distinctive style: similar to what can be observed in Amir's style (see below), Michael tries to integrate the Arabic lexical item *'abāye* into the Hebrew text. This is done by applying the Hebrew syntax and morphology to the Arabic embedded code. For instance, *'abāye* appears with the Hebrew definite article (ה): העביה *ha-'abaye* (1993: 5, 29, 31); it also is found with the Hebrew inseparable preposition (ב) – בעביה *ba-'abaye* (1993: 29; 2015: 29) – as well as the preposition (ל): לעביה *la-'abaye* (1993: 29). In addition, this lexical item takes the female plural with the suffix /ot/: העביות *ha-'abayot* (1993: 21); and עבאיות *'abayot* (2015: 42). Further, it is added to another word using the rules in Hebrew syntax that are applied to female singular lexical items in the case of the adjunct; for instance, עבית משי *'abayet meshi* [an Abaya made of silk] (1993: 30). Michael here uses the borrowing strategy, in which mixing between language systems is involved in conversational or written practices.[13]

The next lexical set after *Clothes* is *Food and Drink*, used in the novels *Viḳṭoryah* three times more than in the novel *Shavim ṿe-shavim yoter* and *Yahalom min ha-yeshimon*. *Music* is only used in the collected sample from the novel *Viḳṭoryah*. The *Insults* set appears in the three novels and it reflects the vernacular Arabic used by the characters in Michael's early writings.

The comparison between the samples gathered from the three novels proves that Michael's use of Arabic lexical sets evinces little variability. In the first novel (1974), the corpus shows the intensive use of two lexical sets *particle* and *interjection*, with less attention to other lexical sets. In the second and third novels (1993, 2015), the analysis of the first fifty pages shows the use of two main Arabic lexical sets associated with Iraqi *Clothes* and *Cuisine*.

According to Figure 3.6, the contextual settings analysis of the sample gathered from the three novels written by Michael shows that the use of Arabic is to some extent related to and associated with highly-charged emotions – categories like *exciting*, *angry*, *sad* and *happy*. The analysis also indicates that in the Hebrew novels the contextual settings in the first Hebrew novel (1974) are greater than in the second novel (1993) in all categories. There is also a place in Michael's style allocated for humour, although it constitutes the lowest frequency in

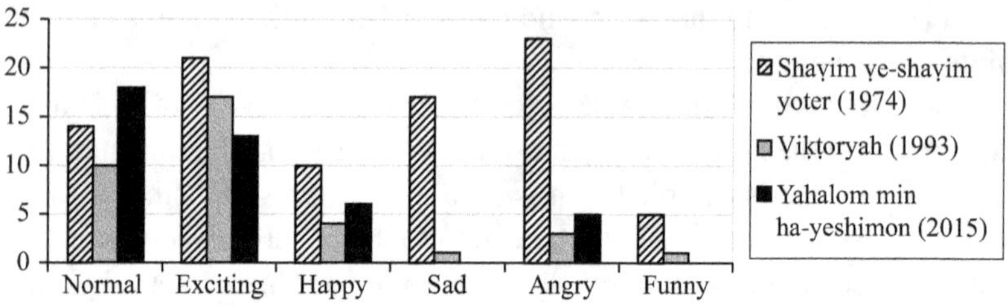

Figure 3.6 Contextual settings in Michael's sample

3.2.3 Eli Amir

According to Table 3.11, Eli Amir's use of Arabic in his novels depends mainly on three parts of speech: noun, interjection and particle. These three parts of speech constitute 54.5 per cent, 20 per cent and 10 per cent respectively of the total Arabic uses in the sample of Amir's style.

Amir has a distinct style of employing some Arabic nouns in his novels. He often uses the Hebrew female plural suffix for Arabic lexical items, e.g. גברים בעביות כהות ובכפיות מנוקדות *gevarim be-'abayot kehot 'u-bekifiyyot menuḳadot* (1992: 17) [Men in dark cloaks and dotted Keffiyehs] (Amir 2010b: 14). Here the two Arabic lexical items *'Abaye* and *Kifiyye* are Hebraised using the Hebrew suffix /ot/ associated with Hebrew female plural terms. The other Hebrew form of plural used for masculine plural, the suffix /im/, is also used by Amir to make the plural of Arabic lexical item וזיר *wazīr* (minster) and 'שֵׁיח *shēkh* (Sheikh) – they appear in Amir's text as: וַזירים ושֵׁיח'ים (1992: 36); this also holds true for the example פינג'אנים *fenjānim* (Amir 1992: 27) which is the plural of the single masculine *fenjān* (cup of coffee). Arabic, in view of this, is more integrated into the Hebrew texts. This was not done only by means of inserting Arabic lexical items, but also in applying Hebrew morphology to them. One should add here that Amir also utilises the Judaeo-Arabic spoken by Jews in Iraq, such as *stādh* [Mister], and *tanu'a* [in reference to the Zionist movement]. Not only does Amir use Arabic lexical items as foreign elements in the texts; he also tries to merge Hebrew and Arabic, creating his own style. This device of Hebraisation of Arabic is used only by Amir, and not by Ballas and Michael.

What also distinguishes Amir's style in employing Arabic lexical items in the Hebrew text is his attempt to merge and integrate Arabic in the texts. Although many lexical items of the total used in the sample are HA-CS, Amir deals with Arabic nouns as if they belong to the Hebrew lexicon. This is obvious, for instance, in his use of Hebrew inseparable prepositions (ל, ב, כ) as well as the Hebrew definite article (ה), e.g. הג'רה *ha-Jārre* [the water jug] (Amir 1992: 7), with Arabic lexical items instead of using the Arabic definite article (ال) like Ballas in אל-מוח'אבראת *al-mukhābarāt* [The Intelligence] (Ballas 1991: 37); בפינג'אנים *be-fenjānim* [cups of coffee] (Amir 1992: 27); בעַמְבָּה *be-'amba* [Amba, an Iraqi traditional dish] (Amir 1992: 35); לחַפְלות הליליות *la-ḥaflot ha-lelyiyot* [to the night parties] (Amir 1992: 36).

Michael also uses this borrowing technique of integrating Arabic lexical items into Hebrew texts used by Amir, e.g. הבָמְיה *ha-bāmye* (Michael 1993: 14) and בעַבָּיות *be-'abāyot* (Michael 1993: 21).

Interjection ranks second in frequency in Amir's style of using Arabic after the use of Arabic nouns. The use of colloquial and vernacular interjections indicates that most characters in Amir's early Hebrew writings belong to the cultural and linguistic life worlds of Iraq and Baghdad. In the present sample of 150 pages from three novels, 18.6 per cent of Arabic uses are interjections, e.g. מאשללה *māshalla* [God bless] (1992: 23); תַבַּארַכּ אללה *tabārak Allā* [God bless] (1992: 52, 53); אהלן וסהלן *ahlan wa sahlan* [welcome] (1983: 19, 1992: 55); יאללה *yalla* [Let's go] (1983: 18); וַאֵילִי *wāwēlī* [what a catastrophe!] (1992: 13, 22).

Amir also uses Judaeo-Arabic spoken by Iraqi Jews in many plots in his works, this is obvious in the style of inserting Arabic in the suggested sample, like this example: כל טיז יסוה אל **עמע'** *kol ṭīẓ yeswā al-'**umegh*** [Each backside is worth a life – what a beautiful ass] (Amir 1983: 19) This is also obvious in the use of constant /gh/ instead of /r/ in the word *'**umegh***, which reflects the Judaeo-Arabic orthography of Iraqi Jews in Baghdad at the time.[14] Other examples confirm this claim, such as סתאד *stādh* [Mister] (Amir 1992: 37, 38, 39,47), in which the Judaeo-Arabic pronunciation rules are applied to the Arabic word أستاذ *ostādh*.[15]

The translation strategy from Arabic into Hebrew distinguishes Amir's style, even though this strategy has been excluded from the statistics. Amir uses this technique mainly with folk sayings and idioms, e.g.: יובַד מאור עיניו *yovad me'or 'enav* (1992: 9) [to lose his eye's light – to get blind]; אללה רחם עלינו *alla raḥam 'alenu* (1992: 13) [Allah have (has) mercy] (Amir 2010b: 8); אללה יאריך ימיך *alla ya'rekh yemekha* (1992: 16) [Allah gives you a long life] (Amir 2010b: 11).

Another distinctive feature in Amir's novels is his style evident in the translation of Arabic songs into Hebrew. Amir puts the first sentence of the Arabic song in Arabic followed by a Hebrew translation. This applies only to the first sentence; Amir then sets the translation of the rest of the song in Hebrew without Arabic (1983: 21):

Table 3.11 Arabic parts of speech in Amir's sample

The novel/parts of speech	**(Amir 1983: 9–58)**	**(Amir 1992: 7–56)**	**(Amir 2010a: 5–54)**	**Total according to parts of speech**
Noun	28	91	6	125
Verb	4	8	–	12
Adverb	2	1	–	3
Adjective	3	9	2	14
Pronoun	–	5	–	5
Conjunction	–	1	–	1
Interjection	23	19	–	42
Particle	8	15	–	23
Sub-total	68	149	8	225

עמי יא ביאע אל ורד
הוי, מוכר ה(**ו**)רדים,[16]
מה מחיר הורדים?

'Omi yā bayyā' al ward
[Oh, rose seller
What is the price of your roses?]
(Amir 1987: 21)

In this example and others (Amir 1983: 38, 57, 1992: 52), Amir tries to connect Arabic to the Hebrew text by means of EA-CS and translation strategies. In this way, the reader finds an Arabic song written in Hebrew script, and then reads the rest of the song in Hebrew.

With regard to Amir's style in connection with strategies of implementing Arabic in the sample, Amir preferred to make the majority of the Arabic codes employed as HA-CS for the outsider reader. According to Table 3.12, 80.6 per cent of the Arabic codes in the sample are HA-CS, compared to only 18.6 per cent EA-CS. Glossing is used only once (1992: 33). Of interest is the use of both HA-CS and EA-CS in Amir's late

Table 3.12 Arabic use strategies in Amir's sample

Novel/ strategies	**(Amir 1983: 9–58)**	**(Amir 1992: 7–56)**	**(Amir 2010a: 5–54)**	**Sub-total**
HA-CS	30	76	2	108
EA-CS	7	16	2	25
Glossing	–	1	–	1
Total	37	93	4	134

Hebrew novel. This is also a distinct feature in his style; Amir still uses, albeit in a very limited way, Arabic codes even in his late literary works.

With respect to the variant use of Arabic in dialogue and narrative modes, Amir uses Arabic with the same proportions in the two modes. It is important to point out that in the novel *Tarnegol kapparot* (1983), Amir used Arabic forty-one times in dialogue mode compared to only nine times in narrative mode. However, in his second novel, *Mafriaḥ ha-yonim* (1992), Arabic appeared seventy times in narrative mode and thirty-seven times in dialogue mode. The total is seventy-nine instances for narrative and seventy-eight for dialogue mode. These findings show that Amir's style regarding dialogue and narrative is variable and even the differences between the use of Arabic in dialogue and narrative modes are not as great as in the case of Ballas and Michael.

Based on the sample, the lexical sets used by Amir show the variety of his selection of Arabic lexical items employed in his works, namely the two early novels (Amir 1983, 1992). Interjections rank first in Amir (1992). *Food and drink* is the most employed lexical set in *Tarnegol kapparot* (1983). Lexical items associated with *Sex* and *Love* are used only in *Tarnegol kapparot* (1983). *Particle* and *Religion* lexical sets are used with a similar frequency in the two novels. There is a significant gap between the two early Hebrew novels of Amir (1983, 1992) with regard to the lexical items related to *Food and drink*, *Music* and *Clothes*. This may because *Mafriaḥ ha-yonim* (1992) is a novel based on events occurring for the most part in Baghdad, where such Arabic lexical items related to Baghdadi cultural life are embodied.

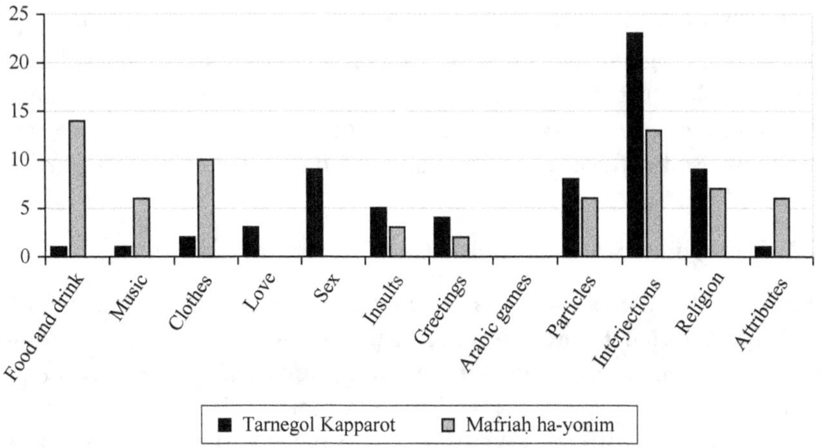

Figure 3.7 Semantic field analysis of Amir's sample

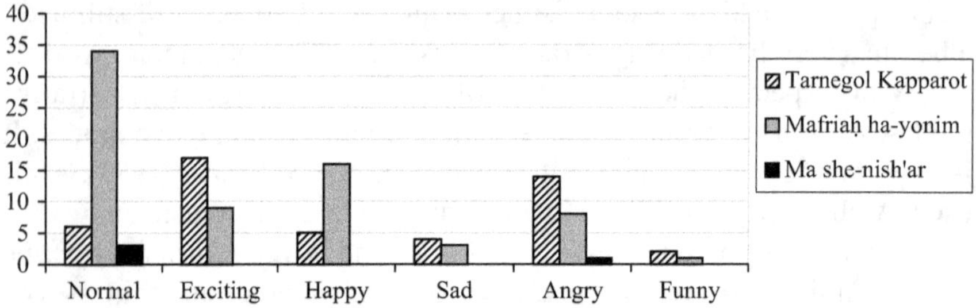

Figure 3.8 Contextual settings in Amir's sample

Contextual settings analysis, in which the context of the scene associated with uses of Arabic is categorised and arranged, can also provide a general picture of the contextual moods in which Arabic is used by means of testing the frequencies of each category. In the sample, as illustrated in Figure 3.8, the use of Arabic is repeatedly related to highly-charged emotions, like *exciting* – sets that also include for example fear and surprise. *Exciting* constitutes a high rank as a set in the Amir sample in both of his early novels (1983, 1992). The same holds true for the *angry* set, the second category associated with highly-charged emotions, represented in the three novels of Amir. The *angry* set is associated principally with the use of Iraqi vernacular insults, e.g.: כוסאֻם אל יהוד *kos um el-yahūd* (1992: 11) [*Kus um-el-yahud*, get the hell up!] (Amir 2010b: 6); אחרא דין בוק *iḥra dīn būk* [wish your father's religion is to be burnt – fuck you] (1983: 14). Sets focused on anger are mainly expressed here by the HA-CS strategy. This observation highlights the mutual relation between the contextual settings and the expected strategy used by the bilingual author. Moreover, the use of Arabic in the angry mode is mainly carried out by inserting hard-access Arabic codes without translation or glossing. *Funny* ranks lowest as a context in which Arabic is used in the sample. The so-called *normal* set, which is associated mainly with the narrative mode, is used extensively in the sample from Amir's novel *Mafriaḥ ha-yonim* (1992).

3.3 Iraqi Judaeo-Arabic and Arabic Dialects in the Novels

After exploring each author's style of employing Arabic in accordance with the selected Hebrew novels, in the following the chapter presents some other unique features in the Iraqi Jewish Hebrew novels concerning Iraqi Judaeo-Arabic and other Arabic dialects that also reflect how Arabic, in different varieties, stylises the literary works of the Iraqis.

3.3.1 Iraqi Judaeo-Arabic

In Amir's novel *Mafriaḥ ha-yonim*, the narrator tells his family's story in Iraq just before their emigration to Israel, and describes his family's feelings of fear and worry of being persecuted by Muslims because of the conflict between Arabs and Jews during and after 1948–51 spilling over into Iraq:

Example 3-1

"אנחנו מוסלמים, מוסלמים, בחיאת מחמד," זעק אדור בהברה שטרח כל-כך לסגל לו.
גם אני ניסיתי לומר משהו בערבית מוסלמית, אבל מרוב הפחד נתמלטו המלים בערבית
יהודית מובהקת.

"we are Muslims, Muslims, beḥiyāt Muḥammad" cried Eduard as strong as he could. I tried to say something in Muslim Arabic dialect too. However, out of fear, clear Judaeo-Arabic came out right away"
(Amir 1992: 44)

Eduard, an Iraqi Jewish young man, and his friend, Kābī, had been chased by a group of Muslims in Baghdad. The two tried to cultivate an Arabic Muslim dialect in order to fool the Muslim group, but they were not successful. This quotation intertwines the fact that there was a difference between Muslim and Jewish Arabic varieties in Iraq.

The use of the Arabic dialect spoken by the Jews in Iraq is also one of the varieties of Arabic used in the Hebrew texts. The Iraqi Judaeo-Arabic employed in the Hebrew novels depends on some lexicon items from biblical Hebrew, or it is formed and follows the way in which some Hebrew lexical items are pronounced. The examples below shed light on the way Iraqi Judaeo-Arabic was employed in some Hebrew texts.

Example 3-2

"הסי־אי־די, הבולשת העיראקית, חודרת לילה־לילה לכל בית ומחפשת נשק ומכשירי
קשר וספרים ללימוד עברית של **הַתַּנוּעַה**, היא המחתרת הציונית"

(Amir 1992: 7)
["Every night the CID, the Iraqi secret service, visited houses in search of weapons, two-way radios, and Hebrew textbooks distributed by 'the Movement', as the Zionist underground was called by us".]
(Amir 2010b: 1)

The use here of הַתַּנוּעַה *ha-tanūa'a*, which the author interpreted in the text to refer to the Zionist movement, replaces the Hebrew equal idiom הַתְּנוּעָה הציונית *ha-teno'a ha-tsyonit*. The comparison below between the origin and the hybrid phonological structure illustrates Arabic/Hebrew phonological interference:

(a) הַתְנוּעָה הציונית *ha-tenu'a ha-tsyonit*
(b) תַנוּעַה *tanūa'a*

Use of this linguistic device and the like in Amir's Hebrew texts foregrounds his literary style. The reader is surprised by the uncommon phonological alteration of a Hebrew lexical item employed by Amir, which reflects his Arabic/Hebrew linguistic background. This background appears in the language of the narrator as well as in the conversations between the characters in the novel. The use here of Arabic language shows that the existence of Arabic is not only assembled in adding Arabic codes to the Hebrew texts; rather it proves that the Arabic influence affects both the phonological and semantic levels; ***tanūa'a*** is not just an alternation of the Hebrew phonological structure of the origin lexical ***tenua'a***; rather it was used in Iraq shortly before 1948 to refer semantically to the *ha-tenu'a ha-tsyonit*.

Iraqi Judaeo-Arabic is also present in Michael's novel. The following example highlights the use of Hebrew lexical items in Arabic spoken by Jews in Iraq:

Example 3-3

ג'מיע אל עאלם יטלבון רזק מן **השם יתברך והוא** יעטיהום, ולאכן פקט תלאת'ה צאחבין מצלחה למן יצלון ט' רזקהום, **השם יתברך** לם יסמע מנהום – אל אולאני, אל חכים. למן ינדעי יריד רזק, ורזקו יעני יתוג'עון אל נאס לחתה ירוח ידאויהום. אל ת'אני, אלד'י עמאל יביע צנאדיק אל יחטון פ'יהא אל מיית, ורזקו יכון ימותון אל נאס לחתה יתרזק. ואל ת', **מחילה**, אל **זונה**. הד'ול אל ת'לאת'ה מן יצלון ט' רזקהום **השמי תברך** לם יסמעהום.

[...] החכם התחיל מפרש את הכתוב. "הבריות כולם," נאמר בפתק, "מבקשים פרנסה מאת **השמי תברך והוא** נותן להם. אבל פעלי שלושה עיסוקים, כשהם מתפללים ומבקשים פרנסה, אין **השמי תברך** שומע להם. האחד הוא המַרפא המייחל לפרנסה, ופרנסתו משמעה שיפלו הבריות למשכב כדי שיטפל בהם. השני הוא מוכר ארונות המתים, שפרנסתו תלויה במותם של הבריות. והשלישית, **במחילה**, היא **הזונה**. אלה השלושה כשהם מתפללים ומבקשים פרנסה **השמי תברך** אינו שומע להם."

(Michael 1993: 67)

["The Ḥakhām began to explain what is written: 'All people', he said in commenting on the text, 'ask for a livelihood from the Blessed Lord, and he gives them. But there are three professions when their practitioners worship and ask for livelihood, but the Blessed Lord does not listen to them. The first is the physician who hopes for livelihood, and his livelihood means that people get ill and he treats them. The second is the seller of coffins, whose livelihood is reliant upon the death of people. And the third, forgiveness, is the prostitute. Those three, when they worship and ask for livelihood, the Blessed Lord does not listen to them.'"]

In Michael's novel *Viḳṭoryah,* three girls found a piece of paper blowing in the air when they were on the roof of the house. Because they were illiterate, they asked for help to know what was written on the paper. They went to *Ḥakham*, who examined the paper and read it to them. The paper was written in Iraqi Judaeo-Arabic followed by a translation into Hebrew on the same page. The influence of the biblical Hebrew on the Arabic text is obvious, as Blanc noted in his study about the dialects in Baghdad (1964: 140–1); for instance: השם יתברך *hashem yetbarekh* (The Blessed Lord); מחילה *meḥila* (forgiveness); *and* אל זונה *al zona* (prostitute). Note here the use of the Hebrew term *meḥela* without the Hebrew preposition /ב/. In addition, note the use of the term *zona* with the Arabic definite article /al/. The Hebrew/Arabic morphological and syntactic interference are obvious in this example.

Example 3-4

"אֻסְתאד נַאוִי, או סְתַאד נַאוי,כמו שביטאנו ביהודית את תואר הכבוד הזה לאיש הרוח, ..."

(Amir 1992: 198)

***'Ustādh** Nawi, 'o **Stādh** Nawi, kemo she-biṭanu bayhudit 'et ha-kavod ha-ze l'ish ha-ruaḥ*

[Ustādh Nawi or Stādh Nawi, as we called him in our Jewish Arabic]

In this example, the author differentiates between spoken Arabic in Iraq and Iraqi Judaeo-Arabic. The different between *'ustādh* and *stādh* is illustrated here by means of the narrative context. Amir wanted to highlight the differences between Jews and Muslims in Iraq in terms of the pronunciation of *'ustādh,* in which the first consonant is not pronounced in Judaeo-Arabic (Yona-Swery 1995: 110).

There is also another literary device employed in Amir's *Tarnegol kapparot* (1983), in which the pronunciation of the consonant /sh/ is replaced by /s/ (Amir 1983: 12, 13, 15, 16, 18, 19, 23, 24, 34, 35, 38, 39, 41, 42, 44, 46, 116, 117, 174):

Example 3-5

"אתה **חדס** ?" שאל. מבטאו היה זר והוא הסתכל בי כאילו הייתי נער מפגר.
"**עכסיו** באת, **עכסיו** ? **חדס** ?" סוף־סוף הבנתי מהוא אומר.
"כן," מילמלתי.
"בוזגלו," אמר והושיט יד.
"נורי." לחיצת ידו היתה איתנה.
"מאיפה ?"
"מן המעברה."

"גם אני. כל המעברות אותו דבר. "איזו ארץ ? אני **סואל**."
"עירק."
"מרוקו," אמר בחיוך חם, רחב. ידו השמאלית גילגלה במהירות מחרוזת של אבנים עגלגלות, חומות.
"אוהו !" בני אפרים שמחליפים שין בשׂין, חשבתי.

(Amir 1983: 11)

['Freth meat! Freth meat!' sang someone next to me.
'Justht arrived?' he asked. He had a strong accent and looked at me as if I was mentally defective.
'Have you justht come? Are you new?' At least I understood what he was saying.
'Yes,' I mumbled.
'Buthaglo,' he said and held out his hand.
'Nuri.' His grip was firm.
'From where?'
'A *ma'abara*.'
'Me too. They're all the thame.' He cut me short. 'What country? That'th what I meant.'
'Iraq.'
'Morocco,' he sid with a warm, broad smile, rolling a string of round, brown beads rapidly through the fingers of his left hand.
Oho! The sons of Ephraim who speak with a lisp, I thought.]
(Amir 1987: 11–12)

Here, the author may have wanted to evoke the biblical story of the Gileadites and the Ephraim tribe in which the Ephraimites were unable to pronounce the shin /sh/ correctly, and pronounced it /s/ instead.[17]

The use of such dialects in the Hebrew text adds to the diversity of using Arabic. Not only is Iraqi Judaeo-Arabic employed in the texts, but also other Arabic dialects. In the following, other Arabic varieties used in the Hebrew texts are shown.

3.3.2 Arabic Dialects

Not only is Iraqi Judaeo-Arabic employed in the Hebrew texts, the Egyptian dialect was also in use. This might be because of the influence of Egyptian media at the time on the Arab world in general through Egyptian cinema as well as famous Egyptian singers, such as Um Kolthom, Farid al-Atrash and Mohamed Abdulmuttaleb. Amir mentioned Abdulmuttaleb in his novel *Mafriaḥ ha-yonim:*

Example 3-6: Egyptian Arabic
The famous Egyptian singer Moḥammad Abd al-Muṭṭaleb was one of the characters in the novel. He sings:

"יַא חַבִּיבְּת אִל־אַלְבּ, אִרְגַעִי, שובי אהובת בלב לגני."

(Amir 1992: 52)
yā ḥabibt-el'alb ergaʻī
[*ya habibat el-'alb, irga'i*, "O thou love of my heart, come back to me"]
(Amir 2010b: 57)

Sami Michael also employed Egyptian Arabic in his Hebrew novel (2011: 194):

Example 3-7

"וָלָה יְהֶמָּכּ"

walā yehemmak
["Take it easy" (= never mind)]

Sami Michael also uses Egyptian dialect Arabic in his first novel published in Hebrew (1974: 191).

Example 3-8: Muslim Iraqi dialect
Michael highlights a wide range of Arabic dialects and varieties in his writings. Not only are standard Arabic, Judaeo-Arabic and Egyptian Arabic employed in his Hebrew novels, but also the dialect of Iraqi Muslims in Baghdad, although in a very limited way:

עזרא הסביר בערבית של מוסלמים: "**ליל הניץ'** הלילה"
'izra hesbir baʻaravīt shel muslemim: "lēl ha-nētch ha-laylah"
Ezra explained in Muslim Arabic: "the night for sex is tonight"
(Michael 1993: 90)

The Muslim Arabic dialect employed by the author is obvious in this example. The Arabic colloquial term *nētch* (نيتش) [sexual intercourse] is the Muslim Baghdadi variant for the consonant /k/. The Muslims of Bagdad used to pronounce the /k/ as /ch/ (Blanc 1964: 25). According to the sentence, here the author points out this feature that distinguishes Muslim and Jewish spoken vernaculars in Iraq at the time.

3.4 Conclusion

To conclude, this chapter has discussed the style of using Arabic in each novel, by each author and in each corpus of the study. Two main comparisons were made concerning the use of Arabic in the nine Hebrew novels, which are divided into three corpora according to the date of publication.

Comparisons concerning the style of using Arabic in the selected nine Hebrew novels yield the following results: from a diachronic perspective, instances of the use of Arabic continue in to decline slightly over the course of about fifty years in the nine selected Hebrew novels by the three Iraqi Jewish authors. The use of Arabic nouns ranks first in the study's Hebrew texts, the interjection comes second, followed by the particle. With respect to the embedded Arabic codes in the Hebrew novels, CS is the most commonly used strategy. The strategy of HA-CS was not affected by the dimension of time. In other words, notwithstanding the long period spent by the authors in Israel, some of their late Hebrew novels written in the 2010s still contain HA-CS.

The three Iraqi Jewish authors employed Arabic in different forms in their Hebrew texts. Their uses of Arabic derive from Iraqi Judaeo-Arabic, Iraqi Muslim dialect and standard Arabic.

4

Final Remarks

4.1 Why Arabic?

> I did not go so very far from the world in which I grew up, I only moved from one country to another within the same region where Arabic is spoken. (Ballas 2009: 65)

> Belonging can be considered a process whereby an individual in some way feels some sense of association with a group, and as such represents a way to explain the relationship between a personalized identity and a collective one. In a purely conceptual way belonging is about the relationship between personal identity and a collective identity. (Delanty et al. 2011: 44)

The above quotations simply summarise the way in which the literary works of the three Iraqi Jewish authors include Arabic. If we agree that language is the most important element in personal and collective identity, then language is strongly connected to the sense of belonging for most individuals. The study of Arabic use in Chapters 2 and 3 shows that instances of Arabic continue to be used by the three Iraqi Jewish authors, even in the late Hebrew novels with some variations. In this regard, this tendency of employing Arabic in the Hebrew works can reflect the attachment of the Iraqi authors to Iraqi and Arabic culture.

This chapter argues that geographic location, as an element of the narrative setting, influences the degree of employing Arabic in the Hebrew novels of the study. Therefore, the book argues that the main reason and motive beyond the use of Arabic in the literary works of the Iraqis is strongly associated with the question of place. The emigration of Iraqi

Jewish authors from Iraq to Israel – which comprises an experience of living in two places, speaking two languages and connecting between two cultures – constitutes a convincing reason for employing and expressing these places with the language/dialects of its characters and protagonists in their writings. In the following, the book extends this argument by means of presenting the question of place in the nine Iraqi Jewish Hebrew novels.

For immigrants, leaving for a new country implies accepting some policies they should follow to be integrated into the new society. The clash between the original and the new culture is likely to occur the more the geographical territories are detached. Despite the typical form of such an emigrational context, people moving from East to West is a dimension represented in the life worlds of all three authors. The Iraqi authors refer to the conflict and the difference between the two places, two cultures and the two languages in which they have experienced both the world of Arabic and Hebrew, Iraq and Israel, oriental culture and Israeli culture, itself more associated with Western culture. Ballas states that he did not cross the sea to reach Israel:

> I did not go so very far from the world in which I grew up, I only moved from one country to another within the same region where Arabic is spoken. In this way, I am also not like other immigrant writers coming from Europe and America to Israel. I did not cross the sea to reach here. Arabic is the language of the region, and it is the second official language in Israel as well. (2009: 65)[1]

Although the surrounding environment in the aftermath of establishing Israel was familiar to the new Iraqi-born emigrants in terms of climate, geographical location and other aspects, the cultural conflict between the newcomers and the 'veterans', between East and West, still permeates the themes their first Hebrew manuscripts contain. The impact of this action on their writings deserves attention. In the following, the chapter will deal mainly with the three authors and their Hebrew manuscripts in terms of writing language and place and language and symbols of belonging. It will also examine the elements in the context of the novels which express the longing for Iraq or/and the oriental culture on the one hand, and the presence of the Arabic language on the other.

4.1.1 Ha-ma'abara: *The Narratives of Baghdad and Israel*

The clash between the newcomers and the new land appears in diverse ways in the first three Hebrew works by the authors under investigation, as they established the so-called '*sifrut ha-ma'abara*', the literature of the *ma'abara* (the transit camp). It is not surprising how they introduce their protagonists to the modern Hebrew literature as a wave of rebellion against the place and its new language and culture.

Ballas's novel *Ha-ma'abara* follows the narrative of some Iraqi Jewish members encountering hardships and difficulties in the transit camp *Oriya* in connection with work, food, medical care, etc. The main character in the novel is Yusuf Shabi, an adult intellectual who takes responsibility for the house, where his mother and brother Said reside but his father is absent. The poverty of the transit camp and the adverse conditions in which the Iraqi members suffer are embodied in the plot; so, for example, the wife of *Na'īm al-Khabbāẓ* was ready to give birth, but the doctor refuses to enter the transit camp because of the obstructed roads leading to the camp. The baby did not survive as a result, and the whole Iraqi group helped and carried the fatigued women to the ambulance. The author wanted to portray the Iraqis' tragic plot in the transit camp on the one hand, and to show to what extent they stood as one united group on the other. The group was furious about what happened; they organised a meeting to put an end to such difficult circumstances. The police, with the help of the three gangsters employed by the director of the transit camp, infiltrated the meeting and the situation ended with the arrest of some members. Yusuf Shabi was one of them.

The majority of the events portrayed by Ballas occur inside the perimeters of the transit camp, a kind of prison camp for the Iraqis. Within this space, there are major components that shape the *ma'abara* and add distinction to it. The café *al-Naṣr* [the victory] is the main place where the people gather. I refer to *al-Naṣr* later because of its connection with the context of language and place. Another point is the *badonim* [the cabins] in which the characters of the novel are housed. They serve as elements to describe the nature of the cruel life associated with the transit camp at the time.

The use of place, however, is more overstretched in Sami Michael's novel *Shavim ẏe-shavim yoter* (1974). This time the transit camp is not the only place where the characters can live; David Asher, the protagonist of the novel, and his family (parents, little sister Hanina and elder brother Shaul) arrive in Israel during the mass immigration in the 1950s. Since the *ma'abara* contains much tragedy and hardship, David Asher and his elder brother Shaul strive to leave the camp for the city. Na'ima and her husband Reuven, the David's neighbours, move to an apartment in Tel Aviv.

The sorrow dominates the tragedy in the novel felt for the old father Abū Sha'ul, who has many maladies. The lack of food, the hardships the family face and the harsh welcome for the new immigrants using DDT constitute typical features in these early Hebrew novels.

Unlike Ballas and Michael, Eli Amir has another conception of place: not only the transit camp or the city but the kibbutz, a fundamental institution in Israel associated with the socialist and the Zionist identity of the state. Nuri, the protagonist of the novel *Tarnegol kapparot* (1983), narrates his experience in the organisation *kiryat oranim.* It involves the search for self-identity in the new land and the inner conflict in the clash between the world of the kibbutz with its all cultural features including secularism, socialism, Zionism and the world of the *ma'abara*, with its religious and family connections and the cultural heritage associated with Baghdad.

After leaving the transit camp for the kibbutz, Nuri and his friends find it difficult to deal with the lifestyle in the kibbutz because they must work in the field. In Iraq, they performed no menial work of any kind but had servants who did the work for them (Amir 1983: 65). However, they start to work in farming. Sacred and secular perspectives motivate the first engagement of Nuri and his friends with the kibbutz. One of the young Iraqis in the group asks where he can find the synagogue, and the answer is a shock for them: 'There isn't any here!' (Amir 1983: 41).

The *ma'abara* in Amir's work serves as a locus or space where Nuri is linked to his past. His religious parents live in the *ma'abara* and not in the kibbutz. The Jewish sacraments are still preserved in an effort to maintain the family traditions. Nuri lies to his parents and brings them a chicken from the kibbutz, which is not slaughtered according to the *kosher* tradition; it was supposed to be prepared for *Yom Kippur*. The parents are upset, and they ascribe the change in Nuri's behaviour to the influence of the kibbutz. The scene constitutes a significant point in the novel, which stresses the conflict between the kibbutz and the family in the *ma'abara* – a conflict in which Nuri is the character most involved.

The place of origin back in Iraq is not just a distant 'other locus' in memory; rather, a simulation of that 'other' place itself may be transferred to Israel. In *Ha-ma'abara*, Ballas uses the café *al-Naṣr*[2] as the hub where most of the members of the Iraqi immigrant community in the transit camp gather, spend their time, make their decisions, listen to Iraqi and Arabic music on the radio, drink Iraqi tea and, of course, speak Arabic. Moreover, the story begins and ends in the *al-Naṣr* café. *Al-Naṣr* is not just a place; rather it is a point in time where two places co-exist, Iraq and Israel, a kind of 'third space' in between. Geographically, the narratives follow the lives of a Iraqi Jewish immigrant group in one of the Israeli transit camps during the 1950s.

On the other hand, the protagonists, the characters and the language of most conversations are connected mostly to Iraqis. One of the characters describes the ma'abara as 'the second Babylon' (1964: 51). In this way, the café *al-Naṣr* serves as this 'third space', belonging neither to 'here' nor 'there'. It is closer to Berg's depiction of the transit camp in Michael's novel *Shavim ṿe-shavim yoter*: 'The camp is a place of transition, a liminal space in which the newcomers are neither here nor there' (2005: 180).

The same holds true for Nuri, the protagonist in *Tarnegol kapparot*. The *ma'abara* exists as an in-between place, between Israel (kibbutz Oranim) and Baghdad. The inner conflict between East and West reaches its peak in Nuri's split sensibility. Nuri is torn between the two places, the two cultures and the two types of music. On the one hand, he wants to adopt the Western style of music to imitate the Ashkenazim, and, on the other, he cannot stop listening to the oriental musical instrument *'ūd* played by his Iraqi friend Masul in the kibbutz. These feelings make him contemplate leaving the kibbutz for the *ma'abara* and then for Baghdad (Amir 1983: 121).

In a very clever way, Amir illuminates the debate between Nuri, Zavik, one of the Ashkenazi members of the kibbutz, and Buzaglo about the definition of normative people and the geographical boundaries:

> ”אתה עוד תלמד, פרימיטיבי.“
> ”מה זה פרימיטיבי, אדון חבר קיבוץ?“ שאל בוזגלו.
> ”זה בדיוק מה שאתה, אסיאט!“
> ”ואני חסבתי (חשבתי), ארץ ישראל זה אסיה,“ חגג בוזגלו את נצחונו הראשון.
> (Amir 1983: 45–6)
> ['You'll learn, primitive'.
> 'What'th "primitive", Mithter kibbutth-member?' asked Buzaglo.
> 'Exactly what you are, Asiatic!'
> 'And I thought that Ithrael was in Athia.' Buzaglo celebrated his first victory.]
> (Amir 1987: 48)

Zavik, the Ashkenazi, describes Nuri as a primitive person simply because he belongs to Asia. Yet Buzaglo, a Moroccan adult and one of Nuri's friends in the kibbutz, reminds Zavik that Israel is also located in Asia. This way the above conversation between the three is an attempt to illustrate the geographical belonging of Israel to Asia, and to the Middle East. In addition, it shows the paradox between the geographical location and the cultural segmentation between Eastern and Western cultures.

4.1.2 Baghdad

After exploring the narrative of the place in the three early Hebrew novels, one can say that through these novels the authors tried to express the feelings of the new immigrants in a new land, in which the representation of two locations, Iraq and Israel, are in the centre of the inner conflict in these three early novels. In the three novels of the 1990s (Amir 1992; Ballas 1991; Michael 1993) the place is more connected to Iraq. This holds true for the late Hebrew novel written by Michael (2015).

Even in Amir's novel *Mafriaḥ ha-yonim*, Israel is described as a place of disappointment for the fresh ambitious immigrant; although he is a Zionist, Abū-Kabī (Mr Immary) is disappointed by the man in charge in the transit camp, who underestimates his ideas and his project for rice cultivation in Israel (Amir 1992: 449–54). In addition, Mr Immary was also upset by not receiving the appropriate support from the Israeli government for his brother Hizkel, the Zionist activist arrested in Iraq who was unable to immigrate to Israel with Immary.

Levy (2006) highlights a very critical theme in the literary works of Iraqi Jewish authors. Speaking of Baghdad as an iconic term in their literary work, she notes: 'The paradox of profound and abiding identification with a place from which the writers were essentially ejected is one of the most intriguing aspects of the Iraqi Jewish experience and of its literary expression' (2006: 169). This is also the case with some of Hebrew novels examined here; Baghdad and Iraq are well represented in four Hebrew novels out of nine.

For Ballas, Baghdad in his novel *Ṿe-hu aḥer* (1991) awakens confused feelings about the place and the issue of attachment and belonging. Soussan, the protagonist of the novel, who is a Jewish convert to Islam in Iraq, asks himself some questions regarding immigration: 'To immigrate? Abandon everything and leave? Cut myself off from my world and seek absorption in an alien society?' (Ballas 2007: 20). This statement reflects the issue of belonging and attachment to the place of origin or Iraq.

In his literary works, Ballas tries to avoid using linguistic terms that are associated with the Zionist narrative. In this novel, for instance, the use of Hebrew lexical items expressing terms related to the place in the novel can substantiate that. The expression לעלות לארץ *la'lot la-aretz*, which used in the Hebrew lexicon to express immigration in the general, word-for-word translation means to immigrate to the *Land* (the land refers here to Israel), is not used in Ballas's novel in the same context. Instead he uses the term הגר *hegger* (Ballas 1991: 21, 56) which gives the same denotation on the one hand, and avoids the Zionist ideology associated with the well-known expression *la'lot la-aretz* on the other.

Amir described a full Jewish world in Baghdad with all its landscapes, geography, smells, customs and traditions, foods, music and language connected with the Jews of Baghdad. In the novel, the reader finds a detailed description of Iraqi and Baghdadi local markets; the description of the place makes the reader feel like she or he is walking in the streets of Baghdad and enjoying its places and its smiles, its corners and its sellers:

> סוק חִנוּנִי, השוק היהודדי, לא נח ולא שקט. שאונו החל שעה ארוכה לפני הזריחה והסתיים שעה ארוכה לאחר השקועה. אילו היה חשמל בכל דוכניו, היה חי ורוגש עד חצות. מאות דוכנים, צבעים ורוחות, סלים מלאים פֵּרות, סבלים עמוסים מזהירים עוברים ושבים"
>
> (Amir 1992: 18)
>
> 'Souk Hinuni, the Jewish marketplace, rarely stopped to catch its breath. Its bustle started well before sunrise and lasted until long after sunset. Only the lack of electric light kept most of its stands from staying open till midnight. There were hundreds of them, each with its colours and smells. The porters beneath their baskets of fruit, shouting at the shoppers to make way.' (Amir 2010b: 15)

The coding of place names in Amir's novel (1992) is notable. Often the author tries to bring the outsider reader closer to the denotation of Arabic place names employed in his text.[3] He does this by using glossing and contextual clarification of the historical and cultural aspects associated with the Iraqi places used in the text, e.g.:

> "למחרת שם את נפשו בכפו והלך אל בַּאבּ אל-שֵׁיח', אל השכונה המוסלמית הארורה שבַּהִיַּה גרה בה, ויהודי שומר נפשו ירחק ממנה."
>
> (Amir 1992: 67)
>
> ['Next day he took his life in his hands and went to **Bab-el-Sheikh**, the Muslim neighbourhood where Bahiya lived and where a Jew did well to steer clear of']
>
> (Amir 2010b: 74–5)

The author sees that the Arab code which refers to *Bāb-al-Sheikh* needs to be clarified and illustrated for the outsider reader. This is why some of the place names are encoded in the Hebrew texts. Other examples of this technique include: the *Karakhāna* [passage, the passage of brothels] (1992: 62, 235); 'In *Share' al-Rashīd,* the main street' (1992: 47); '*Sūq Ḥenuni*, the Jewish market' (1992: 18); and '*Sūq al-Shorja*' (1992: 301).

Translation and glossing are not the only strategies that Amir uses in his texts with Arabic place names, he also applies code-switching, e.g. ['in a speedboat that was waiting to take him safely across the **Shatt-el-Arab**'] (Amir 2010b: 3). Here the author does not define *Shaṭ-al-'Arab* [the word-for-word translation means the Arab shore, referring to the Persian Gulf]. Eli Amir neither translates it into Hebrew in the text nor glosses its meaning in the footnote. In this respect, the Arabic name here serves as a code for the outsider reader.

Arabic place is also used as a metaphor when the lack of cultural background about the place and its historical connotation would make an outsider reader unable to appreciate the metaphoric image that the author wants to present in his text, as in the following example:

> ”הַרון,“ אמר בטלטלו אותי, ”אם תעלה לצריח שוק אל-עַ'זל ותצעק יומם ולילה שרק מאהבת אומת מוחמד התאסלמת, גם זה לא יעזור לך !“
>
> (Ballas 1991: 94)
>
> ["Haroun," he shook me and said, "if you climb to the top of the minaret in the Souk al-Ghazl and yell out day and night that you became a Muslim for no other reason than love of Muhammad's nation, that wouldn't help you either".]
>
> (Ballas 2007: 116)

In this conversation, Kazim, an Iraqi Jew in Baghdad, is not convinced that Haron, the narrator of Ballas's novel (1991), has converted to Islam motivated by love for the religion and its people. In order to convey this opinion, Kazim uses an Iraqi metaphor. The metaphor refers to a famous place in Baghdad at the time, *Sūq al-Ghazl*.[4] This code constitutes the central part of the metaphor, yet its historical and cultural values are hard to translate into Hebrew for the outsider reader.

Michael focused on the Jewish family of Victoria as an example to draw on the Jewish social, economic, family relationship and Jewish and non-Jewish mutual relations in Baghdad. Baghdad, Lebanon, Basra and even Israel are the places about which the author tells his stories. In these words, Michael describes the relationship between Baghdad and Jews:

> ”בגדאד עומדת על תלה יותר מאלף שנים. העיר הגדולה, שהתפתחה מכפר נידח בשולי הממלכה הסאסאנית, חבה הרבה לאבותיה של ויקטוריה.“
>
> ['Baghdad still has remained unruined more than one thousand years. The big city, that was developed from a remote village located of the margins of the Sassanian Empire, owes much to the fathers of Victoria']
>
> (Michael 1993: 59)

Here, the author touches on the historical connection of the Jews to Baghdad. To confirm this strong relationship with Baghdad as a place, Michael adds these words:

> ”היהודים הסתגרו ברובע צר למדי, ורובם נולדו וגדלו והזדקנו ומתו בלי לצאת מתחומיו.“

> ['The Jews have put themselves in a very narrow place, and the majority of them were born, brought up, got old and died without getting out of it (Baghdad)']
> (Michael 1993: 59)

Interestingly enough, the late Hebrew novel by Michael (2015) is based on a love story between Kamāl, a twenty-year-old young man of a wealthy Jewish family in Baghdad, and al-Māsa, an orphaned Jewish girl who became a maid in Kamāl's house. The events of the novel take place in Baghdad during the 1930s. In the novel, Sami Michael describes the city of Baghdad in detail: the River Tigris that crosses the city, the local Iraqi houses, the streets of Baghdad, and even the desert that sieges the city.

In one scene, Michael describes how Kamāl enjoyed the water of the river and its smell and the sounds that came out of his feet while he was sitting and moving them gently in the water (p. 155).

Here, again, the use of Arabic in Michael's novel (2015) is much higher than the use of Arabic in the other two late novels (Amir 2010a; Ballas 2008). Among the main different narrative settings of these three novels is the place. While Baghdad is the only geographic location in Michael's novel, Ballas and Amir choose Israel as the central location for the events.

4.1.3 Israel

> He (the driver) helped me down and said something in a Hebrew that sounded nothing like the language I knew from the prayer book and school. I should never have stopped my Hebrew lessons in the *Movement* after Hizkel's arrest. How did you say, "I have to pee"? Surely it must have occurred to someone that this was one of the first sentences a beginner needed to learn? (Amir 2010b: 484)

With these words, Kābī describes his first meeting with the new land after he leaves Baghdad for Israel. Kābī, the protagonist and the narrator in Eli Amir's novel, discovers that he may encounter some linguistic conflicts just after his immigration to Israel, even though he has learnt Hebrew in a Jewish Baghdadi school.

In two out of three of the late Hebrew novels Iraq is not the central place where the events take place, as in the novels of the other two periods. This is unlike the early and the middle Hebrew novels when Iraq/Baghdad was more involved in the events and the narratives.

In Ballas's novel *Tom ha-biḳur* [End of the Visit] (2008), the protagonist Jacob Sālim goes to Israel for a short visit. Sālim chooses exile based on his own motivation. He lives in London; Israel for him is only a place where some of his relatives live. He believes that he can only have liberty when he is outside the community obligations that are surrounded by conflicts and war among those who have political dreams (Ballas 2008: 63). In this novel, the event of visiting Israel depends more on other places that the author portrays mainly through the technique of flashback memory. Sālim describes how he was able to escape from Iraq to Iran, and how he was forced to go to Israel instead of the UK as planned, and how finally he was able to escape to London. The place for Sālim is the best way to express his refusal to live in a community he does not want to live in or to be forced to live in. Therefore, he searches for escape in the autobiographies of others, who share with him the same feelings of foreignness and alienation (Ballas 2008: 63).

Amir chooses Tel Aviv as a centre of his novel *Ma she-nish'ar* [What's Left] (Amir 2010a), the events there are all connected mainly to Tel Aviv. Baghdad is only mentioned in a few sentences as a memory. This is when the narrator recalls the memory of his parents in Iraq long before emigration to Israe; he says this about his father: 'He was the second son in a low-income family, and when his brother fell down from scaffolding and died, he was also doomed. He had to leave the "Midrash school" and had to work' (Amir 2010a: 105). The narrator also refers, from time to time, to some memories of childhood in Iraq, with his father in Iraqi markets, memories of his teenage experiences and from his school days (Amir 2010a: 138–9).

Each of these memories does not occupy a significant space in the novel that tells the love story of the narrator in Israel extended over about thirty years, and only a small number of memories of Iraq emerge in a very limited way. For instance, even though the novel is based on events in Israel, Arabic songs are still employed by the narrator (Amir 2010a: 273, 307).

Although in the late Hebrew novels Iraq is not the main place where events took place in two novels (Amir 2010a; Ballas 2008), the events of the novel by Michael (2015) are based mainly on a love story that occurred in Baghdad. Moreover, the late Hebrew novels of Amir and Ballas as discussed in Chapter 3 use Arabic in a very limited way compared to their early and middle period's novels. However, Michael employed Arabic extensively in his late novel (2015). That variation in the three Iraqi authors' choices of geographic locations influences, apparently, the way in which Arabic is implemented in the Hebrew texts. Therefore, one can easily claim that the use of Arabic was mostly associated with the choice of geographic location of the narrative setting, and there is no strong evidence of a decline in using Arabic based on a diachronic perspective.

Using Arabic in each novel from a linguistic, literary and sociolinguistic perspective seems to be a tool for verification by which one can judge the Hebrew novels of the study as follows: while Ballas's language challenges the modern Hebrew canon and introduces characters who prefer to engage with the new culture, new place and the new language through their Iraqiness, Amir draws a line around a space in between, with more longed-for acceptance of the new reality. Surprisingly, Amir is the author who employed Arabic more widely in his texts compared to his two counterparts. Michael treads a clever path somewhere in between.

4.2 Summary and Concluding Remarks

The use of Arabic in the nine Hebrew novels of our three Iraqi Jewish authors is the focus of the present study. In order to show the historical implication of the Arabic and Hebrew used in one text, the book presented a short historical introduction and overview relevant to this phenomenon, from the Middle Ages to the present day. In this historical introduction to the project, the three Iraqi Jewish authors are introduced in the light of this socio-political, sociolinguistic and literary perspective.

This study considers the three Iraqi Jewish authors as exophonic authors. 'Exophonic' refers to writing literature in the non-mother tongue and is associated with a bilingual paradigm. The present study argues that there are other linguistic aspects than code-switching that can be found in exophonic texts. This book has also shown what possibilities there are to applying stylistics as a theoretical approach to the exophonic texts (ET). A model based on the stylistic concept of 'choice' has been developed in this study to analyse the selected corpora of nine Hebrew novels. In the following, a summary of the model and the linguistic results are given.

4.2.1 The Model

To begin with, the study of exophonic texts is under-researched. In addition, it tends to follow the sociolinguistic trend in terms of comparing written code-switching (CS) in the literary works to conversational CS. The majority of approaches developed to analyse exophonic texts have been guided mainly by research on bilingualism and/or languages in contact. On the other hand, exophonic texts have deliberate linguistic and literary features including CS and non-CS aspects that stylise them. Because of the author's bilingualism or multilingualism, the choices available to her/him go beyond one language system.

4.2.1.1 WHY STYLISTICS?

Exophonic texts have deliberate linguistic and literary features including CS and non-CS aspects which stylise them. Non-CS aspects include, for instance, loan translation, paradigmatic deviations, syntagmatic deviations and syntactic fusion that are also important to the study of exophonic texts.

Moreover, the function of stylistic analysis as a linguistic tool to investigate aspects on more than one linguistic level in the text is necessary for a better understanding of the linguistic features in exophonic texts. In order to analyse the embedded language uses in the exophonic text the linguistic levels are investigated (linguistic component). In addition, and this adds to the importance of using stylistic analysis to approach the exophonic text, the analysis pays attention not only to the linguistic features in the literary work; rather, it tries to find an objective answer to the question of why? (pragmatic component), and how? (literary-aesthetic component).

The model used in the study is designed to investigate the linguistic phenomena that may be found in the exophonic texts. Both CS and non-CS aspects are taken into consideration in the model.

4.2.1.2 STYLE AS CHOICE AND EXOPHONIC TEXTS

The writer's choice of some linguistic forms as favoured over others has a deep-rooted conceptual basis in stylistic theory. An author's selection and arranging of lexical items and other linguistic levels may be studied stylistically as the authors' linguistic choices drawn from variations and alternatives extant in one language system.

The possibility of varieties which an author can use is likely to be increased according to how many language systems she or he can access. Because of the author's bilingualism or multilingualism the choices available for the author go beyond one language system. For that reason, the study of the style as choice is more appropriate to approach linguistic, literary and pragmatic features of exophonic texts.

4.2.1.3 LITERARY CODE-SWITCHING: NEW PERSPECTIVE

CS in interactive modes (spoken CS) is likely to be more spur of the moment, and the participants in the bilingual conversation are only slightly aware of it. The same may not hold true for the literary text, where less time is spent choosing the codes in the conversations than when the bilingual author is writing the manuscript. The author has both the time and opportunity to edit and review what she or he has written.

Given that an author's decisions and intentions are involved in both the process of inserting codes from outside the Matrix Text Language (MTL) as well as interpreting the text as a message that requires a decoding process, this study divides literary CS into three main types: hard-access code-switching (HA-CS), easy-access code-switching (EA-CS) and ambiguous-access code-switching (AA-CS). The chapter will refer to these three types in more detail later on.

4.2.1.4 NON-CS: SYNTAGMATIC AND PARADIGMATIC DEVIATIONS

It is important for this study to investigate not only CS but also non-CS aspects in exophonic texts using stylistic analysis. Non-CS aspects found in exophonic texts are syntagmatic and paradigmatic deviations. The deviation from the norm is likely to be frequent when there is some interference between two languages. Deviation can also be demonstrated by the author's choice, making it likewise somehow connected to the author's writing style.

4.2.1.5 THE SUGGESTED MODEL

The attempt to regard the linguistic phenomena associated with exophonic texts as the stylistic term 'choice' might serve as a reassessment tool in approaching these phenomena. CS, for instance, will be perceived in connection with the author's readiness to choose codes from another language system (embedded language). Loan translation is to be interpreted as the semantic choices of other linguistic phenomena discussed below. The midpoint in the approach is that the system of the embedded language (EL) has a significant influence on some bilingual authors' choices; not only in terms of using linguistic elements outside the MTL, but also on some linguistic elements that belong to the MTL itself. In view of that, the present study deals with embedded language use in the MTL as:

1. The author's choices within the MTL.
2. Deviation from the norm (paradigmatic and syntagmatic deviations).
3. Code-switching by the author.

Since the bilingual author, as noted, writes her/his literary work consciously, the term 'choice' should be extensively adhered to in the analysis of exophonic texts. The following linguistic patterns are suggested by the study at hand to approach exophonic texts.

To begin with, CS constitutes a dominant phenomenon in the exophonic text. The study suggests that literary CS can be analysed in light of two main types. The first is HA-CS, which refers to any code added by the author that does not belong to the MTL and may be expected to create difficulties for any reader who does not share the author's bilingual and bicultural linguistic background (an outsider reader). This type includes inter-sentential CS and intra-sentential CS. The second type is EA-CS, which refers to the insertion of non-MTL codes by the author, who tries to elucidate these codes to make them decodable to the outsider reader. EA-CS involves both direct translation and glossing. A third type is also put forward to apply to cultural patterns associated with the mother tongue: AA-CS. This can be associated, for instance, with some cases of word-for-word translation, interjections and the use of some character and place names.

Linguistic behaviour towards the non-CS aspects of exophonic texts that resulted in an author's linguistic choices from the varieties in MTL can be primarily categorised along two axes: syntagmatic and paradigmatic. The first category involves the word order of some MTL lexical items structured in a way that violates the MTL norm, on the one hand, and imitates the embedded language norm, on the other. The second category (paradigmatic deviations) includes the lexical selection of varieties existing in the lexicon of MTL, where the influence of embedded language lexicon has a high impact. Paradigmatic deviations are highly expected in cases of loan translation from embedded languages into the MTL as well.

The above three main linguistic features of exophonic texts are connected directly to the authors' ability to access two language systems. The choices here are associated with two main terms: the first constitutes the choices available to an exophonic author between the two language systems MTL/embedded language, which is CS. The second constitutes the selecting of some linguistic varieties within the MTL system in a way that the embedded language influences the choices.

4.2.2 Stylistic Analysis of the Arabic Use of the Iraqi Jewish Authors

This study's data are taken from nine Hebrew novels written by three Iraqi Jewish authors: Sami Michael (1974, 1993, 2015), Eli Amir (1983, 1992, 2010a) and Shimon Ballas (1964, 1991, 2008). The study relies on a manual annotation to the data. All Arabic uses employed by the authors in the suggested corpora are extracted and analysed linguistically. In order to highlight the historical implications of the issue, the study suggests a diachronic analysis based on three periods, in which each period signifies a corpus. The first period is represented through three early novels written in Hebrew by these authors at the beginning of their literary careers (corpus 1). The following middle period is assigned to three Hebrew novels covering the period of the 1990s (corpus 2), while the later literary works of the three authors designate the third period (corpus 3).

Almost 2,000 uses or instances of Arabic have been extracted from the nine Hebrew novels in connection with the model developed by the study. Arabic is used in both CS and non-CS traits. The study has shown with examples from the Hebrew novels the possibility of applying the linguistic categories suggested by the model to be investigated in exophonic texts. Below are general remarks on the style of Arabic use in Iraqi Jewish fiction as well as on the diachronic development of this style over approximately fifty years.

4.2.2.1 THE RESULTS OF THE LINGUISTIC ANALYSIS

The results of the project are based on the extraction of approximately 2,000 instances of Arabic usage in the texts. In all nine novels the noun is used primarily, compared to other parts of speech. The sum of HA-CS in the corpora overall is 1,454 instances, as compared with a total of only 156 instances of EA-CS. This means that of the total number of Arabic codes implemented in the nine Hebrew novels, 90 per cent are HA-CS and 10 per cent are EA-CS. Across all nine novels, HA-CS comprises the major type of coding used. This indicates to what extent the Arabic codes, which are combined into sentences or stand alone in lexical items, could hardly be accessed or were sometimes non-decodable for a reader who is not familiar with Arabic.

It is not only CS which is employed in the suggested corpora; the texts also include a considerable number of cases when Arabic/Hebrew interference was active. This resulted in some syntagmatic and paradigmatic deviations from the modern Hebrew norm. The deviations were categorised mainly along two axes: syntagmatic and paradigmatic. The first category involves the word order of Hebrew lexical items in some sentences in such a way that violence is done to the modern Hebrew norm on the one hand, and there is imitation of the Arabic norm on the other. The second category (paradigmatic deviation) includes the lexical selection of varieties in the Hebrew lexicon that are likely to be more close phonologically to Arabic lexis. Paradigmatic deviations are also highly expected in cases of loan translation from Arabic into the Hebrew texts.

4.2.2.2 GENERAL REMARKS ON THE ANALYSIS OF ARABIC USE

To conclude with some general remarks on the development of the style of Arabic use over approximately fifty years, it is clear from the corpora that Arabic is employed in the Hebrew texts in diverse ways. This claim is derived from the wide range of Arabic parts of speech used, as well as from the variety of strategies employed by the authors discussed in Chapter 3.

The noun is the most favoured part of speech by the Iraqi authors. The use of the noun as the most favoured part of speech has the same ratio throughout the three corpora. Interjections vary: there is a considerable decrease in employing them, from 25 per cent in corpus 1 to 10 per cent in corpus 2, and only 2 per cent in corpus 3. The decrease in the use of interjections, associated mostly with Arabic Iraqi vernacular, sheds useful light on the way in which the employment of Arabic voices in the literary works by the Iraqis was gradually being diminished over the decades. Although the protagonists of the three late Hebrew novels (Ballas 2008; Amir 2010; Michael 2015) are of Iraqi origin, the use of interjections in these novels is minimal compared to Hebrew novels published in the 1990s or to early Hebrew novels that used interjections more widely.

Code-switching continued to be the most commonly used strategy of employing Arabic codes in the three corpora. The ratios of HA-CS to EA-CS, according to the diachronic order, are (7.6:1), (10:1) and (3.1:1) for corpus 1, corpus 2 and corpus 3 respectively. This proves that even in the late Hebrew novels the tendency to use hard-access Arabic codes reflects the main concern in the style of the novels. In all nine novels, HA-CS is used more frequently than the other two strategies of EA-CS and glossing.

Although it is evident from the data analysed through the corpora that the use of Arabic gradually decreased over about fifty years, one can argue that the use of Arabic is likely associated with the geographic location as a narrative setting, i.e. novels that are associated with Iraq/Baghdad.

4.2.3 The Style of Arabic Use According to Each Author

According to a sample of 450 pages from nine Hebrew novels of which the first fifty pages of each novel is analysed, the style of Arabic use regarding each author has been investigated. The strategies of Arabic use, the contextual analysis of Arabic use, the dialogue and non-dialogue cases in which Arabic is used and the diachronic issue of the style of each author are considered in this analysis, presented in tables and examples from the novels. Below are general remarks on the way Iraqi Jewish authors incorporated Arabic in their Hebrew works.

4.2.3.1 SHIMON BALLAS

The ratio of using Arabic in Ballas's sample concerning dialogue to narrative modes is (2:1). This result highlights the variety of Ballas's use of Arabic, not only in the dialogue mode when the characters are expected to reflect their cultural and linguistic backgrounds but also in the narrative mode.

The strategies employed by Ballas prove that his use of Arabic in terms of inserting HA-CS and EA-CS is quite balanced; in the sample, there are twelve instances of HA-CS and ten instances of EA-CS. The majority of these appear in the first of his Hebrew novels in this study (Ballas 1964). This fact reflects the diachronic decrease of Arabic use in Ballas's literary works. Yet one should mention that in his last Hebrew novel to be studied (Ballas 2008), the use of EA-CS and glossing strategies are still maintained.

With regard to semantic field analysis, the sample of 150 pages taken from his three Hebrew novels are to some extent variable, although some lexical sets are not used in Ballas's sample compared to the other two authors, Sami Michael and Eli Amir. Ballas uses Arabic interjection lexical sets widely. The use of lexical sets related to religion is among the most commonly used lexical sets after interjections. These lexemes express both the vernacular and religious sense of belonging of some Iraqi characters in the novels.

With respect to contextual settings in which Arabic is frequently used in the sample, it is clear that Ballas's use of Arabic is associated mostly with the normal mode, in which the author uses mainly the narrative or the non-dialogue technique. The use of Arabic is also associated with emotional contexts, e.g. excitement, happiness and sadness. Yet Arabic use is more pronounced in the contexts of anger and humour.

4.2.3.2 SAMI MICHAEL

Michael's style with regard to the use of Arabic also generally declined over the course of the fifty or so years of his literary career in Israel. However, his late Hebrew novel (2015) employs many instances of Arabic in the first fifty pages. Interestingly, the particle, mainly the use of */yā/*, is the most used item in Michael's style. The use of the Arabic particle exceeds the use of the noun, with 36.5 per cent and 34 per cent respectively.

Michael's Arabic style favours employing interjections. The extensive use of particles and interjections in Michael's style may arise from the tendency in his fiction to employ dialogues rather than narrative. The ratio of dialogue to narrative in Michael's style with respect to an instance of the use of Arabic is (3.8:1). In the light of this ratio, one can certainly say that Michael's style of using Arabic is associated with the conversational mode more than the narrative mode.

Another feature of Michael's style is to avoid the use of EA-CS and glossing strategies. Almost all Arabic codes in the sample from Michael's three Hebrew novels are HA-CS. However, one should mention that some codes used by Michael can also be classified as AA-CS.

The use of Arabic lexical sets evinces little variation in Michael's style. In the first novel (1974), he mainly uses two lexical sets – *particle* and *interjection* – with less attention accorded to other lexical sets. In the second novel (1993), he also uses two Arabic lexical sets, associated mainly with Iraqi *clothes* and *cuisine.*

The analysis of the contextual settings in Michael's sample indicates that the use of Arabic is to some extent related to and associated with highly-charged emotions such as *excitement*, *anger*, *sadness* and *happiness*. The analysis also reveals that in his Hebrew novels there are more contextual settings in the first Hebrew novel (1974) than in the second (1993) in all categories. There is also a place in Michael's style allocated for *humour*, although it constitutes the lowest frequency in the contextual modes in which Arabic is used.

4.2.3.3 ELI AMIR

Eli Amir's use of Arabic in his novels depends mainly on three parts of speech: the noun, the interjection and the particle. These three figures of speech constitute 54.5 per cent, 20 per cent and 10 per cent respectively of the total instances of Arabic use in Amir's sample texts.

What also distinguishes Amir's style when it comes to employing Arabic lexical items in the Hebrew text are his attempts to merge and integrate Arabic in his texts. Although many lexical items of the total used in the sample are HA-CS, Amir deals with Arabic nouns as if they belong to the Hebrew lexicon. Amir also uses Judaeo-Arabic spoken by Iraqi Jews in many plots of his works.

Regarding the strategies of implementing Arabic in his sample texts, Amir preferred to make the majority of inserted Arabic codes HA-CS. According to the sample, 80.6 per cent of the Arabic codes used are HA-CS, compared to only 18.6 per cent EA-CS. Glossing is used only once (1992: 33). Of note is the use of both HA-CS and EA-CS in the late Hebrew novel by Amir. This is also a distinct feature of his style; Amir still uses Arabic codes in his late literary works, albeit in a very limited way.

The translation strategy from Arabic to Hebrew distinguishes Amir's style, even though this strategy is excluded from the statistics. Amir uses this technique mainly with folk sayings and idioms.

Amir uses Arabic in the sample in dialogue and narrative mode, with the same proportions in the two modes. It is important to point out that in the novel *Tarnegol kapparot* (1983), Amir used Arabic forty-one times in dialogue mode compared to only nine times in narrative mode. However, in his second novel, *Mafriaḥ ha-yonim* (1992), Arabic appeared seventy times in narrative mode and thirty-seven times in dialogue mode. The total, then, is seventy-nine for narrative mode and seventy-eight for dialogue mode. This result reveals that Amir's style regarding dialogue and narrative is varied, and even the differences between the use of Arabic in dialogue/narrative modes are not as great as in the case of Ballas and Michael.

According to the sample, the lexical sets used by Amir prove the variety of his selection of Arabic lexical items employed in his Hebrew novels, namely his two earlier novels (Amir 1983, 1992). Interjections are predominant in the 1992 novel. The *foods and drinks* lexical set is represented the most in *Tarnegol kapparot* (1983). Lexical items associated with *sex* and *love* are used only in *Tarnegol kapparot* (1983). *Particle* and *religion* lexical sets are used to the same degree in the two novels.

The findings of the contextual analysis of Amir's sample indicate that Arabic use is repeatedly related to highly-charged emotions – such as *excitement* sets that include, for example, fear and surprise. *Excitement* sets rank highly in Amir's sample in both of his earlier novels (1983, 1992). The same holds true for *anger*, the second category associated with highly-charged emotions observed in Amir's sample. The *anger* set is associated mostly with the use of Iraqi lexical items related to insults. The *anger* set is likewise mainly implemented in the sample by means of the HA-CS strategy. *Humour* constitutes the lowest frequency of use of Arabic in the sample.

Appendices

A List of Arabic Lexical Items with Frequencies

A list of the Arabic lexical items extracted from the nine Hebrew novels is arranged alphabetically with the frequency of each item. Other orthographic formats of the extracted Arabic lexical items are also mentioned in the appendix. It is important to point out that Arabic proper names are excluded from the appendix. The Arabic sentences are divided into lexical units. Only complete sentences, such as folk sayings and interjections, are not divided into single lexical items.

Code-switching Instances in the Hebrew Novels

The two lists below contain the instances of the Arabic codes extracted from the nine Hebrew novels, covering the two main cases of code-switching as suggested by the study, i.e. hard-access code-switching (HA-CS) (Table A.2) and easy-access code-switching (EA-CS) (Table A.3). The extracts are arranged alphabetically with all occurrences (page numbers) listed in the reference column.

Table A.1 List of Arabic lexical items with frequencies

Hebrew script	Arabic script	Other orthographical, and morphological formats	Frequencies
אבו-זקן	أبو ذقن		2
אַבְּנַאְאַל-וַטַן	أبناء الوطن		1
אבן-אל-מאניוקה	ابن المنيوكا		1
אִבְּן עַרַבּ	ابن عرب		2
אַבִּינַא	أبينا		1
אדבח	ادبح	אִדְבַּחוּ	18
אה	اه		7
אהוות ערב	اهوت عرب		2
אַהְלַא וּסַהְלַא	اهلا وسهلا		1
אהלן	اهلاً	אהלן ב אַהְלַן	6
אהלן וסהלן	أهلاً وسهلاً	אַהְלַן וַסַהְלַן	6
אוה	اوه		3
אוהו	او هو		2
אוסכות	اسكت		2
אוף	اوف		2
אחבאבינא	احبابنا		1
אִחְ'וַאן	اخوان		4
אַח'וּיי	اخوي		3
אחרא דין בוק	احرا دين بوك		1
אח'תלט אלחבל באלנאבל	اختلط الحابل بالنابل		1
איבני	ابني		1
אידֵיכּ	ايديك	אִידֵק	2
אידַק באל-דהַן	ايدك بالدهن		1
אינשאללה	انشاء الله	אנשאללה אִנשאללה	11
אינתצרנא	انتصرنا		1
אכון	أكون		1
אלאהווה	الأهوه		1
אלאנקאד	الانقاذ		1
אל-בחרין	البحرين		1
אל-בַּעַת'	البعث		1
אל-בּריד אל-יומי	البريد اليومي		1
אל-גַ'דידה	الجزيرة		1
אלגרעה	الجَرعه		1
אלדאולה	الدولة		1
אל-דעוה	الدعوة		1
אלהזימה	الهزيمة		1
אל-וַדַאע	الوداع		1

Table A.1 continued

Hebrew script	Arabic script	Other orthographical, and morphological formats	Frequencies
אל-וַטַנִיַה	الوطنية		1
אַל-חִזְבּ אַל-וַטַנִי אַל-דִימוקְרַטִי	الحزب الوطني الديمقراطي		2
אלחיא	الحياة		2
אל-חמל	الحمل	חמל	3
אל-חַרַם אלשַרִיף	الحرم الشريف		1
אל-יקד'ה	اليقظة		1
אללַהֲ אַכְּבַּר	الله أكبر	אללה אכבר אללה אכּבּר	31
אל-כֻּפַאר	الكفار		1
אל-מוח'אבראת	المخابرات		3
אלמזעומה	المزعومة		1
אילחמדו-לאיללה	الحمد لله		1
אל-סַפַר	السفر		1
אל-פַּאשַה	الباشا		1
אַלשַרַארַה	الشرارة		1
אשרע	اسرع		2
אל-צַהַאיִנַה	الصهاينه		1
אל-צהיוניה	الصهيونية		1
אל-צַיפִי	الصيفي		1
אלקאנונג'י	الكانونچي	הקאנונצ'י הקאנונג'י מנגן הקאנון הַקאנוּנְצִ'י	5
אל-קֻדְס	القدس		1
אלקווה	القوة		1
אל-שיועיה	الشيوعية	אל-שִׁיוּעִיַה	2
אלשער	الشعر		1
אל-תַקַאסִים	التقاسيم		1
(ה)אִנְגְלִיז	(ها)انجليز	אל-אינגליז	2
אִנְהַגַ'ם בֵּיתוּ	انهچم بيتو		1
אנף נאר אנף דח'אן	انف نارانف دخان		1
אִינְצַאף	إنْصَاف		1
אינתם	إنتم		1
אל-סוּרְמַיַה	الصورمايا		1
אל-סַלַאםֶ אַלְ-מַלִכִּי	السلام الملكي		1
אסלמ עליך	السلام عليك		2
אל-סַלַאם עַלַיכּוּם	السلام عليكم		1
אֶסְתַאד	أستاذ		10

Hebrew script	Arabic script	Other orthographical, and morphological formats	Frequencies
אצַאר בִּיץ' אל־יום יַא ח'וִיַה?	اشصار بيتش اليوم ياخويا؟		1
אִרְגַעִי	ارجعي		3
א-שבאב	الشباب	שבאב	2
אַל-שַהַאדַה	الشهاده		2
אלע'זל	الغزل		1
אצילה	اصيلة		1
בַּאבַּא	بابا	בַּאבּא	27
באיזן אללה	باذن الله		1
בִּבְּלַאש	ببلاش		1
ביג	بيج		1
בידק	بِدَّك		1
בֵּיְת אל-אַעְיַאן	بيت الاعيان		1
בּוּכְּרַה	بكرة		1
בוסתן	بستان		1
בּוּרְגוּל	برغل		2
בחַמְשַׁה	(ب) خمسة		1
ביאע	بياع		1
בִּלְ-אַפְרַאח	بالافراح		1
בלאש	بلاش		1
בלדי	بلدي	בָּלַדי	4
במיה	باميه	הבמיה במיות בַּמְיַה בַּמיה	9
בס	بَس		1
בסטה	بَسْطَه	בַּסטָה	2
בּקְלַאוַה	بقلاوة		1
גַאוּרַג	جاورج		2
ג'את	جت		1
ג'בתיני	جبتيني		1
ג'ין	جن		11
ג'יהאד	جهاد	ג'יהד גיהד גְ'הַאד גִ'הַאד	6
ג'הִאריאק	جهاريك		1
גִ'הֶנַם	جِهنَم		1
גוג'ה	جوچه		3
גַ'זִירַה	جزيرة		2

Table A.1 continued

Hebrew script	Arabic script	Other orthographical, and morphological formats	Frequencies
גזיה	جزية		1
גלביה	جلبية		3
גַ'רַה	جَرَّه	הגַ'רַה ג'רה הג'רה ג'ארה	13
גרוש	جروش		1
דח'ילך	دخيلك	דחילאק דחילק דַחִילַכֹּ	9
דִיר בּאלַכֹּ	ديربالك		1
דיוַאן	ديوان		1
דוֹנְדִרְמַה	دوندرمه		3
דַנְדַח	دَنْدَح		1
דִרהִם	دِرهِم		1
דרויש	درويش		3
דשדאשה	دِشْدَاشَه	דִשְדַאשַה דִשדאשה דִשְדַאַשות	4
הא	ها		2
הדה הוא	هذا هو		1
הַדַה	هَذَا	הַדַא	2
הון	هون	מן הון לאהון	3
הונאכ	هناك		1
הל	هيل		1
הלאהל	هَلَاهِل	הַלַאהִל	10
התַנוּעַה	هتنوعا	תַנוּעַה התַנועה	51
ואללה	والله	וואללה וַאללַה	42
ואילי	واويلي	יא-וואלי יא וואֶלי וואלי וַאוֵילִי וַאוֵילִי עלי וַאוֵילִי	15
ודיני	وديني		2
וואַלאַד	ولد		2

Hebrew script	Arabic script	Other orthographical, and morphological formats	Frequencies
ולא יהימך	ولايهمك	ואָלָא יִהְמַכּ	2
וַזיר	وزير		19
וְחַיַאתַכְּ	وحياتك	וְחַיַאת וחיאת	7
וי	وَيْ		3
וֵינכּום	وينكوم		1
ולאד	ولاد	וְלַאד	4
וַעַלַיכּום	وعليكم		1
זַבַּאנֵה	زبانه		8
זבּון	زبون	הזבּון זבּון השְׂרַד	2
זחלאני	زحلاني		1
זחלאוי	زحلاوي		1
זִיאַרַה	زيارة		2
זְנְגוּלַה	زنجوله		5
חאבובה	حبوبة		1
חאראם	حرام		2
חביבי	حبيبي		13
חַבִּיבְּת אְל-אַלְבּ	حبيبة القلب		3
חביבתי	حبيبتي		4
חַדית	حديث		1
חאוואג'ה	خواجه		1
חילוה	حلوة		2
חַלַאוַה	حلاوة		1
חלס	خلاص		1
חלקון	حلقون		1
חַמַאם	حمام		3
חמדילה עסלאמה	حمدلله عسلامة		5
חפלה	حفلة	החפלה בחפלה לחפלה חַפְלַה בחַפְלַה לחַפְלַה חַפלת אל-וַדַאע החַפְלות בחַפְלות לחַפְלות	35

Table A.1 continued

Hebrew script	Arabic script	Other orthographical, and morphological formats	Frequencies
חראמי	حرامي		2
טאולה	طاولة		1
טאקיה	طقيي		2
טול אל-זַמַן	طول الزمن		
טוּז	طوز		1
טִיז	طيز		3
טפו	تفو		6
תרבוש	طربوش		3
יא	يا	יה יַא יא עיוני יא רוחי יא עיני עלא... יא אללה יא-חרא יא-חביבי יא-מאג'נון יא סַיִדִי יא אבּני יַא סַלַאם	289
יא הַלַא	ياهلا		1
יאהלי אל-ט'לאם חינו עליא	ياهلي الظلام حنو عليا		1
יאללה	يلا		40
יאלילי	ياليلي	יא לילי	3
יאבוי	يابوي		1
יא עיני	ياعيني		6
יבארכ	يبَارِك		1
יַגְרִי	يجري (النهر)		1
יַהוּד	يهود		4
יַהוּדי	يهودي		1
יום	يوم	יום אל עינדך יום אל-קבול אל־יום אל-יומי	4
יזיד פדלכום	يزيد فضلكم		1
יחרב ביתך	يخرب بيتك		4
יכון	يكون		1
ימה	يامه		2

Hebrew script	Arabic script	Other orthographical, and morphological formats	Frequencies
יִנְעַם אללה עַלֵיכּ	يِنْعَم الله عليك		1
יִסְוַה	يِسْوَى	יִסְוַה עַדַאם	1
יעִיש	يعيش		2
יעני	يعني	יַעני	4
כַּמַנְגַ'ה	كمنچه	הַכַּמַנְגַ'ה הכמנג'ה	6
כַּמַנְגַ'אתִי	كمنچاتي		1
כַּבַּאבּ	كباب	כַּבַּאב	12
כִּבַּה	كِبَه	כִּבַּה כבה	15
כַּבְּשְכַּאן	كَبِشْكَان		1
כוסאמו	كس امه	כוסאמו כוסאמם כוסאומכ כוס אֻם אל...	11
כּוּבֶּה	كُبه		1
כושרי	كشري		1
כַּחַל	كَحَل		1
כיפק	كيفك		1
כיף	كيف	כיף חאלק כיף אלאהווה	2
כַּלְבּ	كلب	אל-כַּלְבּ כְּלַאבּ אל-כְּלַאבּ	6
כֻּלַא	كُلا		1
כפייה	كوفيه	כָּפִיוֹת כָּפִייה בכָּפִייה הכָּפייה	21
כַּרְחַ'אנָה	كرخانه	כַּרְחַ'אנה	2
לצאחביהי	لصاحبه		1
לוביה	لوبيا	לוּבְּיה	7
לוֹ וְקַעְת, סִיר רְגַ'אל	لووِقَعت، صيررجال.		1
לוּזִינַה	لوزينه		1
ליל הניץ'	ليل (ها) نيتش		1
ללט'ים	للظيم		1
לַפַּה	لفه	לפה	3
לע'וה	لغايه		1
מאהום	ماهم		1

Table A.1 continued

Hebrew script	Arabic script	Other orthographical, and morphological formats	Frequencies
מאייה	مَيَّه		5
מַאשַׁאלְלַה	ماشاالله	מאשללה	3
מַבְּרוּכּ	مبروك	מאברוק	10
מג'נון	مجنون	מאג'נון מג'נון לילה המג'נון	8
מוּ	مو		1
מואזן	مؤذن		3
מוגליד	مُجلد		1
מוּחְ'תַאר	مختار		1
מֻחְתַשֶׁם	مُحتَشِم		3
מופתי	مُفْتِي		1
מַזַא	مازا		3
מאזֶה	مَزِه		1
מחבוב	محبوب		2
מחטופה	مخطوفه		1
מַחְלַאהַא עִישְׁת אִל-פַּלַאח	محلاها عيشة الفلاحه		1
מיחַ'אנַה	ميخانه		6
מְלַבַּס	مِلَبَس		1
ממנון	ممنون		1
מַן אל-סַמַא	مَـــنّ السما		1
מן עֵיני	من عيني		1
מִסְבַּחַה	مسبحة		10
מסגוף	مسجوف	מַזְגוּף	7
מסטול	مِسْطول		2
מִסְכֵּנָה	مِسْكينة		1
מִסְתַקִי	مِسْتَكي		5
מְעַאינַה	مِعَايْنَه		1
מעאנא	معانا		1
מַעַלֶש	مَعَلِش		1
מפיש	مفيش	מאפיש	3
מַרְחַבַּא	مرحبا	יַא אַלְף מַרְחַבַּא	3
מקאם	مقام	המקאם המקאמאת המקאמה מַקָאמַאת	6
מקברות	مقبروت		1

Hebrew script	Arabic script	Other orthographical, and morphological formats	Frequencies
מע	مع		1
מקטועה	مقطوعة		1
נאצר	نصر		2
נַאדִי	نادي		1
נאס	ناس		1
נַאס תַאכֻּל אַל-תַמַר וּאַנִי אִל-נֻוַאיַה חִצְתִי	ناس تاكل التمر، واني النوايا حصتي		1
נַבִּיל	نبيل		2
נבּוּט	نبوت	נבּוּטים	4
נַחְנוּ	نحن		1
ניפהמהא	نفهمها		1
נעם	نعم	יא נעם נַעַם	4
נַצוּנֶהוּ	نصونه		1
נרגילה	نرجيله		1
סַאדַה	ساده		1
סאלונה	سألونا		1
סואק	سواك		1
סוּלְחה	صُلْحَا		1
סולטאן	سلطان		1
סוּרַת	سورة		1
סחוג	سحوج		2
סִידַארַה	سيداره		3
סַיִדִי	سَيِّدِي		3
סינור	سنور		1
סלאמתך	سلامتك		2
סְלוּק	سلوق		1
סְמְבּוּסַק	سمبوسك	הסְמְבּוּסַק אַבּוּ אל-סְמְבּוּסַק	5
סַמַכּ	سمك	סמק	7
סמרה	سماره		1
סעד	سَعَد		2
סַפַּרְטַאס	سفرطاس		1
סַרְסִי	سَرْسِي		1
סְתַאד	سِتَاذ		22
עארס	عرص	לעארס	2
עאשת	عاشت	עאשְת אִידַכִּי	2
עאשורא	عشورا		1

Table A.1 continued

Hebrew script	Arabic script	Other orthographical, and morphological formats	Frequencies
עביה	عبايي	העביה בעביה לעביה העביות בעביות עֲבָּיה עֲבָּיוֹת העֲבָּיוֹת העבאיה עבית צמר עבית המשי	58
עוד	عود		4
עיוני	عيوني	יא עיוני	6
עיני	عيني	יא עיני מן עיני אבוס עינק	4
עלא	على		5
עַלַא כֵּיפַכ	على كيفك		1
עַלַא ענִי ועלַא רַאסִי	على عيني وعلي راسي		1
עַמְבַּה	عَمْبَه	עמבה	12
עַמִי	عمي	עַמִי	4
עְמַמַה	عِمامه		5
עַסַל	عسل		2
עַקיד	عقيد		1
עקאל	عقال		1
ערוג	عروج		1
עַרַק	عَرَق	ערק ערק זחלאני ערק מִסְתַכִּי	10
פ'אתחה	فاتحة		1
פאצ'ה	پاچة		2
פַאצַ'אצִ'י	پاچاچي		3
פדוה עליץ'	فِدوه عليچ		1
פְדַאִיִין	فدائيين		1
פוּאַד	فؤاد		5
פיין	فين		2
פיתה	بيتا		3
פאלקות	فلاكوت		1

Hebrew script	Arabic script	Other orthographical, and morphological formats	Frequencies
פְלָאו	فلاو		1
פלאח	فلاح		1
פלוס!	فلوس		2
פלפל	فلافل	פלָפל	3
פנאג'ין	فناجين	פינג'אנים	3
פִסטוּק	فستق	פסטוק	2
צ'אי	شاي	צַ'אי	4
צבא	مقام صابا في الغناء		1
צַבַּחְכּוּם אללה באל-חֵ'יר	صبحكم الله بالخير		1
צַבַּחְכּוּם אללה באל-נוּר	صبحكم الله بالنور		1
קאהי	كاهي		4
קאנון	قانون – آلة موسيقية	הקאנון בקאנון בקאנוּן	9
קבב	كباب		1
קובה	كوبه		3
קְטַאן	قطان		1
קַלְבּ	قلب		5
קלֵיצ'ה	كليتشا		1
קֵמַר	قِيَمر		12
רַאַא	رأى		1
רֻבַּעִיַּאת	رباعيات		1
רוחי	روحي		3
רוח מן הון	رُوح من هون		2
רנימה	رنيمه		1
שאייף	شايف		1
שבּאבּ	شباب		1
שהאדה	شهاده		1
שוּכְּרַן	شكراً		1
שורבה	شوربه		1
שט אל ערב	شط العرب		1
שָטָה	شطة		1
שיך	شيخ	שיח' שיח'ים	6
שְלוֹן?	شِلون؟		1
שריעה	شريعة		1
שארמוטה	شرموطه		1
שש בש	شيشبيش		4

Table A.1 continued

Hebrew script	Arabic script	Other orthographical, and morphological formats	Frequencies
ששליק	ششليك	שישליק	3
תַבַּארַכּ אללה	تبارك الله		5
תְבִּית	تبيت		1
תזכיה	تزكيه		1
תַחת אַמְרַכּ	تحت أمرك		1
תמר הינדי	تمر هندي		1
תְסְלַם	تسلم		2
תסאות אל גרעה ואום אל שער	تساوت الجرعة وأم الشعر		
תעאל	تعال	תעאל מן הון תעאל להון	2
תקאסים	تقاسيم	אל-תַקַאסִים	2

List 1: Hard-Access Code-Switching Instances

Table A.2 List 1: hard-access code-switching instances

***Ha-ma'abara* (Ballas 1964)**	
Extracts	**Reference**
אה	159, 163
אהלן באבו-יעגוב	198, 198
אהלן באבו-סבאח	9
אהלן בחיים	99
אוה	70
אוסכות	162
אינשאללה	60, 133
אל-חראמי	113
אללה	33, 35, 181
אל-עמארה	51
א-נאצר	9
דח'ילך	63
הא	13, 191
ואללה	76, 114, 152, 164, 187, 200, 201
ולך	20

***Ha-ma'abara* (Ballas 1964)**

Extracts	Reference
אה	159, 163
אהלן באבו-יעגוב	198, 198
חביבי	31, 137, 162, 164, 201
חג'י חסיין א-נעימי בבאב-לאגה	8
חושו-נא וחלצוני	85
טאולה	11
יא	8, 152
יאבוי	29
יחרב ביתך	67
מבסוט	164
סלאמתך	126
שיך חסן	36
שיך יצחק	16
תפדל	86
Number of CS instances	44

***Shavim ve-shavim yoter* (Michael 1974)**

Extracts	Reference
אבו	28, 48
אבן-אל-מאניוקה	191
אדבח	9, 9, 9, 11, 11, 11
אה	13, 17, 17, 34, 35, 35, 41, 104, 119
אהלאן-וסאהלאן	118
אט-טאריק מקטועה	191
איי	21, 37, 119, 166
אילחמדו-לאיללה	195
אינשאללה	40, 78
אללה	21, 23, 37, 38, 84, 105, 135
אנא מאגרוח	191
אצילה	107
אשרע! אשרע!	191
באקשיש	44
ג'את	26
ג'יהאד	118
דחילאק	31, 73, 130, 132
הונאכ	191
היי	47
וואללה	14, 22, 35, 48, 55, 78, 90, 104, 95, 95, 122
חאבובה	81
חאזוק	78, 78

Table A.2 continued

Shavim ye-shavim yoter **(Michael 1974)**	
Extracts	**Reference**
חאראם	108
חביבי	146
חינא	195
טפו	28
יא	13, 14, 16, 17, 17, 17, 18, 22, 23, 24, 25, 25, 25, 26, 29, 29, 30, 34, 34, 37, 37, 38, 38, 39, 40, 41, 62, 62, 63, 63, 63, 73, 73, 74, 74, 76, 85, 85, 85, 86, 90, 90, 90, 99, 101, 102, 104, 105, 106,106, 106, 106, 106, 106, 106, 106, 106, 106, 106, 106, 106, 106, 106, 106, 106, 106, 106, 106, 106, 106, 106, 108, 196
יא-אבא	13, 13, 13, 24, 33, 38, 38, 39, 39, 90
יא-אבו	13, 17, 17, 17, 21, 35, 72, 72, 118, 119
יא-אחי	103
יא-אללה	32, 104, 142
יא-אללה	13
יא-בני	24, 25, 33, 35, 38, 39, 75
יא-וואלאד	47, 48
יא-וואלי	42, 70, 195
יא-חאראם	104
יא-חבוב	70
יא-חביבי	151, 196
יא-חרא	28, 28
יאללה	33, 46, 58, 87, 136
יאללה	196
יא מאג'נון	201
יה	14, 24
יעני	27
כוס אומכ	221
מאבסוט	40
מאברוק	40, 40, 107, 188
מאייה...מאייה	191, 191, 191
מאפיש מאייה	191
סחוג	26
עארס	48, 119
פיין ?	191
פיין אל-קואת ?	191
קובה	71, 72

קובה-בורגול	188
שארמוטה	24
תעאל לאהון	231
תעאל-מן-הנה	191, 191
תפאדאל	118, 245
תפדאלי	40, 114, 188
Number of CS instances	**217**

Tarnegol kapparot **(Amir 1983)**

Extracts	**Reference**
אהוות ערב	93
אהלן וסהלן	19
אוהו	11, 12
אוף	152, 152
אחרא דין בוק	14
אל -צ'איחנה	152
אללה אכבר	69, 69
אללה יבארכ פיכ על הקפה הזה	148
אלתכ'יה	150
אסלמה עליך	39, 39, 140
בלאש	77
ג'ארה	117
גוג'ה	40, 40
גרוש	151
דחילק	156
הלפה	152
הג'לאלה	91
הדה הוא	58
הלאהל	110, 110, 111, 111
ואללה	40
ואללה מבסוט, יא חואג'ה סלים	147
וי, וי	78
זיפת	117
חביבי	26, 40, 136
חואג'ה	147
חלס	77
חרא	55, 55
טיז	24, 25, 51
יא	19, 18, 55, 101, 106, 130, 196
יא אללה	18, 24, 25, 25, 32, 39, 51, 68, 68, 77, 173
יא אללה, יעיש מצול	123, 124
יא עיני	174

Table A.2 continued

Tarnegol kapparot (Amir 1983)	
Extracts	**Reference**
יאלילי	129
יאללה	18, 30, 30, 31, 44, 104, 194, 194, 194
יחרב ביתהום	111
יעני	38
כוס אמו	27
כרכאנה	58
לוביה	77, 77, 78, 78
מג'נון	136
מג'נון ! ואללה מג'נון	136
מג'נון לילה	137
מן עיני	201
מקאם צבא	111
משמש בלדי	140
נורי! נורי ! אבוס עינק	106
נעם	147
נרגילה	152
עביה	39
עוד	106
עיוני	78, 78, 122, 152, 176
עלא בלדי אל מחבוב	113
ערבאנה	109
פיתה	77, 152
פנאג'ין	148
קבב	193
שארע אל-רשיד	39
ששליק	193
תפד'ל	152
תקאסים	107
תרבוש	39
Number of CS instances	108

Ỵe-hu aḥer (Ballas 1991)	
Extracts	**Reference**
אל-דעוה	156
אל-מוח'אבראת	139, 140, 153
ביג	99
בקהיר אירחו אותי חברי אגודת ''אל־ הִדאיה אל־אסלאמיה"	80

גזיה	76
גשר מוסיב	101
דשדאשה	103
האמונה בספר ולא בסיף	163
הח'ליפים	136
המואזן	102
השריעה	118
חמדילה עסלאמה, חמדילה עסלאמה	104
כפייה ועקאל	52
סואק	139
פ'אתחה	147
פְלָאו וכושרי	52
שהאדה	79
Number of CS instances	19

***Mafriaḥ ha-yonim* (Amir 1992)**

Extracts	**Reference**
אַבּוּ אל-כְּבַּה	223, 394
אַבּוּ אל-סְמְבּוּסַק	345
אבּוּ ג'ורג' אַח'וּיי	246
אִבּן עַרַבּ	66, 97
אבראהים אל ח'ליל	181
אבריק	223
אִדְבַּחוּ אל-כֻּפַּאר	163, 163, 163
אֶה?	32
אַהְלַא וּסַהְלַא	175, 240, 425, 311
אַהְלַן יַא אִחְ'וַאן	54
אוּף, אוּף	146
אורז בחמאה	353
אַח', אַח'	119
אַח'וּיי	246, 246
אַחְלַא גן עדן	415
אינתם יְהוּד?	410
אל הזימה רנימה	8
אַל שַׁרַארַה	152
אל-אינגליז	43
אל-בַּעַת'	401
אל-בּריד אל-יומי	200
אל-גַ'דידה	34
אל-וַטַנִיַּה	207

Table A.2 continued

***Mafriaḥ ha-yonim* (Amir 1992)**

Extracts	**Reference**
אַל-חִזְבּ אַל-וַטַנִי אַל-דִימוּקְרַטִי	63, 401
אל-חַרַם אל שַׁרִיף	72
אללה	11, 11, 13, 17, 27, 54, 58, 62, 64, 64, 67, 79, ,79, 81, 82, 95, 95, 95, 106, 106, 109, 120, 120, 120, 131, 134, 141, 141, 141, 141, 143, 145, 145, 150, 162, 170, 173, 174, 174, 174, 174, 174, 174, 174, 181, 182, 188, 189, 218, 218, 218, 221, 222, 223, 223, 223, 228, 230, 235, 240, 246, 299, 301, 301, 303, 303, 310, 323, 326, 326, 326, 328, 329, 334, 347, 348, 360, 360, 366, 366, 371, 373, 373, 384, 402, 402, 404, 405, 408, 409, 409, 417, 422, 448, 451, 452, 452
אללה אכּבּר	9, 50, 50, 50, 101, 101, 131, 136, 136, 136, 138, 138, 143, 144, 144, 144, 164, 164, 164,164, 174, 174, 232, 232, 338, 400
אללה הגדול	143, 233
אללה יִסְתֻר	159, 186, 186, 277
אללה ירחם עליכם	161
אללה ירחמו	147, 257, 320, 382, 400, 404, 404, 407
אללה כַּרים	159
אַל-מַגְ'לִס אַל-רוּחַנִי ובאל-מַגְ'לִס אֵל-עַאם	103
אל-מַדַאפַּה	272
אל-סַלַאם אַלְ-מַלְכִּי	338
אל-סַלַאם עַלַיכּוּם, יא בֶּק	272
אל-פַאתִחַה	153
אל-צהיוניה	43
אל-צַיפִּי	268
אל-קֻדְס	72
אַל-שַהַאדַה	43, 87, 87
אל-תַקַאסִים	243
אֵם	141, 228, 251, 370, 371, 371
אמיר המאמינים	174
אִמְשִי, עַמִי, אִמְשִי	165
אִנְגְלִיז!	87
אַנדָלוּסי	53

אִנְהַגַ'ם בֵּיתוּ	427
אִנשאללה	169, 169, 256, 292, 392, 404, 429, 444
אֶסְתַאד	70, 70, 70, 70, 70, 70, 168, 168, 169, 198
אִסְתַרְפַר אללה	189
אַפַנדי	425
אצַאר בִּיץ' אל־יום יַא ח'וּיַה?	23
אַשְׁהַדֶ אַלַּא אִלַאהַ אִלַּא אְלְלַאהּ	174
בַּאגִ'לַה	419, 419
בּוּכְּרַה אל-סַפַּר	263
בחיאת אללה	183
בחיאת כּאבּי	311
בחיאת מושה רבּנו	247
בַּיְת אל-אַעְיַאן	244
בְּךְ-אַפְרַאח	213
במיה	124
בני ערב	257
בסורת אל-מאאדה	143
בַּקְלַאוַה	88, 190
גִ'הַאד	86, 256
גִ'הֶנַם	435
גִ'זְיַה	151
גזֵרה	405
ג'יהאד	144
ג'ין	15, 41, 82, 82, 276, 276, 373, 373, 420, 420
גִ'לַאלַה	33, 94
גלביה	52, 54, 60, 116, 335
ג'רה	7, 82, 140, 176, 176, 182, 282, 301, 346, 358
ג'רה	176, 298
דונְדִרְמַה	281, 281
דוֹנְדִרְמַה	135
דַחִילַכּ	173
דחילק	218
דיוַאן	53
דִין מחַמַד בִּאל-סֵיף	136
דַנְדַח	35
דִרהִם	180
דְשדאשה	94, 174, 335, 347

Table A.2 continued

Mafriaḥ ha-yonim (Amir 1992)	
Extracts	**Reference**
הַדַא מוּ אִינְצַאף מְנַכּ	313
הוי אללה	314
הַלַאהִל	79, 280, 289, 336
הַלַאהִל יַא נִסְוַאן	280
המוּאזן	131
ואוֵילִי	84, 138, 331, 332, 342, 388, 415, 415, 417, 422
וַאוֵילִי על אמך	334
וַאוֵילִי עלי	111
וַאוֵילִי עלי ועל החיים שלי	332
וַאללַה	43, 73, 244, 249, 342, 406, 407, 407
וַאשְהַד אַנַּ מחַמַדן רַסוּל אְלְלַאהּ	174
וַזיר	100, 105, 105, 148, 148, 148, 148, 254, 292, 350, 350, 350, 350, 432, 432
וַזירים	204, 263, 270, 385, 432, 450
וחיאת אללה	108
וִחְיַאת אללה	263, 345
וחיאת הנביא?	108
וִחְיַאתִי	250
וִחְיַאתַכְּ	65
וֵינכּוּם?	94
וְלַאד אל-כְּלַאב	190
וְלַאד אל-כְּלַאבּ	167
וְלַכּ	55
וַעלַיכּוּם	272
זַבַּאנַה	29, 98, 99, 103, 184, 184, 372, 394
זבּוּן	123, 148, 396
זיארה	285
זִיאַרַה	121
זְנְגוּלַה ועַסַל	117, 262, 334, 335
חַדִית	145
ח'ליף	167, 178
ח'ליפים	130, 163, 339
חִ'לְפַה	39
חַמַאם	289, 289, 290, 292, 423
חְמַאר	211

חְמַאר אִבְּן חְמַאר	211
חַמְשַׂה	136
חַפְלַה	207, 208, 238, 239, 245, 245, 272, 273, 273, 350, 366, 370, 370, 371, 371, 372, 372, 373, 374, 407, 408, 422, 429, 432
חַפְלַות	36, 271, 294, 317, 366, 386, 403
חַפלת אל-וַדַאע	315
טאקיה	52, 54
טוּגְרַה	210
טֵרפה	129
יא	53, 53, 54, 55, 56, 70, 70, 70, 70, 70, 70, 87, 89, 90, 91, 93, 93, 94, 94, 94, 94, 163, 175, 177, 177, 178, 186, 187, 192, 205, 233, 246, 247, 283, 290, 291, 307, 320, 324, 329, 345, 402, 415
יַא אִבְּן אל-כַּלְבּ	40
יא אח'ואן	189
יא אללה	58, 163, 173, 239, 423
יא אללה	218, 413
יַא אַלְף מַרְחַבַּא	312, 312
יא בן המטונפת	189
יא בן המיובש	189
יַא גִ'ין יַא נַבִּיל	82, 82
יא הלא	325
יא ולאדי	94
יַא חְמַאר	66, 330, 374, 412
יא חרא	341, 341
יא חרא אבן חרא	189
יא לילי, יא עיני	52, 59,
יא מג'נון	222
יא סַיִדִי	185, 187
יַא סַלַאם	55
יא עיוני, יא כאבי	23
יַא פַּתַאח יַא רַזַאק	176, 324
יַא שִׁרַאעַן וַרַאא דִגְלַ'תַ יַגְרִי	267
יאללה	26, 66, 66, 78, 87, 113, 132, 173, 173, 186, 187, 324, 324, 415, 415, 416, 416, 416, 416, 417, 422, 422, 422
יאללה יַא וְלַאד	427
יַהוּד, כופרים	44

Table A.2 continued

***Mafriaḥ ha-yonim* (Amir 1992)**

Extracts	Reference
יַהוּד, כְּלַאבּ	44
יִנְעַם אללה עַלֵיכּ	324
יעני	218, 274, 426
כַּבַּאב	304, 353, 417, 418, 427, 427, 427, 427
כַּבַּאבּ בעַמְבַּה	236
כִּבַּה	29, 29
כִּבַּה בַּמְיַה	77, 297
כִּבּהַ של בּוּרְגוּל	223, 223
כִּבַּה של בַּמיה קרה	126
כַּבְּשְׁכַּאן	298
כּוּבֶּה חמוסטה	351
כוס אם אל יהוד	11
כוס אֻם אל-סִי-אַי-דִּי	326
כוס אֻם אל-פַּאשַׁה	326
כוס אם התַנוּעַה	422
כוס אמם	416
כַּחַל	130
כַּלְבּ אִבְּן כלְבּ	59
כַּמַנְגַ'אתִי	52
כַּמַנְגַ'ה	243
כַּמַנְגַ'ה	52, 61, 267, 267
כָּפִּיוֹת	17, 174, 179, 362
כָּפִּייה	19, 43, 58, 96, 163, 305, 307
כַּרַחַ'אנָה	62, 353
לַא אִלַאהַא אִלַא אללה	81
לא יכּון דבר	246
לַאהִל	94
לוביה	124, 223, 448
לוּזִינַה	262
לחם גַאוּרַג	77
לִיְהוּד גַ'אר אִל־עְמַר	95
לַפַּה כַּבַּאבּ בעַמְבַּה	326
לַפַּה של כַּבַּאבּ ועַמְבַּה	236
מַאשַׁאלְלַה	23, 23, 311
מבסוט	416
מַבּרְוּכּ	180, 211, 211, 230, 277

מֲגַ'אהִדִין	28, 93, 93, 83, 300
מגַ'זִירַה לגַ'זִירַה	317
מַגְ'לִס היהודי	150
מואזינים	50
מואזן	95, 101
מוג'הדין	149
מוּחְ'תַאר	80
מוּסַא	331
מופתי	150
מוּפתי במסגד	143
מַזַא	221, 269
מַחְלַאהַא עִישְת אִל-פַלַאח	130
מֲחְתַשֶם	8, 405, 422
מיחַ'אנַה	85, 220, 222, 224, 259, 286, 330, 365, 365, 346, 369
מן אללה	66
מַן אל-סַמַא ומְלַבַּס	262
מן עֵיני	312
מִסְבַּחַה	162, 250, 250, 254, 295, 425, 435, 439, 441
מִסְבַּחַה	71
מסבחות	299
מִסְכּוּן	41
מִסְכֵּנָה	16
מסתקי	130
מַעַלֶש, יַא אִחְ'וַא	59
מַקַאם צַבַּא	314
מקאמאת	36, 94, 239, 242, 398
מקאמה	245
מַרְחַבַּא	240
מַרְחַבַּא יַא אִחְ'וַאן	425
בַּאדִי אל-זַוְרַאא	362
נבּוּט	139, 141
נבּוּטים	139
נביא אַבִּינַא	410
נַעַם	165
נַעַם, יַא סִידִי	116
סוּלְחה	144
סוּרַת יוּסוּף	386

Table A.2 continued

***Mafriaḥ ha-yonim* (Amir 1992)**

Extracts	*Reference*
סִידַארַה	80, 109, 139, 148
סמבוסַק	18, 18, 108, 262, 346
סַמַכּ מַזְגוּף	57, 122, 129, 242, 387, 417, 417
סַפַּרְטַאס	122
סַרְסִי	91
סְתַאד	37, 38, 39, 46, 199, 201, 201, 202, 202, 317, 446
עַאשְת אִידֵכִּי, אם כַּאבִּי	126
עְבּוּדִיַה	271
עַבָּיוֹת	17, 137, 139, 149, 161, 174, 179, 335, 361
עוד	130, 243, 267
עַלַא עֵנִי ועלַא רַאסִי	116
עליהום	174
עמבה	35, 42, 45, 73, 108, 125, 130, 184, 448
עַמוּ יוּסוּף	387
עַמִי, אל-לְשוֹרְגַ'ה	165
עְמַמַה	28, 104, 123, 137, 150, 396
עָקָל	54, 162, 305
עקָלים	362
ערק	259, 366
ערק ומַזַא	227
ערק זחלאני	236
עַרַק מִסְתַקִי	103, 125, 279, 294, 370
פַאצַ'אצִ'י	318, 326, 418
פַאצַ'ה	125, 162, 318, 321, 322
פְדַאִיִין	259
פִּדְוַה יַא אִבְּנִי	93
פדוה עלִיץ'	54
פוּל	419
פיג'מה	188, 188, 190
פיג'מה	220, 221
פיג'מת פסים	224, 233
פינג'אנים	27, 185
פיתה גַאוּרַג	117
פלאח.	284

פֶּס	123
פִּסטוּק	117
פסטוק חלבי	353
פְרַנְגִ׳י	179
צ'אי	71, 84, 99, 99
צַדַק אללה אל־עַזים	82, 95, 181
צִילוּ כַּבַּאבּ	353
צַ'לְרִי	371, 372
קאנוּן	207
קאנונג'י	36, 243
קַהְוַה סַאדַה	77
קמר	16, 23, 30, 108, 205, 357, 380, 380, 423, 423, 423
רבַּעְיַאת	221
רַחַת לוּקוּם	322
שארִע עלייה	414, 423, 429
שִׁבּוּט וּסְלוּק, קְטַאן ואַבּוּ סְוֵיף	129
שַׁהַאדה	174, 327
שוּכְּרַן, שוּכְּרַן, אַהְלַן וַסַהְלַן	55
שט אל ערב	8
שיח'ים	179
שישליק	417, 418
שָׁרְק	130
שַׁרְקִיַּה	173
שש בש	135, 251, 287
תַבַּארַכּ אללה	52, 53, 81, 83, 83
תְבִּית	123
תוּף	243
תַחְת אל-סוּרְמַיַּה	426
תַחת אַמְרַכּ	169
תַנוּעַה	108
תִסְלַם אידֵיכּ	176, 313
תְפַּדַל	166, 186, 207, 207, 228, 272, 350
תְפַּדַל, עזיזי	19
תְפַּדַלוּ	27, 167, 175,189
תַשְׁרִיבּ	301
תַשְׁרִיבּ של נפתלי קַרְקוּקְלִי	223
Number of CS instances	**837**

Table A.2 continued

Ṿikṭoryah (Michael 1993)	
Extracts	**Reference**
אה, אהה, אההה	181, 181
אינשאללה	265
אללה	80
במיה	12, 14
במיות	14
בסטה	288
גיהד	76
דח'ילך	109
דרויש	69, 110, 131
הסולטאן	77
הקבקב	61
וי	62
זחלאוי	148
חביבתי	253
חלווה	222
חלקון	265
טפו	216, 219, 256
יאללה, קום	196, 297
כבה	26, 48, 200
סאלונה	177
עביה	5, 5, 21, 29, 29, 29, 29, 31, 31, 56, 56, 60, 72, 87, 88, 88, 131, 149, 185, 185, 186, 191, 193, 200, 239, 246, 247, 248, 259, 260, 273, 291, 292, 292
עביות	21, 21, 50, 264
עבית-	7, 30, 30, 46, 55, 170, 186, 273, 289, 291
פרנגים	161
קאהי	25, 25, 25, 25, 26, 26
קאנון	7, 10, 17, 119, 134, 215
קוראיה	81, 82, 82, 82, 82, 83, 92, 206
שש בש	197
תפו, תפו, תפו	74
תרבושו	236
תרחה	56
Number of CS instances	**103**

***Tom ha-bikkur* (Ballas 2008)**

Extracts	Reference
שיח צופי	112, 112
שש ביש	50
Number of CS instances	**3**

Ma she-nish'ar* (Amir 2010*)

Extracts	Reference
אבו זקן	45, 447
אללה	52, 119, 195, 282
אפנדי	170
בלדי	119
בלדר	139
בסטה	105
בפלאווה	358
חילבה	139
סחוג	139
עבאיה	358
ערק	99
פלפל	139, 357
קלב	269
קפה סאדה	170
שטה	138, 138
תמרהינדי	358
Number of CS instances	22

***Yahalom min ha-yeshimon* (Michael 2015)**

Extracts	Reference
אהבל	66
אוּסְתָאד	22, 23, 23, 23, 23, 125, 125
אינשאללה	90, 196, 208
אל-וָוכְּמָה	64, 64
אללה	41, 23
אל-עדא אל-סירייה	70
בחיי אללה	43
בחמאם	26, 26, 28
בְּמָסְטָרָה	125
בָסמוּן	244
בפָּלָקָה	133
בקובה	210
דִשְׁדָאשָׁה	32, 49, 131, 243, 282, 293

Table A.2 continued

Ma she-nish'ar* (Amir 2010*)	
Extracts	**Reference**
דִשְׁדָאשָׁות	117, 123, 293
הבוסתנים	14
הדשדאשה	131, 131, 132, 246, 295, 295
הסמבוסק	20, 21
הפָלָקָה	127
הקובה	204
וויי-וויי	11, 11, 115, 285
וָזִירִים	112
חמאם	26
טוזזזז!	294
יא מאמא	285
יָאבּבּבּוּוּ! יָאבּבּבּוּוּ!	112
יאללה	16, 88, 88, 88, 88, 245
לִיפָּה	28
מאסה	8
משאללה, משאללה	44
סובחאן אללה!	266
סִידָארות	111
סידי	34, 44, 44
סמבוסק	18
סמונים	240, 241, 243
עבאיה	29, 29, 41, 55, 73, 73, 76, 76, 81, 113, 113, 114, 286
עבאיות	42, 111, 262, 263, 285
עבאית המשי	132
פָלָקָה	127
קובה בורגול	204
קובה-במיה	137
ריז בּחליבּ	259
שש-בש	199
תאג'ר	61, 62, 62, 62, 62, 224
Number of CS instances	101

List 2: Easy-Access Code-Switching Instances

Table A.3 List 2: easy-access code-switching instances

***Ha-ma'abara* (Ballas 1964)**

Extracts	**Reference**
אבו-יעגוב	84, 198
אבו-ע'איב	23, 152
אום-אלפלוס	28
אח'תחט אל-חאבל באל-נאבל	52
אלקווה	30
א-שבאב אל-קאומי	11
באיזן אללה אינתצרנא	9
ג'האר יאק	145
הא לך, נזאח	64
הגדיש	156
ובאנו למקברות {ערבית: בית-קברות}	119
ולא יהימך אבו ג'מיל	108
חיים אל-כאתב	53
ח'יר אינשאללה	134, 186
חמדילה עסלאמה	125, 188
יום אלעינדך	33
יזיד פדלכום	86
כובות	180
מסטול	96, 181
מקהא א-מצר לצאחביהי שלמה חמרה	7
נהר דיאלה	122
סינור	162
סעד	16
ענתר אל-עבסי	31
פאצ'ה	28, 77
Number of CS instances	31

***Shavim ye-shavim yoter* (Michael 1974)**

Extracts	**Reference**
NA	-

***Tarnegol kapparot* (Amir 1983)**

Extracts	**Reference**
אבוס עינק	201
אוסכות וחליהא	125

Table A.3 continued

***Tarnegol kapparot* (Amir 1983)**

Extracts	**Reference**
אחבאבינא יא עין מא הום מעאנא	85
אכון ממנון	148
אלחיא חילוה בס ניפהמהא	107
אלפואד אל מג׳רוח	180
אנהג'ם ביתק	79
אנף נאר ואנף דח'אן	87
בידק אהוות ערב מע הל	147
ג'וז מנו	80
גחבה	124, 180
ולאד אללה	66
חפלה	106, 129
יא הלי אל-ט׳לאם חינו עליא	38
יא סמרה רוחי	108
ימה יא ימה ג׳בתיני ללט'ים	57
כיף אלאהווה?	148
כל טיז יסוה אל עמע'	19
לע'וה	122
מחטופה	176
מלעין הדול	149
מפיש פלוס! רוח מן הון	49
סמק מסגוף	48
עאשת אידיק	153
עמי יא ביאע אל ורד	21
פוג-אלנח'ל	173
תסאות אל גרעה ואום אל שער	79
Number of CS instances	29

***Ḥe-hu aḥer* (Ballas 1991)**

Extracts	**Reference**
אתה תיבחר בתזכיה	130
במיה ופלפל	97
יום אל-קבול	108
מגמע אל-בחרין	123
עאשורא	97
ערוג	97
קלֵיצ׳ה	97
Number of CS instances	7

Mafriaḥ ha-yonim **(Amir 1992)**

Extracts	**Reference**
'שבאב אל-אנקאד,' צעירי ההצלחה	32
אידק באל-דהן, לבריאות, לבריאות	320
אל אל-מדאפה, אל טרקלין האורחים	272
אל-דולא אל-מזעומה	8
אללה יחפדכ, אלוהים ישמור אותך	159
אללה יסתר, חס וחלילה	277
אללה כרים, אלוהים נדיב	159
אל-מג'הדין, הלוחמים למען פלסטין	93
אל-ציפי, הקיצי	268
אנא לאללאה ואנא אליהי ראג'עון, אנו לאלוהים ואליו אנו שבים	281
אנא, אני	453
אסתרפר אללה, חס וחלילה	189
בגדד אלג'דידה, החדשה	34
בוכרה אל-ספר, מחר הנסיעה	263
בל-חזב אל-וטני אל-דימוקראטי, המפלגה הלאומית הדמוקרטית.	63
בסורת אל-מאאדה, היא בשורת השולחן	143
גִ'תְם? דְקְעֻדו. לְבַסְתְם לְחְוַאס אל-גִ'דַד? דְשְלְחוּהַא – באתם? היכבדו ושבו נא. לבשתם את הבגדים החדשים? במחילה הורידן נא.	414
דונדרמה, גלידה שלגונית	281
דנדח, גמד	35
הג'ילאלה	33
החמאם, הוא בית-המרחץ	289
הכמנג'אתי, הוא הכנר	52
הכמנגה, הכינור	52
המוגהדין	28
התַנוּעַהה	13
התַנוּעַהה	22
התשריב, מרק הראש	301
ולאד אל-כלאב, בני כלבים	167
זנגולה ועסל בבלאש, זנגולה ודבש חינם	334
יא הלא, ברוך הבא!	325
יא חביבת אל-אלב, ארגעי, שובי אהובת הלב לגני.	52
יא חמאר, הדא טיז כלא חלאוה – חמור, זה תחת שכולו חלווה.	320

Table A.3 continued

***Mafriaḥ ha-yonim* (Amir 1992)**

Extracts	Reference
יא פתאח, יא רזאק, אוי אללה חזן והמפרנס	324
ינעם אללה עליכ, יתן לך אלוהים משלו	324
כבשכאן, בעליית הגג הקטנה שלי	7
כבשכאן, בעליית הגג הקטנה שלי	7
כורדי ראסו בטיזו – הכורדי שכלו בתחת שלו.	289
ל 'שבאב אל-אנקאד', צעירי ההצלחה	21
לו וקעת, סיר רגאל, אם נפלת, תהיה גבר.	443
ליהוד ג׳אר אל-עמר, היהודים שכנינו מאז ומעולם.	95
מן עלמני חרפן מלכני עבדן, מי שלימדני אות אחת עבדו אני כל חיי	40
מסכון, משכן שדים	41
מעלש, יא אח'ואן, אין דבר אחימץ	59
נאס תאכל אל-תמר ואני אל-נואיה חצתי, בני-אדם אוכלים תמרים ןיל משאירים את החרצנים.	79
נחנו אבנא אל-וטן, נצונהו טול אל-זמן – אנו בני המולדת, נגן עליה כל הזמן	337
סוק חנוני	18
סמכ מזגוף, דג על האש	417
על כיפכ, אבני, לאט לאט בני	18
עקיד, אלוף משנה	28
פאסטורמה, פאסטראמי.	92
פאצ׳ה, קיבה של כבש	125
פדוה עליץ', יא בהיה – כפרתך אנחנו, יא בהיה	54
צבחכום אללה בל-ח'יר, בוקר טוב	289
צבחכום אללה בל-נור, בוקר אור	289
צדק אללה אל-עזים, צדק אללה האדיר.	82, 95, 181
קחוה סאדה, פפה שחור מר.	77
שלון טיז, יסוה עדם – איזה תחת, שווה עמוד תלייה.	319
שרקיה, רוח-איש מזרחית	173
תבית, חמיץ של עופות ממולאים נתחי בשר	125

תחת אל-סורמיה, כמו שאומרים פה, תחת הנעל.	426
תחת אמרכ, כרצונך	169
תַנוּעַהה	7
תסלם אידיכ, תבורכנה ידיך	176
תפדל עזיזי, בבקשה יקירי	19
Number of CS instances	66

Yiḳṭoryah **(Michael 1993)**

Extracts	**Reference**
חביבתי, אהובתי	22
ליל הניץ' הלילה	90
מוגליד, כלומר כורך	240
Number of CS instances	3

Tom ha-bikkur **(Ballas 2008)**

Extracts	**Reference**
יאללה, זוז	26
שתקופת ההריון, אל-חמל בערבית	57, 57
Number of CS instances	3

Ma she-nish'ar **(Amir 2010)**

Extracts	**Reference**
קלב	47, 152
פואד	47, 152
Number of CS instances	4

Yahalom min ha-yeshimon **(Michael 2015)**

Extracts	**Reference**
״אל-וָוכְּמָה״, מכסה של סיר לחץ האוטם את העיר על סמטאותיה	64
״מה זה סָמוּן? התעניין חסן	243
״עָלְוָוה״, השוק הסיטוני המרכזי בעיר.	68
אלמאסה, יהלום	217
אלמאסה—יהלום	8, 217
הבּוּזָה, גלידה עיראקית	216
הכּוּפּוּת, סורות עגולות הדומות למגבעות ענק הפוכות	16
כמרזב, כברז שבור	287

Table A.3 continued

***Yahalom min ha-yeshimon* (Michael 2015)**	
Extracts	**Reference**
מָסְטָרָה, מקל ענישה כבד	123
סָמוּן, לחמניות תפוחות כסירה	240
תאג׳ר, סוחר של ממש	133
תַאֲדִיבּ, חינוך	125
Number of CS instances	13

Notes

Introduction

1. For more information about the Farhud, see Kazzaz (1991: 24–5); Rejwan (1998: 146–56); Stillman (1991: 118–19).
2. Jews from non-Ashkenazi origin who emigrated to Israel from the North African lands and the Middle East. They are also known as Oriental Jews, Eastern Jews and Sephardi Jews. For more discussion about this issue, see the introduction of Behar and Ben-Dor Benite (2013).
3. For the original statement of the law in Arabic, see Rejwan (1998: 227–8).
4. See also the interviews of some Iraqi and Mizrahi authors in his book: Alcalay (1996).

Chapter 1

1. For more features of language varieties used by Jews, including Yiddish and Arabic, see Hary (2009: 19–26).
2. There is a claim that Judaeo-Arabic was used by Jewish tribes in Arabia during the pre-Islamic era. This linguistic variety was much the same as the language of Arabs at that time, with some borrowed Hebrew and Aramaic lexical items. See Stillman (2005: 42).
3. For more information about the Judaeo-Arabic manuscripts written in the Middle Ages, see Sirat (2002).
4. For more information about the Jewish newspapers in Iraq, see Al-Ma‘adīdi (2001).
5. Sa‘adya Ga’on al-Fayyūmi (882–942 CE) was one of the most famous Jewish thinkers, philosophers and intellectuals during the Middle Ages in Iraq. He was born in the village of Dilaz in Fayyūm which is located in Upper Egypt. For more information about Sa‘adya Ga’on, see Blau (2001), Brody (2013), Malter (1921) and Vollandt (2015).
6. See, for example, the Hebrew words (עמידה, שבחות, נשמתו) appear in Arabic script respectively: (العميدة، الشباحوث ، نشمتو) in Naqqāsh (1980: 20–1).

7. For more information about the *qeltu-gelet* dialects, see Blanc (1964: 5–8).
8. This centre was founded in 1988. Its main purpose is to collect and preserve the inheritance of Iraqi Jews and to represent Iraqi Jews in Israeli society. The centre also has a museum that contains Jewish monuments from Iraq and publishes *Neharde'a*, a journal of the literature and folklore of the Iraqi Jews. The centre also publishes books and volumes about Iraqi Jews. For more information, see Meir-Glitzenstein (2002). See <http://www.babylonjewry.org.il/new/english/nehardea/nehardea.htm>.
9. The title of his PhD was 'The Arab Literature under the Shadow of War' and he discussed Arab literature written during the period 1948-67. In his dissertation Ballas focused on the study of the Arab man, Arab soldier and of Arab character in the Arabic literature of Iraq, Syria and Egypt. His book, Ballas (1978), was translated into Arabic (Ballas and Darwish 1984).
10. See also the text of the interview with Alcalay (1996).
11. See, for instance, Ballas's description of Iraq and Baghdad in his collections of short stories: Ballas (1969), Ballas (1991) and Ballas (1992). France is also portrayed: Ballas (1984), as is Israel, see for example the trilogy: Ballas (2003).
12. It is important to mention that Ballas's stated tendency in learning Hebrew was to 'narrow the gap between the Israeli public and the Arabic world'. See Ballas (2009: 45).
13. Ballas says that this name had been used for several years as his pen name. The name was modified to 'Adib Kas', without the use of Arabic definite article /al/. See Ballas (2009: 46).
14. This was Michael's name in Iraq.
15. Under the title of the chapter written by Sami Michael in *al-Jadīd*, there is a short introduction that says that, 'Fire ... is a chapter from the Novel *Madinat al-Kharq* which Samir Marid is currently writing in order to be published in Hebrew'. See Snir (2005a: 317); on Sami Michael see Kerbel et al. (2003) and Abramson (2005). See also Sami Michael interviewed by Ruvik Rosenthal: Michael (2000).
16. Michael surveyed water resources between 1955 and 1982, see: Kerbel et al. (2003: 373). The novel *Mayim noshḳim le-mayim* [Water Kissing Water] (Michael 2001), was based on his experience of working in this field (Abramson 2005: 579).
17. See the personal conversation between Sami Michael and Reuven Snir in the footnotes of the book (Snir 2005a: 318).
18. Amir made his literary debut in the mid-1970s; the novel *Tarnegol kapparot* published later in 1983 was among his best-sellers during the 1980s, with eighteen printings. See Abramson (2005: 19).
19. The *ma'abara* (Hebrew: מעברה) was a transit camp for the new Jewish refugees in Israel during the 1950s. The *ma'abarot* (plural) were used as absorption camps, in which accommodation for the newcomers was provided mainly for those who arrived in Israel during the mass immigration of the Oriental Jews. For more information about the *ma'abarot*, see Naor (1986).
20. The journal of the International Federation of Sephardic Jews.
21. On Amir, see Kerbel et al. (2003) and Abramson (2005).
22. This is published in English as *Scapegoat: A Novel* (Amir 1987).

23. This novel was published in an English translation as *The Dove Flyer* (Amir 2010b), and in a German translation as *Der Taubenzüchter von Bagdad: Roman* (Amir 1998).
24. Soussa, historian and engineer, was born in Iraq in 1900 and graduated in civil engineering from Colorado College in 1924. He obtained his PhD in the US in 1930. After finishing his studies in the US he returned to Iraq to work as an engineer. He published more than 100 books and papers. This novel has appeared in an English translation entitled *Outcast* (Ballas 2007).
25. The '*Aḥer – the Other One*' was a rabbi born in Jerusalem before 70 CE. After he was considered heretical by his fellow *Tanna'im*, the rabbis avoided mentioning his name and they referred to him as the 'Other One' (Aḥer). The Other One was the Rabbi Elisha ben Abuya. On Elisha ben Abuya, see for example Rubenstein (1998).

Chapter 2

1. For more information about the question of defining bilingualism, see Baetens Beardsmore (1986: 1–42).
2. Given that the three Iraqi Jewish authors emigrated from Iraq to Israel when they were adolescents, they are treated in the study as bicultural bilinguals.
3. For instance, the *language-spatial relationship* core which investigates the relationship between a particular language or languages in the space of the paper or the sign, i.e. the balance between the involved languages in the text. This core constitutes 25 per cent of the multimodal. Moreover the *units of analysis* themselves – which are divided into three units: (1) grammatical units, (2) genre-specific units relevant to textual structure and cohesion, and (3) visual/spatial units – mark the visual/spatial units as an essential unit when analysing exophonic texts.
4. For more information about the syntagmatic/paradigmatic difference, see Malmkjaer (1991).
5. Some initial ideas of the suggested model have been discussed briefly in Ahmed (2016, 2018).
6. For more information on the shift from Arabic to Hebrew that the three Iraqi Jewish authors of this study experienced in Israel, see section 1.4.
7. Note that according to the Arabic lexical item חאַזוק used here in Hebrew script, the first consonant must be /kh/ and not /ḥ/. It might be that the author uses the Ashkenazi pronunciation, in which the consonant /ח/ is pronounced /kh/. This is also the case with Eli Amir in this lexical item דחילק *dakhīlak* [please – I beg you] (1983: 156). The same lexical item is written with /'ח/ in Hebrew script; note the difference in Ballas's writing style of :1964) דח'ילך 63).
8. For more information about the types of conversational code-switching, see section 2.1.2.
9. It is important to point out here the misuse of the Arabic code (הונאַכּ) (هُنَاك) (*hūnāk*) employed by Michael. This code is supposed to be in Egyptian Arabic. The function of using Arabic in the scene is to to hide Israeli identity to avoid being killed in the war. The protagonist deceives the Egyptian soldiers

using the same dialect they speak. Yet the correct Egyptian Arabic code here should have been inserted as (هِناك) (*henāk*) instead of (هُنَاك) (*hunāk*). Only one phonetic mistake and the expression would be in standard Arabic (*fūsḥa*). This indicates that the author did not pay attention to the Egyptian Arabic.

10. The Turkish title refers to the high-ranking officers; it comes from Turkish, earlier Pasha, from bash 'head, chief'. Please see the online etymology dictionary, available at <http://www.etymonline.com/index.php?term=pasha>.
11. An ancient and very famous marketplace in Baghdad, it is famous for selling and buying birds, and has a market every Friday.
12. See also the term explained in Ben-Jacob (1998: 932). For more examples of Iraqi Judaeo-Arabic folk sayings, see Me'iri (2006).
13. See, for instance, Sagiv (2008: 205, 614); Ben-Yehuda (1980: 1843–4).
14. The Hebrew lexicon differentiates between masculine and feminine forms of the singular lexicon item *ben (banim)* and *bat (banot)*. See, for instance, בָּנֶיךָ וּבְנֹתֶיךָ נְתֻנִים לְעַם אַחֵר:דברים פרק כח.
15. ילד/*yeled* is also used in the Hebrew lexicon to refer to both girls and boys belonging to someone. See, for instance, Kena'ani (1998: 1817).

Chapter 3

1. An Iraqi dish, this is a soup made from certain parts of the meat of a sheep, such as the stomach, tongue, jowl and head. See also the dictionary of Iraqi Judaeo-Arabic in Yosef (2005: 30).
2. This is also an Iraqi Jewish favourite dish, see Yosef (2005: 28).
3. A mode of playing Arabic music using only one instrument. According to the dictionary of Iraqi Judaeo-Arabic, it refers to melody or tune (Yosef 2005: 301).
4. *Karakhāne* is a Turkish term used during the Ottoman Empire to refer to a brothel. Many Arabs borrowed it and it is still used in some Arabic dialects.
5. In the famous Arabian play *Ṭawla* [Backgammon; a board game], this word here refers to the numbers of the dice 1 and 4. This is also a game that Iraqi Jews love to play, see Yona-Swery (1995: 56); Yosef (2005: 150–1).
6. There is only one novel of the nine where the noun comes in third place after particles and interjections, namely Michael (1974).
7. See the summary of the plots of these novels in Chapter 1.
8. See, for instance, the use of such phenomena in Michael (1974) and Amir (1992).
9. See also this term in Me'iri (2006: 289).
10. An Arabic dialect insult related to the action of spitting.
11. An Iraqi interjection meaning 'go to hell', or 'I don't care'.
12. Traditional women's clothing in the Middle East. It is more like a cover and mostly coloured in black.
13. Pfaff (1979: 295–8) distinguishes between code-switching and borrowing by means of surface syntax, lexical inventory and functional load. For more information about the difference between borrowing and code-switching, see Onysko (2012).
14. See section 1.3.2 on the linguistic features of Iraqi Judaeo-Arabic.
15. See also section 1.3.2.

16. A typographical error in the Hebrew text, the correct form is הורדים.
17. See: (ספר שופטים, פרק י"ב פסוק ו'):
"וַיֹּאמְרוּלוֹ אֱמָר-נָא שִׁבֹּלֶת וַיֹּאמֶר סִבֹּלֶת, וְלֹא יָכִין לְדַבֵּר כֵּן, וַיֹּאחֲזוּ אוֹתוֹ, וַיִּשְׁחָטוּהוּ אֶל-מַעְבְּרוֹת הַיַּרְדֵּן"
Judges, 12:6. Then said they to him, say now Shibboleth: and he said Sibboleth: for he could not pronounce it correctly. Then they took him and slew him at the passages of the Jordan.

Chapter 4

1. For more information about the literary representation of crossing the sea in modern Hebrew literature, see Hever et al. (2002).
2. An Arabic name written on a café in one of the transit camps during the 1950s, meaning 'victory'.
3. For more information about the term outsider/insider readers, please see Chapter 2.
4. An ancient and very famous market in Baghdad held every Friday, famous for selling birds.

References

The Novels in the Analysis

Amir, Eli (1983), *Tarnegol kapparot* (Scapegoat), Tel Aviv: ʻAm ʻoved [Hebrew].

—— (1992), *Mafriaḥ ha-yonim* (Farewell Baghdad), Tel Aviv: ʻAm ʻoved [Hebrew].

—— (2010a), *Ma she-nish'ar* (What's Left), Tel Aviv: ʻAm ʻoved [Hebrew].

Ballas, Shimon (1964), *Ha-ma'abara* (The Transit Camp), Tel Aviv: ʻAm ʻoved [Hebrew].

—— (1991), *Ṿe-hu aḥer* (The Other One), Tel Aviv: Zmora-Bitan [Hebrew].

—— (2008), *Tom ha-biḳur* (End of the Visit), Tel Aviv: ha-Ḳibuts ha-me'uḥad [Hebrew].

Michael, Sami (1974), *Shavim ṿe-shavim yoter* (All Men are Equal – But Some are More), Tel Aviv: Hotsaʻat Bustan [Hebrew].

—— (1993), *Ṿiḳṭoryah* (Victoria), Tel Aviv: ʻAm ʻoved [Hebrew].

—— (2015), *Yahalom min ha-yeshimon* (Diamond from the Wilderness), Tel Aviv: Zemorah-Bitan [Hebrew].

Consulted References

Abramson, G. (ed.) (2005), *Encyclopedia of Modern Jewish Culture*, London: Routledge.

Ahmed, M. (2016), 'Arabic Codes in Hebrew Texts: On the Typology of Literary Code-Switching', *Journal of Jewish Languages*, 4(2): 203–30.

—— (2018), 'Codes Across Languages: On the Translation of Literary Code-Switching', *Multilingua*, 37(5): 483–514.

Alcalay, A. (1993), *After Jews and Arabs: Remaking Levantine Culture*, Minneapolis: University of Minnesota Press.

—— (1996), *Keys to the Garden: New Israeli Writing*, San Francisco: City Lights Books.

Al-Maʻadīdi, I. (2001); *Al-Ṣiḥāfah al-Yahūdīyah fī al-ʻIrāq*, Miṣr al-Jadīdah, al-Qāhirah: al-Dār al-Dawlīyah lil-Istithmārāt al-Thaqāfīyah.

Amara, M. (1999), *Politics and Sociolinguistic Reflexes: Palestinian Border Villages*, Amsterdam: John Benjamins.

Amara, M. and Mar'i, A.-e.-R. (2002), *Language Education Policy: The Arab Minority in Israel*, Dordrecht: Kluwer Academic Publishers.

Amir, E. (1983), *Tarnegol kapparot* (Scapegoat), Tel Aviv: Sifriyat ofaḳim.

—— (1987), *Scapegoat: A Novel*, London: Weidenfeld & Nicolson.

—— (1992), *Mafriaḥ ha-yonim* (Farewell Baghdad), Tel Aviv: Sifriyah la-'am.

—— (1998), *Der Taubenzüchter von Bagdad: Roman*, München: Europa Verlag.

—— (2006), 'Ani ḥay be-hermoniya ben ha-tarbiyot ve-sho'ef le-sintasiya ben mizraḥ le-ma'rav', *Kivunim Hadashim*, 14: 103–10.

—— (2010a), *Ma she-nish'ar* (What's Left), Tel Aviv: 'Am 'oved.

—— (2010b), *The Dove Flyer*, London: Halban.

Appel, R. and Muysken, P. (2005), *Language Contact and Bilingualism*, Amsterdam: Amsterdam University Press.

Ashcroft, B., Griffiths, G. and Tiffin, H. (2003), *The Empire Writes Back: Theory and Practice in Post-Colonial Literatures*, 2nd edn, London: Routledge.

Auer, P. (1998), *Code-Switching in Conversation: Language, Interaction and Identity*, London: Routledge.

—— (1999), 'From Codeswitching via Language Mixing to Fused Lects. Toward a Dynamic Typology of Bilingual Speech', *International Journal of Bilingualism*, 3(4): 309–32.

Avishur, Y. (1979), 'Ha-sifrut ha-'mamit shel-yehude bavel be-'aravit yehudit', *Pe'amim*, 3: 83–90.

Backus, A. and Dorleijn, M. (2009), 'Loan Translations Versus Code-Switching', in B. E. Bullock and A. J. Toribio (eds), *The Cambridge Handbook of Linguistic Code-Switching*, Cambridge Handbooks in Linguistics, Cambridge, New York: Cambridge University Press, pp. 75–93.

Baetens Beardsmore, H. (1986), *Bilingualism: Basic Principles*, 2nd edn, Boston, MA: College-Hill Press.

Ballas, S. (1964), *Ha-ma'abara* (The Transit Camp), Tel Aviv: 'Am 'oved.

—— (1969), *Mul ha-ḥomah: sipurim* (In Front of the Wall), Tel Aviv: Agudat ha-sofrim ha-'Ivrim be-Yiśra'el le-yad Hotsa'at Masadah.

—— (1978), *Ha-Sifrut ha-'Arvit be-tsel ha-milḥamah* (Arab Literature under the Shadow of War), Tel Aviv: 'Am 'oved.

—— (1984), *Ḥoref aḥaron* (Last Winter), Yerushalayim: Keter.

—— (1991), *Ve-hu aḥer* (The Other One), Tel Aviv: Zmora-Bitan.

—— (1992), *Otiyot setav: Shalosh novelot* (Signs of Autumn), Tel Aviv: Zmora-Bitan.

—— (2003), *Tel-Aviv mizraḥ: ṭrilogyah* (Tel-Aviv East), Tel Aviv: ha-Ḳibuts ha-me'uḥad.

—— (2005), 'Lo notra beydye ve-lu pisat nayyar aḥat me-hayamim hahem', *Haaretz*, 14 October <http://www.haaretz.co.il/literature/1.1050569>, accessed 6 August 2014.

—— (2007), *Outcast: Translated by Ammiel Alcalay and Oz Shelach*, San Francisco: City Lights.

—— (2008), *Tom ha-biḳur* (End of the Visit), Israel: ha-Ḳibuts ha-me'uḥad.

—— (2009), *Be-guf rishon* (First Person Singular), Israel: ha-Kịbuts ha-me'uhạd.

Ballas, S. and Darwish, Z. (1984), *Al-adab al-'arabi fi ḍel al-ḥarb* (The Arabic Literature under the Shadow of War 1948–1973), Beirut: Dar al-Mashreq.

Behar, M. and Ben-Dor Benite, Z. (eds) (2013), *Modern Middle Eastern Jewish Thought: Writings on Identity, Politics and Culture 1893–1958*, Waltham, MA: Brandeis University Press.

Ben-Jacob, A. (1998), *Otsar ha-meshalim yeha-pitgamim shel Yehude Bavel ba-dorot ha-aḥaronim* (Treasury of Proverbs of Iraqi Jews in the Last Era), Yerushalayim: Yerid ha-sefarim.

Ben-Shammai, H. (1997), 'Jewish Thought in Iraq in the 10th Century', in N. Golb (ed.), *Judaeo-Arabic Studies. Proceedings of the Founding Conference of the Society for Judaeo-Arabic Studies*, Amsterdam: Harwood Academic Publishers, pp. 15–32.

Bensky, T., Don, Y., Krausz, E. et al. (1991), *Yehudé 'Iraḳ be-Yiśra'el be-ḥevrah uve-khalkalah* (Iraqi Jews in Israel: Social and Economic Integration), Ramat-Gan: Universitat Bar-Ilan.

Ben-Yehuda, E. (1980), *Milon ha-lashon ha-'Ivrit ha-yeshanah yeha-ḥadashah* (Complete Dictionary of Ancient and Modern Hebrew), Yerushalayim: Makor.

Berg, N. (1996), *Exile from Exile: Israeli Writers from Iraq*, Albany: State University of New York Press.

—— (2005); *More and More Equal: The Literary Works of Sami Michael*, Lanham, MD: Lexington Books.

Blanc, H. (1964), *Communal Dialects in Baghdad*, 10, Cambridge: Harvard University Press.

Blau, J. (1971), 'Ben 'aravit yehudit le-Quran', *Tarbiz*, 1971: 512–14.

—— (1981), *The Emergence and Linguistic Background of Judaeo-Arabic: A Study of the Origins of Middle Arabic*, Jerusalem: Ben-Zvi Institute.

—— (2001), 'The Linguistic Character of Saadia Gaon's Translation of the Pentateuch', *Oriens*, 36: 1.

Blom, J.-P. and Gumperz, J. J. (1972), 'Social Meaning in Linguistic Structure. Code-Switching in Nerway', in J. J. Gumperz and D. H. Hymes (eds), *The Ethnography of Communication*, New York: Holt, Rinehart and Winston, pp. 407–34.

Bloomfield, L. (1933), *Language*, New York: Henry Holt and Company.

Bloomfield, M. W. (1976), 'Stylistics and the Theory of Literature', *New Literary History*, 7(2): 271–311.

Brenner, R. F. (2001), 'The Search for Identity in Israeli Arab Fiction: Atallah Mansour, Emile Habiby, and Anton Shammas', *Israel Studies*, 6(3): 91–112.

Brody, R. (2013), *Sa'adyah Gaon*, Oxford, Portland, OR: The Littman Library of Jewish Civilization.

Bullock, B. E. and Toribio, A. J. (2009); *The Cambridge Handbook of Linguistic Code-Switching*, Cambridge: Cambridge University Press.

Callahan, L. (2004), *Spanish/English Codeswitching in a Written* Corpus, Studies in Bilingualism, Amsterdam: John Benjamins.

Chetrit, J. (2003), 'Judeo-Arabic', in R. S. Simon, M. M. Laskier and S. Reguer (eds), *The Jews of the Middle East and North Africa in Modern Times*, New York: Columbia University Press, pp. 128–33.

Cortés-Conde, F. and Boxer, D. (2002), 'Bilingual Word-Play in Literary Discourse. The Creation of Relational Identity', *Language and Literature*, 11(2): 137–51.

Coupland, N. (2001a), 'Dialect Stylization in Radio Talk', *Language in Society*, 30: 345–75.

—— (2001b), 'Stylization, Authenticity and TV News Review', *Discourse Studies*, 3: 413–42.

Delanty, G., Wodak, R. and Jones, P. (eds) (2011), *Identity, Belonging and Migration*, Liverpool: Liverpool University Press.

Elazar, D. J. (1989), *The Other Jews: The Sephardim Today*, New York: Basic Books.

Enkvist, N. E., Spencer, J. and Gregory, M. J. (1964), *Linguistics and Style*, Oxford: Oxford University Press.

Gardner-Chloros, P. (2009), *Code-Switching*, Cambridge: Cambridge University Press.

Gat, M. (1997), *The Jewish Exodus from Iraq, 1948–1951*, London: Frank Cass.

—— (1998), 'The Immigration of Iraqi Jewry to Israel as Reflected in Literature', *Revue Européenne des Migrations Internationales*, 14(3): 45–60.

Ghunayma, Y. R. A. (1924), *Nuzhat al-mushtāq fī tārīkh Yahūd al-'Irāq* (A Nostalgic Trip into the History of the Jews of Iraq), Baghdad: Maktab al-'Arabiyyah.

Goldenberg, G. (2013), *Semitic Languages: Features, Structures, Relations, Processes*, Oxford Linguistics, 1st edn, Impression 1, Oxford: Oxford University Press.

Grosjean, F. (1982), *Life with Two Languages: An Introduction to Bilingualism*, Cambridge, MA: Harvard University Press.

—— (2010), *Bilingual: Life and Reality*, Cambridge, MA: Harvard University Press.

—— (2013), 'Bilingualism: A Short Introduction', in F. Grosjean and P. Li (eds), *The Psycholinguistics of Bilingualism*, Malden, MA and Oxford: Wiley-Blackwell, pp. 5–25.

Gumperz, J. J. (1977), 'The Sociolinguistic Significance of Conversational Code-Switching', *RELC Journal*, 8(2): 1–34.

Hary, B. H. (1992), *Multiglossia in Judeo-Arabic, with an Edition, Translation and Grammatical Study of the Cairene Purim Scroll*, Leiden: Brill.

—— (2009), *Translating Religion: Linguistic Analysis of Judeo-Arabic Sacred Texts from Egypt*, Leiden: Brill.

Haugen, E. (1953), *The Norwegian Language in America: A Study in Bilingual Behavior Dialects of Norwegian*, Philadelphia: University of Pennsylvania Press.

Heinrichs, H.-J. (1992), *Sprich Deine Eigene Sprache, Afrika!: Von der Négritude zur afrikanischen Literatur der Gegenwart*, Berlin: D. Reimer.

Henkin-Roitfarb, R. (2011), 'Hebrew and Arabic in Asymmetric Contact in Israel', *Lodz Papers in Pragmatics*, 7(1).

Henshke, Y. (2013), 'Sara Shilo's No Gnomes Will Appear', *Hebrew Studies*, LIV: 265–84.

Hever, H. (1987), 'Hebrew in an Israeli Arab Hand. Six Miniatures on Anton Shammas's Arabesques', *Cultural Critique*, 1987: 47–76.

—— (2002), *Producing the Modern Hebrew Canon: Nation Building and Minority Discourse*, New York: New York University Press.

—— (2007), *Ha-sipur ye-ha-li'om* (Narrative and the Nation), Tel Aviv: Resling.

Hever, H., Shenhav, Y. A. and Motzafi-Haller, P. (2002), *Mizraḥim be-Yisra'el* (Mizrahim in Israel), Yerushalayim: Mekhon Van Lir be-Yerushalayim; ha-qibuts ha-me'uḥad.

Ibhawaegbele, F. O. and Edokpayi, J. N. (2012), 'Code-Switching and Code-Mixing as Stylistic Devices in Nigerian Prose Fiction. A Study of Three Nigerian Novels', *Research on Humanities and Social Sciences*, 2(6): 12–19.

Jakobson, R. (1960), 'Closing Statement. Linguistics and Poetics', in T. A. Sebeok (ed.), *Style in Language*, London: John Wiley & Sons.

Jakobson, R. and Halle, M. (1956), *Fundamentals of Language*, 'S-Gravenhage: Mouton.

Jastrow, O. (1990), *Der arabische Dialekt der Juden von 'Aqra und Arbīl*, Wiesbaden: O. Harrassowitz.

Jeffries, L. and McIntyre, D. (2010), *Stylistics*, New York: Cambridge University Press.

Jonsson, C. (2005), *Code-Switching in Chicano Theater: Power, Identity and Style in Three Plays by Cherríe Moraga*, Umeå: Institutionen för moderna språk, Umeå universitet.

—— (2010), 'Functions of Code-Switching in Bilingual Theater. An Analysis of Three Chicano Plays', *Journal of Pragmatics*, 42(5): 1296–1310.

Kayyal, M. (2008a), 'Arab Dancing in a New Light of Arabesques. Minor Hebrew Works of Palestinian Authors in the Eyes of Critics', *Middle Eastern Literatures*, 11(1): 31–51.

—— (2008b), 'Salim al Dawudi and the Beginnings of Translation into Arabic of Modern Hebrew Literature', *Target: International Journal of Translation Studies (Holanda)*, 20(1): 52–78.

—— (2010), 'Al-tadākhol al-lughawey al-'ibrey fi al-adab al-Falastini al-maḥalley', *Magma' al-Lugha al-Arabiyah*, 1: 167–186 <http://www.arabicac.com/?mod=book&ID=339>, accessed 12 February 2015.

—— (2011), 'From Left to Right and From Right to Left. Anton Shamas's Translations from Hebrew into Arabic Vice Versa', *Babel*, 57(1): 76–98.

Kazzaz, N. (1991), *Ha-Yehudim be-'Iraḳ ba-me'ah ha-'eśrim* (The Jews in Iraq in the Twentieth Century), Yerushalayim: Ben-Zvi Institute.

Keller, G. (1976), 'Toward a Stylistic Analysis of Bilingual Texts', in M. A. Beck (ed.), *The Analysis of Hispanic Texts. Current Trends in Methodology: 1st York College Colloquium*, New York: Bilingual Press.

Kellman, S. G. (2000), *The Translingual Imagination*, Lincoln: University of Nebraska Press.

Kena'ani, Y. (1998), *Ha-Milon ha-'ivri ha-male: Otsar makif ye-shimushi shel ha-lashon ha-'ivrit ha-yeshanah ye-ha-hadashah* (The Complete Hebrew Dictionary), Yerushalayim: Milonim la-'am.

Kerbel, S., Emanuel, M. and Phillips, L. (2003), *Jewish Writers of the Twentieth Century*, New York: Fitzroy Dearborn.

Khan, G. (2007), 'Judaeo-Arabic', in L. Edzard and R. de Jong (eds), *Encyclopedia of Arabic Language and Linguistics*, Leiden: Brill, pp. 526–36.

—— (2013), ‘Transcriptions into Arabic Script. Medieval Karaite Sources’, in G. Khan and S. Bolozky (eds), *Encyclopedia of Hebrew Language and Linguistics*, Leiden: Brill, pp. 792–9.

Kiwān, M. (1996), *Al-Yahūd fi al-Sharq al-Awsaṭ: Al-khrūg al-akhīr mina al-getto al-jadīd* (Jews in the Middle East: The Last Exodus from the New Ghetto), ʻAmmān: al-Ahliyya.

Koplewitz, I. (1990), ‘The Use and Integration of Hebrew Lexemes in Israeli Spoken Arabic’, in D. Gorter (ed.), *Fourth International Conference on Minority Languages*, Vol. 2, Clevedon, UK: Multilingual Matters.

Kraus, P. (1930), ‘Hebräische und syrische Zitate in ismāʻīlitischen Schriften’, *Der Islam*, 19(4): 243–63.

Kressel, G. (1965–7), *Leksiḳon ha-sifrut ha-ʻivrit ba-dorot ha-aḥaronim* (Encyclopedia of Modern Hebrew Literature), Merḥavyah: Sifriyat Poʻalim.

Kūriyah,Y. (1998), *Yahūd al-ʻIrāq: Taʼrīkhuhum, ahwāluhum, hijratuhum* (The Jews of Iraq: History, Life, Immigration), ʻAmmān: al-Ahliyya.

Lachmanovitz, A. (2011), ‘Ani kotev ladam she-betokhi’ <http://www.israelhayom.co.il/site/newsletter_article.php?id=10968&newsletter=22.04.2011>, updated 22 April 2011, accessed 6 August 2014.

Leech, G. (2008), *Language in Literature: Style and Foregrounding (Textual Explorations)*, 1st edn, London: Routledge.

Leech, G. N. and Short, M. (1981), *Style in Fiction: A Linguistic Introduction to English Fictional Prose*, London, New York: Pearson Longman.

Lefkowitz, D. (2004), *Words and Stones: The Politics of Language and Identity in Israel*, New York: Oxford University Press.

Levy, L. (2003), ‘Exchanging Words. Thematizations of Translation in Arabic Writing from Israel’, *Comparative Studies of South Asia, Africa and the Middle East*, 23(1–2): 106–27.

—— (2006), ‘Self and the City. Literary Representations of Jewish Baghdad’, *Prooftexts*, 26(1): 163–211.

—— (2014), *Poetic Trespass: Writing Between Hebrew and Arabic in Israel/Palestine*, Lawrenceville, NJ: Princeton University Press.

Lipski, J. M. (1977), ‘Code-Switching and the Problem of Bilingual Competence’, in M. Paradis (ed.), *The Fourth LACUS Forum*, Columbia, SC: Hornbeam Press.

—— (1982), ‘Spanish-English Language Switching in Speech and Literature. Theories and Models’, *Bilingual Review/La Revista Bilingüe*, 9(3): 191–212.

—— (1985), *Linguistic Aspects of Spanish-English Language Switching*, Tempe, AZ: Center for Latin American Studies, Arizona State University.

McClure, E. (1981), ‘Formal and Functional Aspects of the Code-Switched Discourse of Bilingual Children’, in R. P. Duran (ed.), *Latino Language and Communicative Behavior*, Norwood, NJ: Ablex Publishing Corporation, pp. 69–94.

Mackey, W. (1993), ‘Literary Diglossia, Biculturalism and Cosmopolitanism in Literature’, in R. Sarkonak and R. Hodgson (eds), *Writing ... in Stereo. Bilingualism in the Text*, Providence, MJ: Rhode Island School of Design.

McMenamin, G. R. and Choi, D. (2002), *Forensic Linguistics: Advances in Forensic Stylistics*, Boca Raton, FL: CRC Press.

Malmkjaer, K. (ed.) (1991), *Linguistics Encyclopedia*, London: Routledge.

Malter, H. (1921), *Saadia Gaon: His Life and Works*, Philadelphia, PA: The Jewish Publication Society of America.
Mansour, J. (1991), *The Jewish Baghdadi Dialect: Studies and Texts in the Judeo-Arabic Dialect of Baghdad*, Or-Yehuda: The Babylonian Jewry Heritage Center, The Institute for Research on Iraqi Jewry.
Meir-Glitzenstein, E. (2002), 'Our Dowry. Identity and Memory among Iraqi Immigrants in Israel', *Middle Eastern Studies*, 38(2): 165–86.
Me'iri, Y. (2006), *Hedim mi-Bavel: Biṭuyim, imrot ṿe-haṿai shel Yehude Bagdad: be-shiluv minhagim, folḳlor, emunot ṿe-sipurim me-haṿai Yehude Bavel* (Echoes of Babylon), Yerushalayim: Hotsa'at Re'uven Mas.
Michael, S. (1974), *Shavim ṿe-shavim yoter* (All Men are Equal – But Some are More), Tel Aviv: Hotsa'at Bustan.
—— (1984), 'On Being an Iraqi-Jewish Writer in Israel', *Prooftexts*, 4: 23–33.
—— (1993), *Ṿiḳṭoryah* (Victoria), 392, Tel Aviv: 'Am 'oved.
—— (2000), *Gevulot ha-ruaḥ: Shiḥot 'im Rubiḳ Rozenṭal* (Unbounded Ideas: Ruvik Rosenthal Talks with Sami Michael), Kaṿ adom, Tel Aviv: ha-Ḳibuts ha-me'uḥad.
—— (2001), *Mayim noshḳim le-mayim* (Water Kissing Water), Tel Aviv: Sifriyah la-'am.
—— (2011), *Me'of ha-barburim* (Flight of the Swans), Or-Yehuda: Kineret.
—— (2015), *Yahalom min ha-yeshimon* (Diamond from the Wilderness), Or-Yehuda: Kineret.
Montes-Alcala, C. (2000), 'Two Languages, One Pen. Socio-Pragmatic Functions in Written Spanish-English Code-Switching', PhD thesis, Santa Barbara, University of California.
—— (2012), 'Code-Switching in US-Latino Novels', in M. Sebba, S. Mahootian and C. Jonsson (eds), *Language Mixing and Code-Switching in Writing. Approaches to Mixed-Language Written Discourse*, Routledge Critical Studies in Multilingualism, New York: Routledge, pp. 68–88.
Mukařovský, J. (1964), *Standard Language and Poetic Language*, Washington: Georgetown University Press.
Müller, H. M., Feinberg, A. and Kolo, Kamal Y. Odisho (2011), *Das Ende des Babylonischen Exils: Kulturgeschichtliche Epochenwende in der Literatur der letzten irakisch-jüdischen Autoren*, Wiesbaden: Reichert.
Muysken, P. (2000), *Bilingual Speech: A Typology of Code-Mixing*, Cambridge: Cambridge University Press.
Myers-Scotton, C. (1993a), *Duelling Languages: Grammatical Structure in Codeswitching*, Oxford: Clarendon Press.
—— (1993b), *Social Motivations for Codeswitching: Evidence from Africa*, Oxford: Clarendon Press.
—— (1998), *Codes and Consequences: Choosing Linguistic Varieties*, New York: Oxford University Press.
—— (2002), *Contact Linguistics: Bilingual Encounters and Grammatical Outcomes*, Oxford: Oxford University Press.
—— (2006), *Multiple Voices: An Introduction to Bilingualism*, Malden, MA: Blackwell Publishing.
Naor, M. (1986), *'Olim u-ma'barot, 1948–1952* (Immigrants and Transit Camps), Yerushalayim: Yad Yitshak Ben-Tsevi.

Naqqāsh, S. (1980), *Yawm ḥabilat wa-ajhaḍat al-dunyā: Qiṣaṣ 'irāqīyah* (Day in which the World has been Conceived and Miscarried), al-Quds: Matba`at al-Sharq al-`Arabiyah.
Onysko, A. (2012), *Anglicisms in German: Borrowing, Lexical Productivity, and Written Codeswitching*, Berlin: Walter de Gruyter.
Özdamar, E. S. (1990), *Mutterzunge: Erzählungen*, Berlin: Rotbuch.
Perloff, Marjorie (2010), 'Language in Migration: Multilingualism and Exophonic Writing in the New Poetics', *Textual Practice*, 24(4): 725–48.
Pfaff, C. W. (1976), 'Functional and Structural Constraints on Syntactic Variation in Code-Switching', in B. Steever et al. (eds), *Papers from the Parasession on Diachronic Syntax*, Chicago: Chicago Linguistic Society, pp. 248–59.
—— (1979), 'Constraints on Language Mixing. Intrasentential Code-Switching and Borrowing in Spanish/English', *Language*, 55(2): 291–318.
Poplack, S. (1980), '"Sometimes I'll Start a Sentence in Spanish Y TERMINO EN ESPAÑOL". Toward a Typology of Code-Switching', *Linguistics*, 18(7–8): 581–618.
—— (1981), 'Syntactic Structure and Social Function', in R. P. Duran (ed.), *Latino Language and Communicative Behavior*, Norwood, NJ: Ablex Publishing Corporation, pp. 169–84.
Reif, S. C. (2000), *A Jewish Archive from Old Cairo: The History of Cambridge University's Genizah Collection*, Richmond, UK: Curzon Press.
Rejwan, N. (1985), *The Jews of Iraq: 3000 Years of History and Culture*, Boulder, CO: Westview Press.
—— (1998), *Mujaz tarikh Yahūd al-'Irāq: Min saby Bābil ila nuzuḥihim 'ām 1951* (A Summary of the Iraqi Jewish History), al-Quds: Rābitat al-Jami'iyin al-Yahūd al-Nāziḥin min al-'irāq.
Rubenstein, J. L. (1998), 'Elisha ben Abuya. Torah and the Sinful Sage', *The Journal of Jewish Thought and Philosophy*, 7: 139–225.
Sagiv, D. (2008), *Milon Sagiv: 'Arvi-'Ivri, 'Ivri-'Arvi* (Sagiv Dictionary), Yerushalayim: Shoken.
Sarkonak, R. and Hodgson, R. (1993), *Writing ... in Stereo: Bilingualism in the Text*, Providence: Rhode Island School of Design.
Saussure, F. de (1986), *Course in General Linguistics*, New York: Open Court.
Sebba, M. (2013), 'Multilingualism in Written Discourse. An Approach to the Analysis of Multilingual Texts', *International Journal of Bilingualism*, 17(1): 97–118.
Shanon, B. (1991), 'Faulty Language Selection in Polyglots', *Language and Cognitive Processes*, 6(4): 339–50.
Shenhav, Y. A. (2003), *Ha-Yehudim-ha-'Arvim: Leumiyut, dat ve-etniyut* (The Arab Jews), Tel Aviv: 'Am 'oved.
Shiblak, A. (2005), *Iraqi Jews: A History of the Mass Exodus*, London: Saqi.
Shlonsky, U. (1997), *Clause Structure and Word Order in Hebrew and Arabic: An Essay in Comparative Semitic Syntax*, Oxford Studies in Comparative Syntax, New York, Oxford: Oxford University Press.
Shohat, E. (1999), 'The Invention of the Mizrahim', *Journal of Palestine Studies–Berkeley*, 29(1): 5–20.
Siebers, S. (2010), *Der Irak in Israel: Vom zionistischen Staat zur transkulturellen Gesellschaft*, Göttingen: Vandenhoeck & Ruprecht.

Simon, R. S., Laskier, M. M. and Reguer, S. (eds) (2003), *The Jews of the Middle East and North Africa in Modern Times*, New York: Columbia University Press.

Simpson, P. (2004), *Stylistics: A Resource Book for Students*, London: Routledge.

Sirat, C. (2002), *Hebrew Manuscripts of the Middle Ages*, Cambridge: Cambridge University Press.

Snir, R. (1991), '"We Were Like Those Who Dream". Iraqi-Jewish Writers in Israel in the 1950s', *Prooftexts*, 11: 153–83.

—— (1993), 'Source and Translation by the Borders', in S. Somekh (ed.), *Targum be-tside ha-derekh. 'iyunim be-targumim min ha-sifrut ha-'Arvit le-'Ivrit be-yamenu*, Tel Aviv: ha-Makhon le-limudim 'Arviyim, pp. 21–39.

—— (1995), '"Hebrew as the Language of Grace". Arab-Palestinian Writers in Hebrew', *Prooftexts*, 15: 163–83.

—— (2005a), *'Arviyut, Yahadut, Tsiyonut: Ma'avaḳ zehuyot bi-yetsiratam shel Yehude 'Iraḳ* (Arabness, Jewishness, Zionism: A Clash of Identities in the Literature of Iraqi Jews), Yerushalayim: Yad Yitshak Ben-Tsevi.

—— (2005b), 'When Time Stopped. Ishaq Bar-Moshe as Arab-Jewish Writer in Israel', *Jewish Social Studies*, 11(2): 102–35.

—— (2015), *Who Needs Arab-Jewish Identity?: Interpellation, Exclusion, and Inessential Solidarities*, Leiden: Brill.

Somekh, S. (ed.) (1993), *Targum be-tside ha-derekh: 'iyunim be-targumim min ha-sifrut ha-'Arvit le-'Ivrit be-yamenu*, Tel Aviv: ha-Makhon le-limudim 'Arviyim.

Spillner, B. (1974), *Linguistik und Literaturwissenschaft: Stilforschung, Rhetorik, Textlinguistik*, Stuttgart: Kohlhammer.

Stahl, A. (1979), 'Adapting the Curriculum to the Needs of a Multiethnic Society. The Case of Israel', *Curriculum Inquiry*, 9(4): 361–71.

Steinschneider, M. (1902), *Die arabische Literatur der Juden: Ein Beitrag zur Literaturgeschichte der Araber, grossenteils aus handschriftlichen Quellen (Bibliotheca Arabico-Judaica)*, Frankfurt am Main: Verlag von J. Kauffmann.

Stillman, N. (1991), *The Jews of Arab Lands in Modern Times*, Philadelphia, PA: The Jewish Publication Society.

—— (2005), 'The Judeo-Arabic Heritage', in Z. Zohar (ed.), *Sephardic and Mizrahi Jewry. From the Golden Age of Spain to Modern Times*, New York: NYU Press, pp. 40–54.

Stockwell, P. (2006), 'Language and Literature. Stylistics', in B. Aarts and April McMahon (eds), *The Handbook of English Linguistics*, Oxford: Blackwell, pp. 742–58.

—— (2012), 'Textual Analysis and Stylistics', in D. Clayton and The English and Media Centre (eds), *Language. A Student Handbook on Key Topics and Theories*, London: The English and Media Centre, pp. 150–62.

Talmon, R. (2000), 'Arabic as a Minority Language in Israel', in J. Owens (ed.), *Arabic as a Minority Language*, Berlin: Mouton de Gruyter, pp. 199–220.

Tannenbaum, M. (2014), 'With a Tongue Forked in Two. Translingual Arab Writers in Israel', *International Journal of Bilingualism*, 18(2): 99–117.

Thomason, S. G. (2001), *Language Contact*, Edinburgh: Edinburgh University Press.

Thornborrow, J. and Wareing, S. (1998), *Patterns in Language: An Introduction to Language and Literary Style*, London: Routledge.

Timm, L. A. (1975), 'Spanish-English Code-Switching. El Porque and How-Not-To', *Romance Philology*, 28: 473–82.

Tobi, Y. (2014), 'Sociolinguistic Aspects of Printed Judeo-Arabic Literature in Tunisia. The North (Tunis and Sousse) Versus the South (Djerba)', in Y. Hanshaka, A. Maman and T. Zvi (eds), *Keramlim*, Yerushalayim: Mekhon Van Lir be-Yerushalayim.

Torres, L. (2007), 'In the Contact Zone. Code-Switching Strategies by Latino/a Writers', *MELUS*, 32(1): 75–96.

Vollandt, R. (2015), *Arabic Versions of the Pentateuch: A Comparative Study of Jewish, Christian, and Muslim Sources*, Leiden: Brill.

Wales, K. (1994), *A Dictionary of Stylistics*, 3rd impression, London: Longman.

Weinreich, U. (1968), *Languages in Contact: Findings and Problems*, The Hague: Mouton & Co.

Wright, C. (2008), 'Writing in the "Grey Zone". Exophonic Literature in Contemporary Germany', *German as a Foreign Language*, 3: 26–42.

—— (2010), 'Exophony and Literary Translation. What it Means for the Translator when a Writer Adopts a New Language', *Target, International Journal of Translation Studies*, 22(1): 22–39.

Wulfinsūn, I. (1927), *Tā'rikh al-Yahūd fi bilād al-'Arab fi al-Jāhiliyya wa-ṣadr al-Islām* (The History of Jews of Arab Lands in the Pre- and Post-Islamic Era), Cairo: Matba'at Al-I'timad.

Yaar, E. and Shavit, Z. (eds) (2003), *Megamot ba-ḥevrah ha-Yisra'ilit*, 2, Tel Aviv: The Open University of Israel.

Yona-Swery, G. (1995), *Milon imrot u-meshalim shel lahag Yehudé Bavel* (The Dictionary of Iraqi Jewish Dialect), Yerushalayim: Agudat ha-Aḳadema'im Yotṣ'é 'Iraḳ be-Yisra'el.

Yosef, D. (2005), *Sefat ha-em: Milon ha-nosṭalgyah shel ha-'Iraḳim be-lahag ha-safah ha-'Iraḳit ha-Yehudit* (The Mother Tongue: A Nostalgic Dictionary of Spoken Iraqi Judeo-Arabic), Tel Aviv: Y. David.

Index

Abdulmuttaleb, Mohamed, 30, 104
al-Afghānī, Jamāl al-Dīn, 22
al-Atrash, Farid, 104
Alcalay, Ammiel, 6, 21, 89
al-Farhūd/Farhud, 4, 30, 161
Alliance Israélite Universelle schools, 3, 21, 34
al-Qatl al-Ghāmiḍ, 21
al-Rashīd, 113
al-Yahūdiyya, 11
'Aqra, 14, 17
Aramaic, 11–14, 17, 18, 161
Arbīl, 14, 17
Ashkenazi, 19, 20, 21, 25, 26, 27, 29, 63, 64, 65, 111, 161, 163
Auer, Peter, 45

Bāb-al-Sheikh, 113
Babylon, 12, 15, 16, 20, 72, 110, 162
Babylonian Jewry Heritage Centre, 20
Backus, Ad, 76
Baetens Beardsmore, Hugo, 40
Baghdad, 1, 3–4, 6, 16, 17, 19, 21, 22, 23, 24, 25, 29, 30, 31, 32, 34, 37, 71, 83, 94, 97, 99, 101, 103, 105, 108, 110, 111–15, 116, 122, 162, 164, 165
Bar Moshe, Ishac, 20
Ben-Gurion, David, 4
Bensky, Tova, 20
Berg, Nancy, 2, 5, 6, 18, 19, 111
bicultural-bilingual, 41
bilingual authors, 6, 8, 38– 41, 119
bilingualism, 2, 3, 5, 6, 9, 38, 39, 40, 43, 49, 52, 57, 117, 118
Blanc, Haim, 17, 103
Bloomfield, Leonard, 40, 50
borrowing, 12, 45, 76, 87, 95, 97, 164

Callahan, Laura, 45
Cambridge Handbook of Linguistic Code-Switching, 44
Chetrit, Joseph, 13
Cisneros, Sandra, 47
classical Arabic, 3, 17, 18
code choice, 50, 55, 56
code-mixing, 45–6, 66
code-switching, 3, 6, 9, 10, 13, 38, 43, 55, 57, 60, 113, 117, 119, 122, 126, 164
- ambiguous-access code-switching, 52, 55, 68–73, 79, 119
- conversational code-switching, 38, 43–4
- easy-access code-switching, 51, 60, 61–5, 79, 83, 119, 126, 155
- hard-access code-switching, 9, 51, 55, 60, 65–8, 119, 126, 138
- inter-sentential code-switching, 44, 45, 65, 66, 120
- intra-sentential code-switching, 44, 45, 52, 55, 56, 65, 66, 67, 68, 120
- literary code-switching, 2, 51–2, 118
- non-code-switching aspects, 3, 38, 47, 53–4
- spoken code-switching, 9, 46

tag-switching, 44, 52
written code-switching, 9, 38, 43, 45–7, 117
Cohen, Jacob, 15
Conrad, Joseph, 41

DDT, 109
De Saussure, Ferdinand, 53
Dorleijn, Margreet, 76

Edokpayi, Justina N., 46
El Huitlacoche, Gary, 39
Enkvist, Nils Erik, 53
Ephraim tribe, 104
exile, 2, 5, 18, 19, 35, 36, 41, 115
exophony, 38
bilingual literary texts, 2, 39, 43
exophonic writers, 41, 58
exophonic texts, 2, 3, 6–7, 8, 38–43, 45–8, 50–7, 73, 117–21, 163
exophonic writing, 2–3, 6, 38, 41

Farhi, Eliezer, 15
Fatal, Nasim, 18
Flah, Chalom, 15
France, 21

Ga'on, Sa'adya, 16–17, 161
Gat, Moshe, 6
gelet dialects, 17
Grosjean, François, 39, 40

ḥarīq, 22, 23
Hārūn, Aḥmad, 35
Hary, Benjamin, 13
Haugen, Einar, 40, 41
Hever, Hannan, 6

Ibhawaegbele, Faith O., 46
Ibn-'Arab, 23–4
insider reader, 52, 165
Iraqi Judaeo-Arabic, 3, 15–18, 64, 78, 100–6

Jakobson, Roman, 44, 51
Jerusalem, 24
Jonsson, Carla, 45
journal *al-Jadīd*, 22, 23, 162
journal *Bma'arakha*, 24
Judaeo-Arabic texts, 11, 13–15, 16
Judaeo-Arabic, 8, 10, 11–16, 18, 80, 96–7, 124, 161, 164; *see also* Iraqi Judaeo-Arabic

Karakhāna, 113
Keller, Gary, 39
Kellman, Steven G., 41
Khan, Geoffrey, 11
kibbutz, 24–6, 61, 110–11
Kol ha-'am, 21

language contact, 6, 43–4, 45
languages in contact, 38, 44, 57, 117
Latino, 46, 51, 61
Lebanon, 33, 114
Leech, Geoffrey, 48, 49, 53
Levi, Sameh, 15
Levy, Lital, 6, 112
Linguistic Encyclopaedia, 40, 76
London, 115, 116

Malter, Henry, 16
Markedness Model, 49
mass immigration, 1, 4, 5, 15, 16, 24, 109, 162
Matrix Language Frame, 45, 52
Matrix Text Language, 52, 57, 118
melting pot, 19, 20
Mesopotamia, 17
Middle Arabic, 11, 13
Mishnaic Hebrew, 18
Mizrahi Jews, 4, 6, 9, 19–20, 26
monoculture bilingual, 41
Montes-Alcala, Cecilia, 45
Moritz Steinschneider, 11
Mosul, 17
Mutterzunge, 41
Myers-Scotton, Carol, 40, 44, 45, 49, 52

Naqqāsh, Samir, 16, 20
North Africa, 4, 9, 12, 14, 15, 161
Algiers, 15
Morocco, 15, 104
North African lands, 15, 161
Tunisia, 15

outsider reader, 52, 60, 69, 83, 88, 98, 113–14, 119, 120
Oxford English Dictionary, 53
Özdamar, Emine S., 41

Palestine, 4, 12
paradigmatic deviations, 3, 38, 56, 59, 73, 74–8, 79, 118, 119, 120, 121
Paris, 21
Passover Haggada, 16
Pentateuch, 16

Persian, 18, 113
philosophy, 12, 14, 16
Poplack, Shana, 44

qeltu dialects, 17
Quran, 13

Rabbi Elisha ben Abuya, 163
Rejwan, Nissim, 4
Rivera, Eduardo, 39
Roman period, 12
Roni, Henkin-Roitfarb, 9

science, 12, 14
Sebba, Mark, 46, 47
Semah, David, 22
Semitic languages, 2, 12, 36, 64, 74
sharḥ, 14
Shlonsky, Ur, 73
Short, Mick, 22, 48, 49, 53
Siebers, Stefan, 6
sifrut ha-ma'abara, 108
Sir Sassoon Eskell, 4
Snir, Reuven, 6
Somekh, Sasson, 22
Sorbonne, 21
Soussa, Aḥmad Nasīm, 34, 163
Spain, 13, 14
Spillner, Bernd, 48, 50
Stockwell, Peter, 50
stylistic analysis, 7, 47–8, 50, 53, 57, 118–20
stylistics, 2, 3, 6, 8, 38, 39–56, 117, 118
Sūq al-Ghazl, 71, 114
Sūq al-Shorja, 113
Sūq Ḥenuni, 113
syntagmatic deviations, 38, 54, 55, 73–4, 118, 119

Tanakh, 17
ṭasqīt law, 4
Tel Aviv, 109, 116
The Black Panthers, 20
The Middle East, 4, 14, 15, 16, 20, 111, 161, 164
Thomason, Sarah Grey, 44, 45
Torres, Lourdes, 51, 61,
Turkish, 18, 164

Umm Kulthum, 20
US, 24, 30, 31, 34, 36, 37, 46

Wādī Ṣalīb, 20
Weinreich, Uriel, 44
Western Jews, 4
Wright, Chantal, 41, 42

Yom Kippur, 26, 110